Learn the Bible in 24 Hours
Book Endorsements

"My friend Chuck Missler has spent a lifetime teaching the Word of God. This unique book is an outgrowth of that teaching and is the best way I know to learn the entire Bible in the shortest period of time. It can truly be a life-changing experience for anyone who seriously wants to know how to 'rightly divide the word of truth.'"

— Tim LaHaye
Author

"Anyone familiar with Chuck Missler will know what to expect from this volume: A tight, to-the-point, provocative, and challenging journey through the Bible from a man who does his homework to help the rest of us do ours."

— Frank E. Peretti
Author

"I have just received Chuck's new book, *Learn the Bible in 24 Hours,* and I am enjoying it tremendously (not that I understand the physics part)."

— Hugh Hewitt
Author, Radio Show Host,
and Attorney

"The CD program *Learn the Bible in 24 Hours* was pretty amazing, but I never thought you could capture its contents in a 329-page book. Maybe you should rework the title—'Learn the Bible in Less Than 350 Pages.' It is a colossal effort and will become a standard text in the very near future for all new, developing and mature Christians—a four-star effort!"

— Warren Duffy
Radio Show Host

"Learn the Bible in 24 Hours is the finest introduction to God's Word available. Chuck Missler has done a masterful job. My wife and I use it in our own Bible studies."

— JOSEPH FARAH
WorldNetDaily.com

"Chuck—only you could do this!"

— JOSH MCDOWELL
Author and Speaker

"Chuck's *Learn the Bible in 24 Hours* synopsis of the Bible is the best aid to learning the Bible I have seen."

— HAL LINDSEY
Author

"Chuck Missler's new book is an adventure of discovery from beginning to end. *Learn the Bible in 24 Hours* is an excellent survey of the Bible. Chuck hits all the highlights with solid overview reinforced by several unique features found nowhere else. Don't miss it!"

— DR. ED HINDSON
Liberty University, VA

"Chuck's love for the Scriptures is contagious! His wealth of biblical knowledge and keen insight into God's Word is attractively presented in his new book, *Learn the Bible in 24 Hours*. Those who read it will gain a greater understanding of God's glorious attributes and man's unique opportunity to live a victorious life in Christ Jesus."

— MIKE GENDRON
Author and Speaker

"Thank you for the copy of your new book, *Learn the Bible in 24 Hours*. What a brilliant idea. I love it. I was able to glance through the book immediately and know I am going to benefit by reading it through."

— WOODROW KROLL
Back to the Bible Ministry

DR. CHUCK MISSLER

LEARN THE BIBLE
in
24
HOURS ®

THOMAS NELSON
Since 1798

NASHVILLE   DALLAS   MEXICO CITY   RIO DE JANEIRO

Published in Nashville, Tennessee, by Thomas Nelson. Thomas Nelson is a registered trademark of Thomas Nelson, Inc.

Thomas Nelson, Inc., titles may be purchased in bulk for educational, business, fund-raising, or sales promotional use. For information, please e-mail SpecialMarkets@ThomasNelson.com.

Scripture quotations are from THE KING JAMES VERSION.

ISBN 978-1-4185-4918-3 (TP)

Library of Congress Cataloging-in-Publication Data

Missler, Chuck.
    Learn the Bible in 24 hours / Chuck Missler.
      p. cm.
    Includes bibliographical references.
    ISBN 978-0-7852-6429-3 (pbk.)
     1. Bible—Introductions. 2. Bible—Study and teaching. I. Title: Learn the Bible in twenty-four hours.
  II. Title.
BS475.3 .M57 2002   2002011415
220.6'1—dc21

Printed in the United States of America

15 16 17 18 RRD 18 17 16 15 14 13

This book is dedicated to Pastor Charles Schmitz, Pastor Theodore B. Hax, and William E. Biggs, who instilled my early passion for the Holy Scripture, and to Pastor Chuck Smith, Walter Martin, and Hal Lindsey, who, as my personal mentors, patiently endured my growing pains.

Contents

INTRODUCTION

WE ARE ABOUT TO EMBARK on the ultimate literary adventure. And we hope that this excursion will result in practical, strategic awareness of the entire Bible—a perspective from which you can navigate your own personal adventure that will enrich a lifetime and even more. It's not just a fascinating read; it's a participation that will determine your eternal destiny.

We're going to reach far beyond the earth's prehistory, behind the mists of legend and folklore to discover the greatest drama of all literature. We'll encounter the greatest evil—betrayals, revenge, deceptions, and the ultimate Prince of Darkness. We'll also encounter the greatest good, the highest achievements, the greatest courage and sacrifice; in fact, the ultimate sacrifice—the Kinsman Redeemer of all mankind!

We'll find ourselves in a courtship between a sovereign God and His rebellious offspring. We'll explore the ultimate ironies of all literature—hidden surprises on every page. We'll experience the rise of the great empires, as well as their fall, through dreams and visions and secret encrypted messages.

We'll discover letters written to great leaders from extraterrestrial sources, outlining their careers and achievements in advance, giving them instructions on how to proceed. We'll thrill to the hero conquering enemies against impossible odds, betrayals of thrones and retributions, vendettas and conspiracies extending to many generations.

We'll also probe the greatest mysteries ever to confront mankind—the nature of time, the issue of predestination versus free will. We'll explore the purity of God and the frustrations of man, the search for good and the reign of evil; the nature of evil—where it comes from and why.

We'll discover that this ancient record anticipates the most modern discoveries of particle physics and cosmology, hyperspace and time travel. We'll discover that we are part of a virtual reality that is transcended by a larger one, that both benevolent and malevolent beings intervene in our lives from other dimensions.

We'll stand in awe of the biography of a Superman: His origin, His mission, His manifest destiny, His understated powers, and His betrayal by which He will accomplish His "Mission Impossible"—the Creator Himself entering His creation to repair the damage introduced by a dark intruder who previously ruled planet Earth.

We'll also discover that we're participants in a cosmic war. And we'll discover that we're in possession of an integrated series of messages from an extraterrestrial source that describes the origin, career, and destiny of the superbeings behind the scenes of our physical universe and the political events we see.

REALITY IS NOT WHAT IT USED TO BE

The field of particle physics has totally altered our conceptions of reality. Scientists now tell us that the universe is a digital simulation within a much larger reality and consists of at least ten dimensions. Some investigators believe that much of what we call "paranormal phenomena" is simply transdimensional episodes within that larger reality. But we will see that all of this has been anticipated by the message of the Bible. We'll discover that each of us is both a pawn and a prize in a cosmic warfare—a hyper-dimensional conflict between good and evil that will come to a climax soon. In fact, we believe we are being plunged into a time of conflict unlike any other. It's the ultimate adventure, involving each of us in the interval between the miracle of our origin and the mystery of our destiny.

What are the secrets that have created empires and tumbled thrones? Has an intergalactic warfare caused the scars on the planets in our solar system? Is it still going on? If God is good and created us, where did evil come from? Are demons simply super-hackers attempting to penetrate the gateways of the software we call *soul* and *spirit*? Where did we come from and why are we here? If we are objects of design, what is the purpose of it all? Where are we headed?

> *It is impossible to rightly govern the world without God and the Bible.*
>
> —GEORGE WASHINGTON

There is only one Book on earth, only one Book in the history of mankind that can answer those cosmic questions and demonstrate its transcendence over time and space. It has the audacity to hang its credibility and authenticity on its record of recording history before it happens. Only one Book holds the key to your eternal destiny: the ultimate love story, written in blood on a wooden cross erected in Judea some two thousand years ago.

What an ambitious project—going through the entire Bible in twenty-four hours! Of course, this brief series will not exhaust the inexhaustible. But we can learn the Bible sufficiently to navigate among its many adventures and the many discoveries it contains. If this book is successful, it should ignite in each of us a passion—perhaps an obsession—that will inflame a lifetime of adventure, excitement, insight, and satisfaction not available through any other means. But you are the deciding factor; you are going to determine the end of the story—on the precipice of cosmic doom, or on the threshold of eternity.

> *I believe the Bible is the best gift God has ever given to man. All the good from the Savior of the world is communicated to us through this book.*
>
> —ABRAHAM LINCOLN

Approaching the "Hours"

You will probably find that you will be able to read each "Hour" in less than sixty minutes. We suggest that you use any additional time reviewing the endnotes provided and exploring the relevant texts directly. There is no substitute for plunging into the Bible itself. The more you learn, the more each segment of the text will become clearer. You will find that even the simplest texts will prove inexhaustible in their yield of insights. And that's what you would expect from the Word of God Himself.

Enjoy your journey to the most fantastic adventure imaginable.

The poet Henry Van Dyke wrote:

> Born in the East and clothed in Oriental form and imagery,
> the Bible walks the ways of the world with familiar feet
> and enters land after land to find its own everywhere.

It has learned to speak in hundreds of languages to the heart of man. Children listen to
   its stories with wonder and delight,

and wise men ponder them as parables of life.

The wicked and the proud tremble at its warnings,

but to the wounded and penitent it has a mother's voice.

It has woven itself into our dearest dreams;

so that Love, Friendship, Sympathy, Devotion, Memory, Hope,

put on the beautiful garments of its treasured speech.

No man is poor or desolate who has this treasure for his own.

When the landscape darkens,

and the trembling pilgrim comes to the Valley of the Shadow,

he is not afraid to enter;

he takes the rod and staff of Scripture in his hand;

he says to friend and comrade, "Goodbye; We Shall Meet Again"; and, comforted by
   that support, he goes toward the lonely pass

as one who walks through darkness into light.

Hour 1

AN OVERVIEW OF THE BIBLE

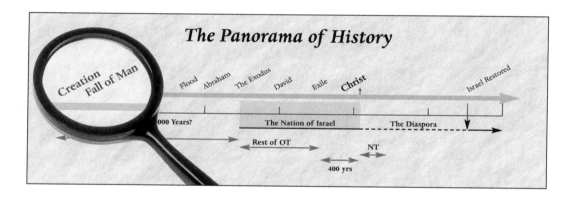

TO BEGIN OUR LIFELONG study adventure, we will need a solid foundation. Actually, our exploration will build on three foundations. First, although the Bible consists of sixty-six separate books penned by over forty authors over a period of several thousand years, it is an integrated message system. Every passage, every word, every number, and every place name is there for a specific reason. A skillful design pervades the whole.

The second foundation is that this message system is from outside our dimensions of space and time. It is literally of *extraterrestrial* origin.

Third, every word and every phrase of the Bible turns around a central theme. The Old Testament theme is the account of a nation—its origin, destiny, ups and downs, and its history yet to unfold. The New Testament is the account of a man, the Creator of the universe whose appearance is the central event of all history.

The Timeline of History

A timeline through Biblical history would start at creation and the fall of man and would span approximately six thousand years. The progress of major events on the line would be the flood, then the call of Abraham, then the exodus from Egypt, and the birth of the nation, Israel. Following these events are the dynasty of David and then Solomon's kingdom after David's death.

A civil war broke out after Solomon's death and the nation split in two. The Northern Kingdom was eventually destroyed by the Assyrians, and the Southern Kingdom went into exile for seventy years—a very important watershed in Israel's history which will be key to many of the things we consider.

An interesting fact about the book of Genesis is that it covers the creation up to, but not including, the Exodus, a period of about twenty-five hundred years. The rest of the Old Testament covers a small fraction of that—from the exodus to just beyond the exile and the return.

After the events of the Old Testament, there was a four hundred year period called "the silent years." No prophet's voice was heard. God appeared to be silent until He sent His messenger, John the Baptist, who ushered in the New Testament period. A fascinating contrast is that the Old Testament was compiled over several thousand years; all the New Testament was compiled and published within one lifetime.

The central theme in the entire panorama is the advent of Jesus Christ who came, ministered, and went to the Cross. Then, after the New Testament period, came the Diaspora when Israel was scattered all over the world. Finally, miraculously, just as predicted in the Bible, on May 14, 1948, Israel was again restored. For centuries scholars debated whether prophesies in the Old Testament and the New were literal or symbolic (would Israel ever be regathered?). Those debates should have ended in 1948 when Israel became a nation again.

LAYING THE GROUNDWORK: AN OLD TESTAMENT OVERVIEW

The Old Testament consists of thirty-nine books. The most venerated portion of the Old Testament is the *Torah*, the five books of Moses known also by the Greek word, *Pentateuch*. The Torah consists of five books:

1. **Genesis** is the book of beginnings—the word itself means "the beginnings."
2. **Exodus** follows, and it describes the birth of the nation.
3. **Leviticus** details the laws of that nation.
4. **Numbers** tracks the wanderings in the wilderness—the forty years before the new nation was able to enter the land that God had set aside for them.
5. **Deuteronomy** is a review of the laws; it is also the book that Jesus quotes from the most.

The Torah is pivotal to everything we will be dealing with.

The Torah is followed by twelve historical books which are divided by a major event in Israel's history—the Babylonian captivity. Joshua to 2 Chronicles are pre-exile (or pre-Babylonian captivity); Ezra, Nehemiah, and Esther are post-exile.

6. **Joshua** succeeded Moses and conquered Canaan.
7. Then came the three hundred years known as the period of the **Judges.**
8. During this time a fascinating little four-chapter book called **Ruth** was written. Ruth is one of the most important books in the Old Testament. You won't understand the book of Revelation unless you understand the book of Ruth.

After the Judges are the records of the kingdom itself:

9. **1 Samuel**—the birth of the kingdom.
10. **2 Samuel**—the reign of King David.
11. **1 Kings**—the kingdom divided after David dies, the death of Solomon and the civil war which follows, dividing the kingdom permanently.

3

12. **2 Kings**—the history of the divided kingdom.

13. **1 Chronicles**—the reign of David.

14. **2 Chronicles**—the history of the southern kingdom.

The post-exile history books include:

15. **Ezra**—the return from the Babylonian captivity.

16. **Nehemiah**—the rebuilding of the city of Jerusalem.

17. **Esther**—the escape from extermination under the Persian Empire.

The five books of poetry—Job, Psalms, Proverbs, Ecclesiastes, Song of Songs—are the poetry, hymns, and wisdom of the nation.

18. **Job**—"peaking behind the curtain."

19. The book of **Psalms** (which is actually five books) is the hymnbook of the nation, which not only contains beautiful hymns and praise but includes some incredible prophesies.

20. **Proverbs** contains, but is not limited to, the Wisdom of Solomon.

21. **Ecclesiastes,** also written by Solomon, talks of the vanity of life.

22. **Song of Songs** is a mystical book about wedded love and other topics.

Next in line are the five Major Prophets:

23. **Isaiah** is the Messianic prophet.

24. **Jeremiah** deals primarily with the desolation of Jerusalem.

25. **Lamentations** is Jeremiah's dirge over the loss of Jerusalem. These three books are mostly pre-exile, though Lamentations splits the pre- and the post-exile Major Prophets.

26. **Ezekiel** is in captivity, but in his book he talks about the rebuilding of the Temple and the restoration of Israel when they return to the land. He also describes what appears to be a nuclear war—when Israel is invaded from the north (this is yet to happen).

27. **Daniel's** theme is "the times of the Gentiles." Daniel is unique in portraying an overview of all Gentile history—from Babylon until the day that God sets up His own kingdom on earth.

The Major Prophets are followed by twelve Minor Prophets: Hosea, Joel, Amos, Obadiah, Jonah, Micah, Nahum, Habakkuk, Zephaniah. The last three of the twelve—Haggai, Zechariah, and Malachi—prophesied after the return from Babylon.

28. **Hosea** focuses on the apostasy of the Northern Kingdom (many of the situations are similar to modern-day America).

29. **Joel** speaks of "the day of the Lord," a climax which is also in the future.

30. **Amos** speaks of the ultimate rule of the dynasty of David on the planet earth.

31. **Obadiah** focuses on the destruction of Edom.

32. **Jonah** is a warning to Nineveh, capital of the pagan world empire at the time.

33. **Micah** is best known for prophesying that Bethlehem would be the birthplace of the Messiah.

34. **Nahum** describes the destruction of Nineveh. Like Jonah, Nahum was sent to Nineveh, but this time they didn't repent.

35. **Habakkuk** contains, among other things, the very interesting phrase "the just shall live by faith," which becomes the cornerstone of three New Testament epistles.

36. **Zephaniah** prophesies many things, one being that when Israel is restored they will again speak Hebrew, and since May 14, 1948, they have.

37. **Haggai** predicts the rebuilding of the Temple.

38. **Zechariah** has a number of fascinating prophecies about the Second Coming of Christ.

39. **Malachi** has a final message to a disobedient people, and he sets the stage for John the Baptist who comes in the spirit and power of Elijah.

That's the Old Testament. The key idea is of a single, integrated design. You'll find that the more you know about these books, the more inseparable they are. As you begin to develop respect for the integrity of the whole, you'll be amazed at how any confusion, the many seeming paradoxes, and quibbles evaporate.

LAYING THE GROUNDWORK:
A NEW TESTAMENT OVERVIEW

The New Testament consists of twenty-seven books. The first five are historical books—the four Gospels and the book of Acts. Twenty-one interpretive letters called the Epistles are next. The New Testament ends with the climactic book, the book of Revelation. Thirteen epistles were written by the Apostle Paul and eight were written by and to Hebrew Christians.

The four Gospels—Matthew, Mark, Luke and John—are parallel yet distinctive.

1. **Matthew** presents Jesus Christ as the Lion of the tribe of Judah.

2. **Mark** presents Jesus Christ as the Suffering Servant.

3. **Luke** presents Jesus Christ as the Son of Man.

4. **John** presents Jesus Christ as the Son of God.

Each of the four Gospels presents a particular perspective—they overlap in many ways yet they each have distinctive vocabularies, emphases, and genealogical perspectives. Each is very skillfully designed to present a particular aspect.

5. **Acts** describes the formation of the church in the first thirty years. The book of Acts could really be called "The Acts of the Holy Spirit."

The Pauline Epistles are interpretive. They explain the relevance of what has gone before—including both the Old and New Testament. Romans, 1 and 2 Corinthians, Galatians, Ephesians, Philippians, Colossians, and 1 and 2 Thessalonians are one group, each book was written to churches with the intention that they would be circulated. Paul also wrote four letters to pastors called the Pastoral Epistles: 1 and 2 Timothy, Titus and Philemon.

6. **Romans,** called by some the "Gospel According to Paul," is the definitive statement of Christian doctrine in the New Testament; it is comprehensive, well-organized, and one of the most profound books in the New Testament.

7–8. **1 Corinthians** and **2 Corinthians** are letters Paul wrote to help establish order in the church.

9. **Galatians** was probably the key book in the Reformation, distinguishing between law and grace—it is by grace that we are saved, not by keeping the law.

10. **Ephesians** could be considered the high ground of the New Testament. It could be called "The Church in the Heavenlies."

11. **Philippians** is "joy through suffering."

12. **Colossians** teaches that Christ is pre-eminent above all things.

13. **First Thessalonians** declares the mystery of what we call the "Rapture."

14. **Second Thessalonians** clarifies some confusion about the Rapture. Both letters focus on Second Coming aspects; they are end-times epistles.

15–17. **First Timothy, Second Timothy,** and **Titus** give pastoral advice.

18. **Philemon,** though a short letter, is a model of intercession on behalf of a runaway slave. There are many lessons in this one-chapter book.

These are followed by eight Jewish epistles: Hebrews; James; two by Peter; three by John; and one by Jude.

19. **Hebrews** amplifies the New Covenant. The authorship of Hebrews has been a question among many scholars. Many people believe Hebrews was written by Paul; others notice that it seems deliberately anonymous. One clue may be Habakkuk 2:4: "the just shall live by faith." Romans quotes from this passage and specifically deals with justification: Who are "the just"? How do you become just before God? Galatians discusses how the just "shall live," a call out of religious externalism. Hebrews tells us the just shall live "by faith." Habakkuk 2:4 is the cornerstone of each of these three epistles, which implies that Paul really was the writer of Hebrews. Even more remarkable is how the Holy Spirit guided the structure of these epistles.

20. **James** talks about faith demonstrated.

21. **First Peter** talks about the persecuted church.

22. **Second Peter** talks about the coming apostasy and the end times.

23. **First John** is the classic epistle on love.

24. **Second John** warns about false teachers.

25. **3 John** speaks on the preparation of helpers.

26. **Jude,** like 2 Peter, discusses the apostasy, except Jude has some Old Testament roots that are fascinating in their own right.

The final book and, in fact, the climactic book of the entire Bible, is the book of Revelation.

27. **Revelation** is more than just the close of the Bible; it is the consummation of all things. Everything that started in Genesis finds its end in the book of Revelation. It is the only book in the Bible that has the audacity to pronounce a special blessing on the reader. The book's 404 verses contain over eight hundred allusions from the Old Testament. So if the book seems strange to our understanding, it's because we haven't done our homework in the Old Testament. It's in code, but every code is unraveled for you somewhere else in Scripture, and that's the challenge of this incredible Book.

The New Testament is in the Old Testament concealed; the Old Testament is in the New Testament revealed.

LET THE ADVENTURE BEGIN!

It is absolutely astonishing how many controversies about the Bible evaporate once you recognize two things: the Bible is designed as a whole, not just in broad terms but down to the very letter, and time is not linear and absolute but a physical property that varies with mass, acceleration, and gravity.

God has more than simply "lots of time" since He is outside the dimensionality of time altogether! In the next chapter, we'll talk about the nature of time, the controversy about the speed of light, the concept of entropy and how all these impact the Scripture. You may be surprised to discover that some of the world's greatest scientists of the past and today take the Biblical record very seriously. Sir Isaac Newton, one of the greatest scientists who ever lived, wrote over a million words of commentary on Daniel and Revelation. Contemporary scientists, nuclear physicists, and others have written extensively about the first two chapters of Genesis in terms of what we know today about particle physics.

Many Christians are apologetic about the Scripture because they haven't connected the dots, a situation we will attempt to remedy on this Grand Adventure.

Hour 2

GENESIS 1:1–3
THE BEGINNING OF BEGINNINGS

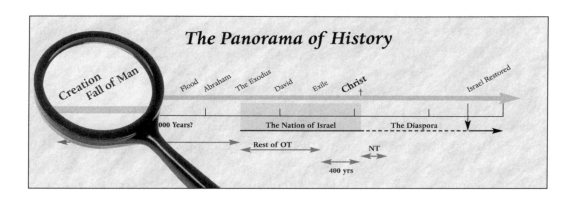

GENESIS HAS FIFTY CHAPTERS. The first two chapters deal with creation. Genesis 3 is the seed plot of the Bible and records the Fall of Man. Chapter 4 is the story of Cain and Abel, the first murder. Genesis 5 contains the genealogy of Noah, which includes some interesting surprises. Genesis 6–9 record the Flood of Noah, and Genesis 10–11, the Tower of Babel. The first eleven chapters of Genesis constitute prehistory, before the call of Abraham. Chapters 12–20 record the call and service of Abraham. Chapters 21–26 tell of his son Isaac. Chapters 27–36 record the story of Isaac's son, Jacob, and the Twelve Tribes. Chapters 37–50 contain the incredible saga of Joseph.

THE BEGINNING OF ALL THINGS

All the major doctrines in the Bible have their roots in the book of Genesis: sovereign election, salvation, justification by faith, the believer's security, separation, disciplinary chastisement, the Rapture of the Church, divine incarnation, death and resurrection, the priesthoods—both the Aaronic priesthood and the Melchizadek priesthood—the antichrist, the Palestinian Covenant, and many more.

All the false philosophies are answered in the book of Genesis. Atheism claims there is no God; Genesis asserts that all Creation is by God. Pantheism says that God is everything; Genesis teaches that God is transcendent and distinguishable from His creation. Polytheism claims there are many gods; Genesis emphasizes the one God. Materialism claims the universe is eternal; Genesis shows that even matter has a beginning. Humanism asserts that man determines the ultimate reality; Genesis says God does. Evolutionism says that everything evolved gradually; Genesis asserts that God created all things. Uniformitarianism claims that everything is moving along as it always has; Genesis shows God's interventions in history.

IN THE BEGINNING

Genesis, chapter 1, opens, "In the beginning, God created the heaven and the earth." If you embrace and accept that verse, it will unlock every other problem in the rest of Scripture.

Verse 2 continues, "And the earth was without form, and void; and darkness was upon the face of the deep. And the Spirit of God moved upon the face of the waters. And God said, Let there be light: and there was light. And God saw the light, that it was good: and God divided the light from the darkness. And God called the light Day, and the darkness He called Night. And the evening and the morning were the first day."

These opening verses immediately confront us with some fundamental questions: Is the universe really fifteen billion years old? Was it created in just six days? What do we mean by "six days"? Does the Scripture mean twenty-four-hour days? Since the stars are so far away, is it possible that God just created the light already in transit? Some say that the aging factors were built into the initial creation. Others say if that's the case, God would be a liar (He made the universe look old when it's not). Were these first days of Genesis geologic eras?

CLUES FROM THE NATURE OF TIME

You and I take for granted that time is linear and absolute—something starts and ends. We assume eternity is like a line that is infinitely long, starting at infinity on the left and going to infinity on the right. When we think of God, we probably envision someone who has lots of time. This is colorful and poetic, but it's bad physics.

Albert Einstein formulated his Theory of Relativity in 1905. He theorized that length, mass, velocity and time are relative to the velocity of the observer. It was very radical insight. Among other things, his theory recognizes that there is no distinction between time and space and that we live in a four-dimensional continuum—three spatial dimensions and time.

There is an atomic clock at the National Bureau of Standards in Boulder, Colorado, and an identical one at the Royal Observatory in Greenwich, England. They are accurate to within one second in a million years. But each year they differ by about five microseconds (five millionths of a second). The one in Colorado ticks five microseconds per year faster than the one in Greenwich. Which one is correct? They *both* are. The one in Colorado is 5,400 feet above sea level; the one in Greenwich is 80 feet above sea level. The clocks are not wrong; time itself differs due to the difference in gravitational attraction.

Physics textbooks will often use the hypothetical example of twin brothers, one of which is sent to our nearest star, Alpha Centauri, as an astronaut. The star is four and a half light years away. Assuming that he is sent at fifty percent of the speed of light, his round trip would take eighteen years. However, when he returns, he would be two years and five months younger than his twin brother.

You may be stunned to realize that time is a *physical* property. But we need to realize that we live in more than three dimensions. We all experience a three-dimensional geometry (length, width, height) and this strange dimension we call time. But God is not subject to

You may be stunned to realize that time is a physical property. But we need to realize that we live in more than three dimensions.

gravity. He is not limited to the constraints of mass, acceleration, or gravity. So God is not somebody who "has lots of time;" He is someone who is *outside* the physical constraints of time itself. And He uses that very attribute to authenticate His Word.

My favorite Einstein quote is, "People like us, who believe in physics, know that the distinction between the past, the present, and future is only a stubbornly persistent illusion." This is exactly what Isaiah says in Isaiah 57:15: "For thus saith the high and lofty One that inhabiteth eternity . . . " He is not in our time domain—He is outside our time altogether.

The Geometry of Eternity

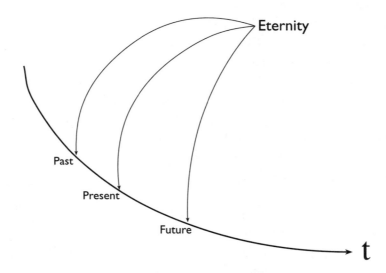

Imagine a line drawn to represent three-dimensional space. We're right in the middle called the present, behind us is the past, and a little ahead of us is the future. For us, life is a *sequence* of events since we are within that time line. But someone who is outside our linear time could see the past, present, and the future simultaneously. For instance, if you were sitting on a curb watching a parade, you would experience each event as it happened to go by. But someone outside of the parade's plane of existence, say in a helicopter above the parade, could see the beginning, the middle, and the end simultaneously.

This is the attribute that God exploits to authenticate His message. If God has the ability to create us in the first place, He certainly has the ability to get a message to us. But how does He authenticate it? How does He let us know that the message we have is really from Him, and not some kind of contrivance or fraud, or simply an ancient tradition? One way

The Velocity of Light

Light is the most mysterious fundamental in the entire field of physics. Until the 17th century, Kepler, Descartes, and others believed that light did not travel but was instantaneous. In 1677, Olaf Roemer, a Danish astronomer, measured the elapsed time between eclipses of Jupiter with its moons in such a way that he could detect the speed of light in finite terms. He published the idea that light traveled about 300,000 meters/second; he was laughed at for fifty years. Then in 1729, James Bradley, an Englishman, reconfirmed Roemer's work and the physics community finally admitted that light was not instantaneous—it has a finite speed. Over the last three hundred years, the speed of light has been measured 164 times by sixteen different methods. Roemer thought that the speed of light was 308,600 kilometers per second (km/sec).

In 1875 at Harvard, using the same method more precisely, scientists found the mean to be slightly smaller. In 1983, the National Bureau of Standards used laser techniques and pinned it down to 299,792.4586 +/-.00003 km/sec. In examining the data from each of these measurements, Barry Setterfield, a physicist, and Trevor Norman, a mathematician, noticed that the speed of light seems to be getting slower. There have been other confirmations. In 1927, a French astronomical journal based results on measurements taken over seventy-five years; Troitskii at the Radio Physical Research Institute in Gorky, Russia, 1987 (independent of Setterfield), published papers along the same lines; Tom Van Flandern, of the U.S. Naval Observatory, also noticed something (1981)—that the atomic clocks are beginning to slow down relative to orbital clocks.

There have been more recent publications where scientists are finally, rather reluctantly, beginning to recognize that the speed of light is not a constant as had been previously assumed.

is to demonstrate that the origin of His message is from outside time itself. Isaiah alludes to this in several places. In chapter forty-six, verse ten, he speaks of God: "Declaring the end from the beginning, and from ancient times, the things that are not yet done." The Bible is the only book that hangs its entire credibility on its ability to write history in advance, without error.

DAY ONE OF CREATION

"In the beginning, God created the heaven and the earth." Let's take a closer look at that. In Hebrew the words are, *"Beresheet bara Elohim, et ha-Shamayim et ha-Eretz."* The word, Barasheet, is the name of the book—Genesis. *Bara* is a verb meaning to create out of nothing—only God can do that.

Scientists now know that the universe is finite and that it had a beginning. The Big Bang theory is their attempt to explain a beginning without acknowledging a creator. It has many different varieties. The original Big Bang theory was Einstein's Steady State Model, and he later admitted it was his biggest mistake. The Hesitation Model was refuted in the Sixties. Entropy laws and the lack of adequate mass refuted the Oscillation Model. The Inflation Model requires anti-gravity forces that have never been observed. These are all variations of what we would collectively call the Big Bang. They're all in major trouble for various reasons.

Two other important verbs are *asa,* which means "to make, fashion or fabricate," and *yatsa,* "to form." Isaiah 43:7 uses all three of these, but *bara* is used very rarely. "Creating out of nothing" is quite distinct from "forming" or "shaping." Creating the clay is quite different than simply sculpting it.

The third word, *Elohim,* is one of the several names of God; it's interesting because it is a *plural* noun. Certain Hebrew nouns end with *im,* indicating a plural (*cherub* and *cherubim,* for example). *Elohim* is a plural noun, but even within the rigors of the Hebrew language, it's used as if it's singular. In the third word of the Bible is our first hint of the Trinity.

Genesis 1:2 says, "The earth was without form, and void; and darkness was on the face of the deep. And the spirit of God moved upon the face of the waters." Sounds straightforward enough, right? But there's a little problem tucked away in this verse. In 1814, Thomas Chalmers noticed something interesting in the term for "without form and void," *tohu v'bohu.* Isaiah 45:18 reads, "For thus saith the LORD that created the heavens; God himself that formed the earth and made it; he hath established it, he created it not in vain, he formed it to be inhabited: I am the LORD; and there is none else." This verse seems to indicate that the earth was not originally created "without form and void" but subsequently *became* that way. In fact, the verb in that sentence translated "was"—*haya*—means "became;" it is a transitive verb implying action. Lot's wife became *(haya)* a pillar of salt—same verb.

So verse 2 could be translated, "But the earth became without form and void." The word for "but" here is an adversative in both the Septuagint (ancient Greek translation) and the Vulgate (Latin). One suggestion is that from this hint in verse 2, possibly there is a gap, an interval of time (maybe billions of years), between verses 1 and 2. Some people dismiss this "Gap Theory," but it could be a hint of a precedent catastrophe, possibly associated with the rebellion of Satan prior to the events of chapter 3.

Satan was originally the number one angel, in charge of everything. Through pride, he rebelled and took one third of the angels with him. His seat was not in heaven; it was on the earth. The earth was his domain. The "Gap Theory" suggests that God judged the earth

Hubble's Law

The reason we think the universe has been expanding is because of Hubble's Law. Edwin Hubble postulated that the more a star's color spectrum shifted to red, the further away it was. Because astronomers assume that the red shift is very similar to the Doppler Effect (when an ambulance is coming at you, the pitch of the siren seems to be going up, when going away, it seems to be going down), the theory suggests that the universe is expanding.

Two men—Halton Arp in Germany and William Tifft at the University of Arizona—have discovered some interesting facts about red shifts in the last couple of decades. They've discovered that some shifts don't shift to the red, they shift to the blue. That would mean stars are not getting further away, but coming closer to us. William Tifft, particularly, has discovered something very intriguing: the shift of the red is always in discreet steps. He doesn't postulate any conclusions, but this has profound implications. This may be evidence of a change in the very properties of space itself and a fundamental atomic effect rather than a recessional velocity effect.

and it became without form and void—ruined and uninhabitable. Verse 2 and forward may describe a re-creation, a reconstruction of the earth after eons of helplessness where Satan couldn't repair his mess. "And the Spirit of God moved on the face of the waters"—and rather than wipe out the earth, God chose to undertake a plan of redemption.

Although not a certainty or a doctrine, the Gap Theory is something to consider.

Verse 3: "And God said, Let there be light: and there was light. (v. 4) And God saw the light, that it was good: and God divided the light from the darkness. (v. 5) And God called the light Day, and the darkness he called Night. And the evening and the morning were the first day."

The word for "darkness" is *choshek,* and it's suggestive of the existence of black holes—things that are dark and have mass, so much mass that light cannot escape. The two words to pay attention to are *erev* and *boker.* The word *erev* originally suggested chaos or disorder. As the sun went down and the night fell, things were confusing and dark, so *erev* also came to mean "evening." The other is *boker,* which suggests "orderly or discernible." As morning twilight approaches, as the sun starts to come up, you can begin to discern things and things start to take order. So the root word that meant "orderly or discernible" also becomes the word for "morning."

"And the evening and the morning were the first day" is a very important phrase. The phrase *yom echad,* which is "day one," is an absolute phrase, not a relative one as all the subsequent references are. All the rest of the days (second day, third day, etc.) are relative to this first day. It's Day One; a real anchor point is suggested in the grammar.

THE SECOND DAY

The second day involves the stretching of space. We usually think of space as being empty, but it isn't. Genesis 1:7-8: "And God made the firmament, and divided the waters which were under the firmament from the waters which were above the firmament: and it was so. And God called the firmament Heaven. And the evening and the morning were the second day."

The word "firmament" is a problem. What is the firmament? Nobody knows. What are the waters? Nobody knows. In Hebrew, *raqia* (for "the firmament") means an extended surface, a *solid* expanse, and the opposite of empty space. The Greek word, *stereoma,* means firmness; from this comes the Latin, *firmamentum,* which means three-dimensional solidity or firmness. Is this more than a metaphor?

Job 9:8 speaks of "God who alone stretches out the heavens"; Psalm 104, "stretching out the heaven like a tent curtain"; Isaiah 40:22, "stretches out the heavens like a curtain and spreads them out like a tent to dwell in"; Jeremiah 10:12, "He has stretched out the heavens"; Zechariah 12:1, "the Lord who stretches the heavens," and another dozen verses which speak of God stretching the heavens.

Another method might be *unraveling* the 3-dimensional object into 2 dimensions:

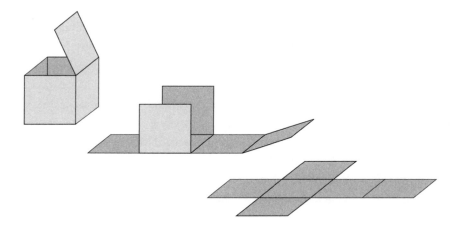

Space is not simply an empty vacuum. Isaiah 64:1 says it can be torn; Psalm 102 says it can be worn out like a garment; Hebrews 12:26, Haggai 2:6, and Isaiah 13:13 say it can be shaken; in 2 Peter 3:12, it can be "burnt up"; in Revelation 6:14, "it split apart like a scroll." Hebrews 1:12 says it can be "rolled up like a mantle." What is meant by "rolled up"? Let's think that through: In order for space to be rolled up, there must be some dimension in which it's *thin*. (If it's not thin, you can't roll it up.) Also, if it can be rolled up, it can be bent. If it can be bent, there must be some *direction* toward which it can be bent. The whole idea of being rolled up implies thinness and *an additional dimension* in which to roll it up, which begins to indicate that space has more than three dimensions, which we now know today from particle physics.

But the Scripture has said all along that we have additional, spacial dimensions. Nachmonides, a Hebrew sage of the twelfth century, concluded from studying Genesis, chapter 1, that the universe has ten dimensions. Four of those are directly "knowable" and six of them are "not knowable" (in his vocabulary). Particle physicists in the 21st century now believe that the universe has ten dimensions but only four of them are directly measurable.

THIRD THROUGH SIX DAYS

Land and vegetation appear on the third day. Genesis 2:9 "Out of the ground made [not "created"] the LORD God to grow every tree that is pleasant to the sight, and good for food; the tree of life also in the midst of the garden, and the tree of knowledge of good and evil." The verses from Genesis 1:29 to Genesis 2:9 are *encrypted*: behind those verses are the names of the twenty-five trees that show up in the Bible. Some think that this is simply a statistical accident of the alphabet, but I find that hard to accept. The fact that certain words may occur randomly with equidistant letter sequencing can occur in any large corpus of text, but for them to cluster with relevance to the plain text above implies a deliberate design.

On the fourth day, the sun, moon, and stars become visible. "God said, Let there be lights in the firmament of the heaven . . . and let them be for lights in the firmament . . . and God made two great lights; the greater light to rule the day, and the lesser light to rule the night . . . And God set them in the firmament of the heaven to give light upon the earth" (Genesis 1:14–17).

Sea creatures and birds were created on the fifth day (Genesis 1:20–23); land animals and man on the sixth day (Genesis 1:20–31). This brings up the issue of fossils. Paleontology has a sordid history of frauds and deceit. In 120 years since Darwin, no one has found a fossil of a legitimate intermediate stage of any kind. The textbook examples of our supposed ancestors have all been discredited, some of them as deliberate frauds. The Heidelberg Man was built from a jawbone; the Nebraska Man (1922) was made from just one tooth that was later discovered to be part of an extinct pig; the Piltdown Man (1912) was made from the jawbone of a modern ape and was filed and treated with iron salts to make it look old. Neanderthal Man was found in the Neander valley near Dusseldorf. The International Congress of Zoology (1958) determined that it was just an old man suffering from arthritis. The Java Man (1922) was built by an 1891 skull cap and a femur; the teeth were from an orangutan. These well-documented frauds continue to be promoted in most school textbooks, however.

To summarize the creation:

Day 1: "Let light be"

Day 2: Stretching of space

Day 3: Land of vegetation

Day 4: Sun, moon, and stars

Day 5: Sea, animals, and birds

Day 6: Land animals and mankind

Day 7: The Sabbath Rest

ISSUES FROM SCIENCE

Microbiology. I encourage you to explore the advances in microbiology, which demonstrate that even the simplest cell is complex beyond our imagining. The advances in microbiology are finally dealing a deathblow to Darwinism. Information science has underscored the role of design in the creation. The Darwinists cannot explain the origin of life because they cannot explain the origin of information. In the beginning was information from an external source to make it all happen. Michael Behe, Philip Johnson, William Dembski, Steven Meyer, and others have turned the intellectual world upside-down by demonstrating that Darwinism is simply bad science.

Thermodynamics. The first law of thermodynamics is the conservation of matter and energy (you cannot create matter and energy). Conservation of matter and energy is all throughout the Scripture, starting on the seventh day when God ended His work. The works were finished from the foundation of the world according to Hebrews 4. In Nehemiah 9, "All the things that are therein, you preserve them all." The first law of thermodynamics is confirmed all through Scripture; we also know it as a law of science.

The second law of thermodynamics is called *entropy*, the "bondage to decay." It says that all thermodynamic processes are inefficient (whenever you transfer energy, you always lose a little). Entropy is sort of a synonym for randomness. Entropy is also in the Scripture: "They shall perish, grow old as a garment" (Psalm 103); "The earth will grow old like a garment" (Isaiah 51:6); "Heaven and earth will pass away" (Matthew 24:35). Romans 8:21 says "the creature itself also shall be delivered from the bondage of corruption into the glorious liberty of the children of God." That passage seems to indicate that when the creation is relieved from its present bondage, the entropy laws may be nullified. That's a very controversial idea, but a provocative one. Do you recognize the ostensible contradiction between these two fundamental laws of science?

Let's take a look at the week from an entropy point of view. We know that each day is defined by an *erev* and a *boker* (*erev* meaning evening and chaotic; *boker* meaning morning, or orderly and discernible); from disorder to order. Each day is another step of entropy reduction, or another introduction of design. But on the seventh day, there is no evening and morning. Exodus 20:11 says, "For in six days, the LORD made heaven and earth, the sea, and all that in them is, and rested the seventh day: wherefore the LORD blessed the sabbath day, and hallowed it." Some of the rabbis believe that it was at the end of the six days that God solidified the laws of physics.

THE FALL OF MAN

This leads us to the next primary cataclysm on the planet earth: the Fall of Man. From that point on, history changes. We don't know what Adam was like; the Psalms imply that he was clothed with light. We can't imagine what the world was like prior to the curse. But in Genesis 3, the seed plot of the entire Bible, we immediately encounter the Shining One, the *nachash,* who will become the Serpent.

Adam and Eve were targets of deception of this Super Being. It is instructive to note his methodology because it has not changed. His first step was to create doubt. He asked, "Yea, hath God said?" or, Did God really say that? He uses that today. Once he created the doubt, his next step was direct denial: "Ye shall not surely die." These are the basic ingredients of Satan's strategies, even today, to cause us to stumble and fall. The result of this deception was God's declaration of war against Satan. And in that declaration, I want you to notice the seed of the woman and the seed of the serpent.

Verse 14: "And the LORD God said unto the serpent, Because thou hast done this, thou art cursed above all cattle, and above every beast of the field; upon thy belly thou shalt go, and dust shalt thou eat all the days of thy life." Verse 15 is the key verse for many of us: "And I will put enmity between thee and the woman, and between thy seed and her seed; it shall bruise thy head and thou shalt bruise his heal. Unto the woman he said, I will greatly multiply thy sorrow and thy conception; in sorrow shalt thou bring forth children; and thy desire shall be to thy husband, and he shall rule over thee" (Genesis 3:15-16).

We can't begin to imagine the effects of God's declaration of war. He cursed the ground since from that point Adam would get his food from working the ground. Thorns were then the symbol of the curse. On the Cross, Jesus bore those thorns, which were literally thorns, but also were emblematic of bearing the curse for all of us.

Something else is suggested by some: entropy may have been introduced then. Physical laws may have substantially changed. We have no concept of the depth of change caused in chapter 3 and onward. Some suggest that the basic structure of the universe may have been fractured at that time, separating the physical and spiritual world, which had previously been unified. But that is what the Plan of Redemption is out to repair. The Redemption Plan of God involves more than just mankind. We'll see time and again the phrase, "I saw a new heaven and a new earth." Heaven also is going to be redeemed; earth is going to be redeemed.

The first act of religion is recorded in Genesis 3. Remember what Adam and Eve did when they first discovered they had sinned? Genesis 3:7: "And the eyes of them both were opened, and they knew that they were naked; and they sewed fig leaves together, and made themselves aprons." (The word for "aprons" actually means "covering" or "armor.") We think of them being just nude but it may mean much more than that: they were no longer sheathed in light. This has far more profound implications than we can know. The first thing they tried to do was to cover themselves, to cover over their sin by the work of their hands. "Religion" is always man's attempt to cover himself. But the central message of the Bible is that God Himself has taken care of it as only He can—if we but accept it.

God's Plan of Redemption was hinted at earlier in verse 21, "Unto Adam also and to his wife did the LORD God make coats of skins, and clothed them." It may sound like God simply gave them more durable garments, but once you read through the Torah, through the book of Leviticus, through all the Scriptures, and you look back, you realize what God was doing: He was teaching them that by the shedding of innocent blood on another tree, in another garden, they would be covered.

The Scarlet Thread began from the "seed of the woman" mentioned in Genesis 3, which became a title of the Messiah; it was a hint of the Virgin Birth. It continued in the call of Abraham, in chapter 12, where God began to set out a people for Himself, and through the call of Judah. Through the dynasty of David, God began to reveal through whom the seed of the woman would come; in the Virgin Birth in Bethlehem, which was predicted by Isaiah and fulfilled with Christ.

Something else is suggested by some: entropy may have been introduced then. Physical laws may have substantially changed.

The Scarlet Thread finally ended on another tree in another garden—when Jesus went to the Cross to redeem you and me, to pay the price for the first Adam's failure. In Jesus, also called the Last Adam, God Himself became man and fulfilled the requirements that we, as members of a fallen race, could not. Adam fell, and there's nothing we can do to repair that—the Law is there to show us our shortcomings, to let us recognize that we need a Redeemer.

The Good News is that He paid the price and He has a destiny for you. There's nothing we can do to earn it; we simply have to receive it as a free gift. To try to add to it is blasphemy, because He did it *all*.

GENESIS 4-11
FROM THE FALL OF MAN TO THE
TOWER OF BABEL

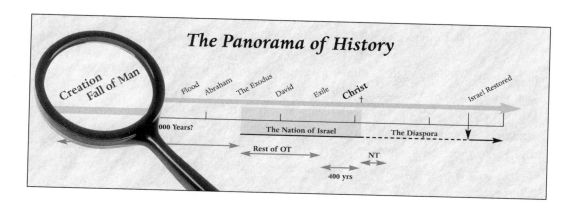

ADAM AND EVE WERE TOLD that from their offspring would come the Messiah. You can imagine that they thought their first baby would be that Messiah. Their first children were Cain and Abel.

The story of Cain and Abel deals with their offerings. Cain was a farmer and his offering was the fruit of his own labor, the fruit of the ground (as some would point out, the cursed ground). Abel's offering was a lamb; he was a shepherd. Many people presume that it was natural for a shepherd to give a lamb and for a farmer to give the fruit of his hands. But the fact that Abel was a shepherd is merely coincidental. Remember that before Genesis 3 closed, God had replaced the first couple's aprons of fig leaves with coats of skins. He was teaching them that by the shedding of innocent blood they would be covered.

Abel was giving the offering that God had specified; however, Cain was doing what he thought best and seemed reasonable. Cain's offering was rejected, probably because it did not meet the specifications ordained in Eden, namely, the offering of a lamb. (Some of the things which we associate with the Levitical offerings were codified under Moses but were originally ordained in Eden.) The concept of the shed blood of a lamb permeates all the Scriptures. Abraham recognized it long before Moses.[1] John the Baptist, when he first introduced Jesus Christ publicly in John, chapter 1, declared, "Behold the Lamb of God, which taketh away the sin of the world," (v. 29) which was an echo, not only of the Passover Lamb of the Exodus, but of the basic concept first introduced in Eden.

Because Cain could not handle his offering being rejected, he murdered Abel—the first murder. (It is actually the second murder since Satan, in effect, had effected the death of Adam and his progeny by deceiving them into sin.)

HIDDEN MESSAGES IN GENESIS 5

This section will begin with a riddle: Methuselah is well known as the oldest man in the Bible; yet he died before his father. How can that be?

Enoch, Methusaleh's father, didn't die; he was transferred directly to heaven without passing through death ("raptured," as some would say). It is interesting that the oldest prophecy in the Bible was uttered by Enoch before the flood of Noah and concerned the Second Coming of Christ. (It is not found here in Genesis but in the next-to-last book of the Bible, Jude.)

Another fact about Enoch is that at age sixty-five, something very special happened in his life. From that day on, for over three hundred years, he "walked with God." It seems that when his son was born, he was told that as long as his son was alive, the forthcoming judgment of the flood (the flood of Noah) would be withheld.

Enoch thus named his son using two Hebrew roots: *muth,* which means "his death," and *shelac,* which is a verb form that means "bring," or "sent forth." So the name Methuselah means, "his death shall bring." The flood of Noah did not come as a surprise; it had been predicted for four generations.

This significance behind the name Methuselah also hints that a message might be hidden behind these other names found in chapter 5. Adam had a son named Seth, Seth had a son named Enoch, and so on. The problem with Genesis 5 is that these proper names are not translated for the reader from their Hebrew meanings, so you have to unravel these by digging into the meaning of the Hebrew roots that make up the names.

- **Adam:** *(adomah)* "man"
- **Seth:** "appointed" (Genesis 4:25)
- **Enosh:** (from root *anash,* "to be incurable") "mortal," "frail," "miserable"
- **Kenan:** "sorrow," "dirge," "elegy"
- **Mahalal'el:** "the Blessed God"—*(mahalal)* "blessed"; *(El)* the name for God
- **Jared:** (from the verb *yaradh*) "shall come down"
- **Enoch:** "commencement" or "teaching"
- **Methusaleh:** "his death shall bring"—*muth,* a root that means "death"; *shalach* means "bring" or "send forth"
- **Lamech:** "despairing" (from which we get "lament" or "lamentation")
- **Noah:** (derived from *nacham*) "comfort" or "rest" (Genesis 5:29)

We now can look at the genealogy with more insight. The sequence—Adam—Seth—Enosh—Kenan—Mahalaleel—Jared—Enoch—Methusaleh—Lamech—Noah—reads, in English, "Man [is] appointed mortal sorrow; [but] the blessed God shall come down teaching [that His] death shall bring [the] despairing rest."

There are several profound lessons here. First, here is a summary of the New Testament Gospel tucked away in a genealogy in the Torah. This demonstrates something we will encounter throughout all the Scripture: *every detail is there by design.* It also tells us that God's plan of redemption was not a knee-jerk reaction to chapter 3. God had ordained it before the foundation of the world.

Yes, there are hidden messages in the Bible, and I don't mean just the equidistant letter sequences that have caused such controversies in recent years. There are dozens of other kinds of codes that don't require a computer to decipher; they are there if you know how to look. The Scripture is inexhaustible—you can never get to the bottom of its depth. And that's what you would expect from the Word of God.

Let me remind you: the New Testament is in the Old Testament concealed, and the Old Testament is in the New Testament revealed. Many things in the Old Testament do not seem to make sense until you illuminate them with the New Testament.

THE DAYS OF NOAH

In the New Testament, four disciples came to Jesus and asked Him about His Second Coming. He gave them a confidential briefing, and in that briefing Jesus made a very strange remark, saying, "As the days of Noah were, so shall the coming of the Son of man be" (Matthew 24:37). Most people do not fully understand the Flood of Noah because they have no grasp of the real problem it was sent to resolve.

There was much more to the Flood of Noah than simply a lot of water: the entire climate of the earth changed; our whole creation changed. There was a major discontinuity. We believe there was much more behind it than just the sinfulness of man.

EXTRATERRESTRIALS CORRUPT THE EARTH

Genesis 6:1-2 is a single sentence. It says, "And it came to pass, when men began to multiply on the face of the earth, and daughters were born unto them, that the sons of God saw the daughters of men that they were fair; and they took them wives of all which they chose."

The understanding of this passage hangs on the Hebrew term that has been translated "sons of God," *Bene HaElohim*. In the Old Testament this term refers exclusively to angels. Many similar terms are used for other things, but this specific term always refers to a direct creation of God, and it alludes to angels whom we find in Job chapters 1, 2, 38, and other places. (We also find it in the New Testament, specifically in Luke 20:36.)

Perhaps our most authoritative source is the Greek translation of the Old Testament from the third century B.C., known as the Septuagint. Greek is a very precise language, and the seventy scholars who produced the Septuagint (a fancy word for seventy) help us understand the Hebrew from which it was translated. The Septuagint clearly translates this term as "angels."

Another important phrase is "the daughters of men" (*benoth adam*). They are the daughters of Adam, not just the daughters of Cain.

Genesis 6:4 says, "There were *Nephilim* in the earth in those days; and also after that, when the sons of God came in unto the daughters of men, and they bare children to them, the same became mighty men which were of old, men of renown." The word "*Nephilim*" means "the fallen ones." It comes from a verb, "to fall away," "to cast down," or "desert." These were the hybrids that resulted from the mischief between the fallen angels and human women. Another unusual term, "the mighty ones," the *HaGibborim*, is mentioned here. That was translated into the Greek Septuagint as *gigantes,* which does not mean "giant" but "earth-born," from the Greek *gigas.* Although the word is translated into English as "giants"—and they did happen to be very large—it is not true to the original text. This has caused a lot of confusion.

Later, in chapter 6, we read, "These are the generations of Noah: Noah was a just man and perfect in his generations, and Noah walked with God" (verse 9). The word *perfect* is a term to mean "without blemish," "sound," "healthful," "without spot," or "unimpaired." It is always used with regard to physical defects. The Scripture is telling us that Noah was distinctive in that his genealogy was not blemished.

As we begin to put this together, it leads us to the strange idea that there were fallen angels that, somehow, began this strange business of generating a hybrid group called "Nephilim." This bizarre view is confirmed in the New Testament in Jude 6-7: "And the angels which kept not their first estate, but left their own habitation, he hath reserved in everlasting chains under darkness unto the judgment of the great day. Even as Sodom and Gomorrha, and the cities about them in like manner, giving themselves over to fornication, and going after strange flesh, are set forth for an example, suffering the vengeance of eternal fire." Jude made an allusion to these events in Genesis 6 and clearly he was writing about angels who, for whatever reason, went after "strange flesh."

As we begin to put this together, it leads us to the strange idea that there were fallen angels that, somehow, began this strange business of generating a hybrid group called "Nephilim."

Peter, in his second letter, chapter 2:4-5, also says, "For if God spared not the angels that sinned, but cast them down to hell, and delivered them into chains of darkness, to be reserved unto judgment; and spared not the old world, but saved Noah . . . " Peter wrote much the same thing as Jude, but he even tied it specifically to the days of Noah. He also used a term for hell that was only used in the New Testament: *tartarus,* a term used in Greek literature for "a dark abode of woe" or "a pit of darkness of the unseen world." In Homer's *Iliad,* it is thought to be as far below Hades as the earth is below heaven.

The idea that renegade angels came down to the earth and cohabited with women to produce a hybrid offspring is pretty strange. But that notion is found in the legends of virtually every ancient culture on earth, including Sumer, Assyria, Egypt, the Incas, the Mayans, the Gilgamesh epic of Babylon, the Persians, Greece, India, Bolivia, South Sea Islands, and the Sioux Indians in the United States. They all have stories about "star people" or gods of some kind who produced offspring on earth.

For example, in Greek mythology, the Titans were partly celestial, partly terrestrial. They rebelled against their father Uranus, and after a prolonged contest, they were defeated by Zeus and condemned into Tartarus. Atlas and Hercules were also Nephilim. They presumably were the hybrid offspring of the gods mixing with human women.

Many students of the Bible have encountered an interpretation of these passages known as "the lines of Seth" view. This interpretation assumes that "the sons of God" refers to the leadership of the line of Seth and tries to distinguish between the line of Seth and the line of Cain. The "sons of God" are thought to be from the line of Seth, and the "daughters of Adam" are thought to be those from Cain. And, according to this view, the sin involved was their failure to maintain separation—the two were not to mix. This theory started in the fifth century A.D. Celsus and Julian the Apostate used the traditional belief, which we call the angel view, to attack Christianity. Julius Africanus resorted to the Sethite theory as a more comfortable way of dealing with this.

The problem with the Sethite view is that it violates the text. The phrase, "sons of God," is never used of believers in the Old Testament. Furthermore, Seth was not God and Cain was not Adam. Blurring those distinctions imposes on the text. The idea that they were supposed to stay separate is strange because individual lines don't show up until Genesis 11. Isaac was the first one to be told to remain separate, not Ishmael or any of the others. In any case, in chapter 6, "all flesh are corrupted," which included the Sethites. If they were supposed to represent the good guys, why did they drown in the flood? The inferred godliness of Seth turns out to be wrong because only Enoch and the eight people in the Ark were spared in the Flood.

The real problem is the Nephilim. When believers and unbelievers marry, they do not yield offspring that are physiologically different. The Scripture indicates that the offspring were distinctive: the *HaGibborim*, the mighty ones. And what made Noah's genealogy so distinctive was that his family tree was uncontaminated with these strange intrusions.

In summary, the Sethite view violates the text itself. It depends on inferred separation that the text does not support. It infers the godliness of the Sethites, which the text does not support. It infers a Cainite subset of the Adamites, which is reading into the text. The result of this is unnatural offspring, which is unexplained by the Sethite view. The New Testament confirms the angel view.

THE COSMIC WARS

I used to believe this was just a peripheral issue. Then while preparing another book I was startled to realize that one cannot understand major portions of the Old Testament and major prophetic issues unless you recognize the reality of this strange passage in Genesis 6:4. The passage says, "There were giants in the earth in those [Flood] days; and also after that." So there were some occurrences of this kind even *after* the Flood. In Genesis 14 and 15 and later in the Old Testament, certain tribes—the Rephaim, the Emim, the Horim, the Zamsummim—are *Nephilim*. Arba, Anak and his seven sons were the Anakim. They were encountered in Canaan in Numbers 13 when Moses sent the twelve spies. The ten who came back terrified said, "There are giants in the land" (the word is *Nephilim*). Og, the king of Bashan, is the King of the Giants in Deuteronomy 3 and Joshua 12. Goliath had four brothers who also were a derivative offspring of the *Nephilim*.

From cover to cover, the Bible is a drama about Satan trying to thwart the plan of God. As God revealed His plan in more detail, Satan was able to focus his attack. Here, in Genesis 6, we find Satan attempting to corrupt the human line. If God was going to redeem His creation through the descendants of Adam, by corrupting that line Satan could prevent the birth of the Messiah. That was apparently his strategy, and God used a barge and eight people to thwart that strategy.

Later, Abraham's seed was targeted. This led to the famine in Genesis 50, and the destruction of the male line in Exodus 1. Pharaoh's pursuit of Israel after the Exodus was an attempt to wipe them out. When God told Abraham that after four hundred years his descendants would return to Canaan, that gave Satan four hundred years to lay down a minefield of *Nephilim*. Since God says in 2 Samuel 7 that the Messiah would come from David's line, David's family was singled out for attacks. Again and again, the drama has somebody attempting to wipe out all the heirs to the throne, but a servant hid one of the babies, and the tale goes on. Even in the Persian Empire, Haman attempted to wipe out the Jews. Over and over we see Satan attempting to wipe out the Jews. All prejudice is wrong and evil, of course, but the focus on the Jewish line, specifically, has a particular satanic twist to it because of Satan's continued attempts to thwart God's plan.

In the New Testament we find Joseph's fears in Matthew 1. Herod attempted, in Matthew 2, to kill all the male babies in Bethlehem. There were two storms on the sea in

Mark 4 and Luke 8 that were more than just natural storms. And of course, the ultimate strategy was the Cross. And Satan is not finished. He's still at it.

With that weird background, we confront the strange, rather extreme remedy that God used—the Flood of Noah.

THE FLOOD

Similar flood narratives are found in Egyptian, Babylonian, Persian, Greek, Hindu, and Chinese cultures. Also the Druids, Polynesians, Mexicans, Peruvians, and American Indians all have legends of a flood on the Earth where certain people were saved by an ark or a boat. Some of these legends even have two doves.

Noah's Ark was about 450 feet long, 75 feet wide and 45 feet high (using a cubit of approximately 18 inches). This would give it a displacement of about 20,000 tons, very similar to the Titanic. Its 1.5 million cubic feet would hold about 522 standard livestock railroad cars. Assuming 240 sheep per car, that is equivalent to 125,000 sheep-sized animals. Some people estimate it could accommodate over 18,000 species.

Noah was told to take seven of each of the clean animals and two of the unclean. How did Noah know which were clean and which were unclean? These definitions were codified in the book of Leviticus, which is one of the books of Moses, many generations after Noah. The answer is pretty obvious: these ideas were originally ordained in Eden.

The flood itself was more than just a lot of rain. The fountains of the deep were opened. Unleashed on the earth were sources of water that were apparently reserved for this purpose. Some scientists who specialize in inter-planetary catastrophes argue that perhaps the planet Mars was involved. There are some very strange things on the planet Mars—it has no water and yet there are clear signs of erosion by large bodies of water. It has also passed near the earth. (This will be explored in Hour 6.)

> *The flood itself was more than just a lot of rain. The fountains of the deep were opened. Unleashed on the earth were sources of water that were apparently reserved for this purpose.*

The waters prevailed for about 150 days. Noah and his family were in the Ark for 371 days, five months floating and seven months on the mountain. God provided a singular opportunity: one ark, one door. There were no births or deaths; all in the ark were saved. How did God do it? I have no idea. Did he put those animals in hibernation? Possibly. Many competent scientists have explored these possibilities.

There have been a number of apparent sightings of the Ark reported throughout history. As early as 275 B.C., a Chaldean priest made record of it. In A.D. 70 Josephus records a sighting. In 1993, CBS produced a prime-time special with alleged photographs of the Ark. None of these sightings has been confirmed, but they still remain provocative. In 1916, some Russian aviators thought they saw the Ark. They got the Czar interested, but the Russian revolution interfered. In the early 1900s, George Hagopian made some trips in search of the Ark. Many people have gone to Ararat to search for the Ark and have returned with all kinds of sketches and pieces of wood, but it's still a subject of much debate. There are some that believe that the actual site is in Iran rather than in Turkey.

I do believe, for lots of biblical reasons, that the Ark will ultimately be discovered. And it will once again serve as testimony of a coming judgment to an unbelieving world.

THE FLOOD ENDS

On about the 264th day Noah sent out a raven; the raven did not return. On the 271st day he sent out a dove, and the dove came back. On the 278th day, dove number two was sent out and returned with an olive branch. On the 285th day, the third dove was sent out and did not come back. So on the 314th day, Noah removed the roof and on the 377th day they disembarked after fifty-three weeks in the Ark.

Genesis 8:4 says, "And the ark rested in the seventh month, of the seventeenth day of the month, upon the mountains of Ararat." If you're a typical Bible reader, you might just continue reading; but once you realize that everything is there by deliberate design, you may wonder, *Why did God record the exact day of the Ark's landing?*

The Jews have two calendars. Their civil calendar starts at *Rosh Hoshana*, in the month of Tishri, in the fall. However, in Exodus 12:2, when the Passover was being instituted, God instructed Moses, "This month (the month of Nisan, in the spring) shall be unto you the beginning of months: it shall be the first month of the year to you." Thus, the Jews actually have two calendars: They have the old "Genesis" calendar, which starts at the first of Tishri, and they also have a religious calendar which begins with the month of Nisan (in which Tishri turns out to be the seventh month).

Jesus was crucified on Passover, which is on the fourteenth of Nisan. He was in the grave three days, resurrected on the seventeenth day of the seventh month of the "Genesis" calendar. God's new beginning on the Planet Earth under Noah was on the anniversary, in anticipation of our new beginning in Jesus Christ!

A NEW ORDER

In Genesis 9, we now have a new beginning, a new order, after the Flood. Capital punishment was expressly ordained. Human government was established. Sinful man had been wiped out, but not sin, as we'll quickly discover. Noah had three sons, Ham, Shem, and Japheth, and he prophesied (verse 27), "God shall enlarge Japheth [which is a pun since Japheth means "enlarge" and out of Japheth came the Europeans and others], and he shall dwell in the tents of Shem [Shem is the line we are particularly interested in]; and Canaan shall be his servant [which is, in effect, a curse on Canaan, the son of Ham]."

There is a new physical order, too. Apparently a thermal blanket that had protected the earth was gone. Prior to the Flood there was a universal climate, which is now gone. I believe the atmospheric pressure has been reduced by half because pterodactyls could not fly without an atmospheric pressure twice what it is today. The incredibly long lifetimes recorded, not just in the Bible but in a lot of other ancient records, began to decline.

THE TABLE OF NATIONS

Seventy nations spring from Noah's three sons, from Ham, Shem and Japheth. They are listed in chapter 10, known as the "Table of Nations." All of us are descendants of Noah through one of his three sons.

Ham's sons included Mizraim (which is the name for what we know as Egypt—Upper and Lower) from whom came the Philistines. Another son of Ham was Cush, who settled south of the second cataract of the Nile. It is sometimes translated Ethiopia in our Bibles but it is much broader than that—it really speaks of most of the inhabitants of central and southern Africa. Nimrod was of Cush and he became the first world dictator. Put settled west of Egypt, therefore it is often translated Libya, but really refers to all of North Africa. And of course, Canaan settled from Sidon to Gaza to Sodom and Gomorrah. Also, from Canaan came Khittae, from which we get "Cathay," and the Sinites whose descendents are the Chinese. They moved very far east and, because of the separation of the mountains and deserts, developed their own culture. China is one of the few countries on earth that can trace a history of more than five thousand years.

One of Shem's sons was Elam, settling a land known today as Persia (Iran). Other sons were Asshur, Arphaxad (who is important because out of him came Salah, Eber, and Peleg, from whom came Reu, Serug, Nahor, Terah, Abraham, and Joktan), Lud, and Aram.

The last son was Japheth, whose sons were Gomer (whose descendents were Ashkenaz, Riphath, and Togarmah), Magog (who will be very important to us when we get to Ezekiel 38 and 39 and was the father of the Scythians), Madai (who became the Medes who are the Kurds of today), Javan (Ionia or Greece), Tarshish (there are some who link this to the British Isles), and Tiras (who are the Etruscans of Italy and others).

THE TOWER OF BABEL

God told the people to spread out and populate the world, but they wanted to do just the opposite: coalesce and make a superstate. Led by the first world dictator, Nimrod (whose name means "we will rebel"), they tried to put together a godless confederacy. On the Plain of Shinar they built a tower, which was supposed to be a gateway to God or a tower to Heaven: Bab-El. ("Bab" means gateway; "el" is a name for God.)

These ancient people were probably far brighter than we think. They weren't trying to climb to Heaven by a ladder; this was an astrological temple on seven levels. This is where the original Zodiac became corrupted. The whole thing was a pagan rebellion against the living God. At that time, the Scripture says there was one language (which I believe was Hebrew), so God confused their language, forcing them to disband. This is the beginning of Babylon, which also became a major power center in later history.

The history of the Bible can be viewed as a Tale of Two Cities: Babylon as the City of Man; Jerusalem as the City of God. Both of them have their beginnings in Genesis and both of them are prominent in the climax of the book of Revelation. They represent ideas, not just locales.

The Bible focuses on three primary promises: God's covenant with Abraham—which will be taken up in the next section—"that in His seed all the nations will be blessed"; God's covenant with the nation Israel, that if they faithfully served Him they'd prosper and if they forsook him they'd be destroyed; God's covenant with David, that his family would produce the Messiah who would reign over God's people forever.

Hour 4

GENESIS 12-50 ABRAHAM, ISAAC, JACOB, AND JOSEPH

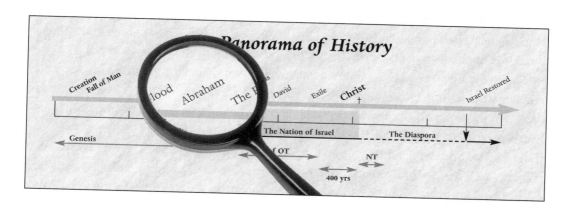

GENESIS 12 IS ONE of the key milestones of the entire Bible: the call of Abraham.

Genesis 12:1 "Now the LORD had said unto Abraham, Get thee out of thy country, and from thy kindred, and from thy father's house, unto a land that I will show thee." From Stephen's discussion in Acts 7, we learn that Abraham was called out of his kindred and father's house, but all he did was move up river. He left Ur of the Chaldees and moved up to Haran and settled with his father. It wasn't until his father died that he followed through to a land that God had set out for him.

The second and third verses of chapter 12 are among the most important commitments in the Scripture. These two verses consist of seven "I will" statements by God:

1. I will make of thee a great nation
2. and I will bless thee
3. and make thy name great
4. and thou shalt be a blessing
5. I will bless them that bless thee
6. and curse him that curseth thee
7. and in thee shall all the families of the earth be blessed

All of God's program, from Genesis 12 to the end of the book, derives from these two verses. Abraham will be a blessing not just to Israel, but to all nations. His name will be great.

Chapter 14 is the Battle of Nine Kings. Four Shemite kings—Amraphel, king of Shinar; Arioch, king of Ellasar; Chedorlaomer, king of Elam; Tidal, king of the nations—go to battle against five Hamite kings—Bera, king of Sodom; Birsha, king of Gomorrah; Shinab, king of Admah; Shemeber, king of Zeboiim; and the king of Bela (also Zoar).

The five kings served Chedorlaomer for twelve years, but in the thirteenth year, they rebelled. Chedorlaomer defeated the rebels and took spoil. This wouldn't be significant to us except he took Lot, Abraham's nephew, who lived in Sodom. Abraham and his nephew had separated in the previous chapter. Abraham gave him the choice to go where he thought was the most prosperous, and Lot went to Sodom. In fact, he even became a councilman. But when Sodom was attacked, Lot was captured and taken up north. One person escaped and got the message to Abraham, and we begin to see that Abraham was probably one of the most powerful, wealthiest men on the earth at that time. He had 318 trained servants born under his roof, so to speak, who were his army, and they rescued Lot and the people of Sodom. These four kings had just defeated five other kings, but they were no match for Abraham's leadership and the training of his servants!

On the way back, they met a very significant person in a very famous place: Melchizedek, king of Salem (at the base of Mount Moriah, later called Jerusalem) and priest of the Most High God. He received Abraham's tithes and administered bread and wine to him. This little incident, which is just a couple of verses in chapter 14, would probably have fallen into obscurity except for the fact that there are very important allusions to this event in Psalm 110 and in three chapters in the book of Hebrews.

What makes Melchizedek so unique is that he is both a king and a priest. Later in the Torah, Judah was the royal tribe from which the king came; Levi was the priestly tribe, and they were not to mix. Jesus is singled out in the Scripture as being a ruling priest—He's our high priest, not after the order of Aaron, but after the order of Melchizedek, who represents a priestly order that also rules. There are many theories about Melchizedek, but he's certainly, idiomatically at least, a very key figure.

CHAPTER 15

The next chapter also elaborates God's unconditional covenant with Abraham. A very unusual event takes place. There was a divinely ordered ritual called a *barath:* "to cut a covenant." The procedure was as follows: two participants would divide a sacrifice into two parts and would walk a "figure of eight" pattern together between the elements while reciting the terms of the covenant. What makes Genesis 15 so interesting is God first put Abraham in a deep *sleep* (the same term was used of Adam when Eve was taken from his side in Genesis 2). Then God, in the form of a fire, a smoking furnace, went through the covenant procedure *by Himself.* The two of them did not go together; God went alone. The point is the covenant was unconditional and unilateral to Abraham's benefit. He didn't make a commitment; he was in a deep sleep! Even to this day, many churches fail to appreciate that the Abrahamic covenant was unconditional. This is an important undergirding for the Book of Romans as well as many other major doctrinal passages.

First, God committed the land to Abraham and his descendants. This is particularly interesting since he had no descendants at this point in time. The land committed to Abraham and his descendants was "from the river of Egypt to the great river Euphrates."

Abraham was also told that his descendants would be estranged from the land for four hundred years and they would be afflicted. This was fulfilled during the bondage in Egypt. But the good news was that they would return and with great possessions. For Abraham this was a prophecy, but Satan was looking over his shoulder. Satan knew he had a four-hundred-year interval to lay a minefield down before those descendants returned. So he populated the land with *Nephilim* that were intended to be a barrier. That will be important to us when we get to the Book of Joshua because Joshua will be told to wipe out every man, woman, and child of certain tribes. We're shocked when we read those passages. It seems so barbaric because we don't understand that the same problem was evident there that caused the Flood of Noah in the first place: it's called a gene pool problem.

The covenant was declared eternal and unconditional. It was reconfirmed by an oath in Genesis 22. The New Testament declares it immutable in Hebrews 6 and elsewhere.

CHAPTER 16

In this chapter, Abraham himself tried to remedy the problem of having no heir. Sarah was barren, so as the procedure was in those days, she let her handmaid be a surrogate bearer of children for the head of the household. So Hagar, the Egyptian handmaid, gave birth to Ishmael. Abraham thought that was the answer since God said he would have descendants. But God had a different plan.

GENESIS 17

In Genesis 17, God changed Abram's name to Abraham. He also confirmed His covenant to Abraham—that he would be the father of many nations, not just the Jewish people.

God also changed Sarai's name to Sarah. And He promised Abraham a son. Abraham thought, "Hey, I have Ishmael"; no, in a year Sarah herself would bear. (All God did, in effect, was to add a *heh* to the letters to Sarai and Abram's names—a "breath." It was added as a representation of the Holy Spirit being given to these two for the supernatural birth of Isaac.)

God also instituted circumcision as a sign of this special covenant, and descendants of Abraham, not just Jews, are circumcised because of that. But why does the Scripture instruct that boys are to be circumcised the eighth day? First, clotting agents are not optimized until then. Vitamin K is not formed until the fifth through the seventh days, so the eighth is the first safe day. Second, prothrombin (which facilitates clotting) is below normal until the eighth day when it peaks to 110 percent of normal for a day or so, then drops back to its normal value. We know that now from modern medicine, but during the time of Abraham only the Creator was privy to such information.

GENESIS 18-22

In Genesis 18, while camped on the plains of Mamre, Abraham and Sarah were visited by three men—the Lord (a pre-incarnate manifestation of Jesus, called by some a Christophany) and two angels. Abraham commanded that three measures of meal be prepared for these three visitors. From that day on, in Arab as well as Jewish cultures, three measures of meal are known as the fellowship offering.

Among other things, the Lord confirmed that Sarah would have a son. She overheard this in her tent and laughed. She was ninety! But they scolded her for laughing. They also indicated they were passing by because the two angels had an errand to run in a place called Sodom and Gomorrah: They were going to wipe out those towns because of the rampant wickedness there. Of course, Lot, Abraham's nephew, was living there. So Abraham "bargains" with God concerning Sodom and Gomorrah, asking God to preserve the town if fifty righteous are found, then forty . . . thirty . . . finally down to ten, but none but Lot could be found.

In chapter 19, the two angels visited Lot, who lived there with his daughters—two of whom were unmarried, virgins. All the homosexuals of the town, young and old, were after the visitors. The visitors planned to spend the night out in the square, but Lot wouldn't let them because he knew they would be at great risk. The homosexuals pounded on the door, demanding that Lot deliver these two visitors to them. It is shocking, but to protect his visitors, Lot even offered his virgin daughters to them instead. Meanwhile the angels blinded the townspeople and then urged—in fact, required—Lot to get his family out of town. When they were gone, fire and brimstone rained down and destroyed the towns.

> *The sin of Sodom and Gomorrah was not homosexuality; it was the open, public condoning of homosexuality. And God dealt with it.*

Historically, one of the symptoms of cultural decay is the rise and condoning of homosexuality (e.g. the Roman Empire). We see it here in Sodom and Gomorrah and we see it in the chronicles of other great empires as they decay and, of course, we see it today. The sin of Sodom and Gomorrah was not just homosexuality; it was also the open, public condoning of homosexuality. And God dealt with it.

By Genesis 22, one of the pivotal chapters in Genesis, Abraham has learned a lot of lessons. Isaac was probably in his thirties when God said to Abraham, "Take now thy son, thine only son Isaac, whom thou lovest, and get thee into the land of Moriah; and offer him there for a burnt offering upon one of the mountains which I will tell thee of" (verse 2). Here's a strange phrase, "take thy son, thine only son." Abraham had two sons including Ishmael through Hagar, but not as far as God was concerned. For God's purposes, Abraham had one son.

There is a principle in Scripture study called *the law of first mention*: always note the first place something is mentioned. Genesis 22:2 is the first place in the Bible where the word *love* appears. As we see here, it echoes John 3:16: "For God so loved the world that he gave his only begotten son, that whosoever believeth in Him should not perish but have everlasting life."

Here is the passage from verses 2-8:

> And he said, Take now thy son, thine only son Isaac, whom thou lovest, and get thee into the land of Moriah; and offer him there for a burnt offering upon one of the mountains which I will tell thee of. And Abraham rose up early in the morning, and saddled his ass, and took two of his young men with him, and Isaac his son, and clave the wood for the burnt offering, and rose up, and went unto the place of which God had told him.
>
> Then on the third day Abraham lifted up his eyes, and saw the place afar off. And Abraham said unto his young men, Abide ye here with the ass; and I and the lad will go yonder and worship, and come again to you.
>
> And Abraham took the wood of the burnt offering, and laid it upon Isaac his son; and he took the fire in his hand, and a knife; and they went both of them together. And Isaac spake unto Abraham his father, and said, My father: and he said, Here am I, my son. And he said, Behold the fire and the wood: but where is the lamb for a burnt offering? And Abraham said, My son, God will provide himself a lamb for a burnt offering: so they went both of them together.

God will provide whom? Himself. I believe that Abraham assumed that Isaac would be resurrected because he was promised that Isaac would have children.[1] Abraham's attitude was that it was God's problem because He had to keep His promise regarding Isaac's children.

GENESIS 23–34

In chapter 23 Sarah died, and in chapter 24 Abraham commissioned his eldest servant, Eliezer, to gather a bride for Isaac. Eliezer was not a menial but a business partner: if Abraham had no children, Eliezer would have inherited everything. Eliezer took the mission, went to the far country, qualified the candidate by a well and she agreed to marry the bridegroom she had never met. He arranged to bring her back and gave her gifts on the way. Here again, we have a type: Eliezer is a type of the Holy Spirit gathering a bride for the son; Rebecca is a type of the Bride (Church). What makes this even more provocative is that Eliezer means "comforter." The Holy Spirit is always in the role of an unnamed servant. (You have to look elsewhere to discover his name.[2]) Jesus points out in John 16 that the Holy Spirit will not testify of Himself.

Topography of Mount Moriah

Mount Moriah is a ridge system between two other mountains. There is a ridge running north and south; to the east is the Mount of Olives, separated by the Kidron Valley. About 600 meters above sea level is a place that was called Salem, and later, Ophel. At about 741 meters above sea level is a saddleback that was the threshing floor of Arunah later purchased by David that ultimately became the site of the Temple Mount. But that's not the peak. Further up, at 777 meters above sea level, is a place called Golgotha. Abraham offered his son, Isaac, on the very spot that, two thousand years later, another Father offered His Son as an offering for all of us.

Just as Abraham was ready to strike with a knife, an angel intervened. They substituted a ram and that substitutionary ram later gets codified in the Law of Moses. What's interesting is that Abraham knew he was acting out prophecy. Verse 14 in chapter 22 says, "And Abraham called the name of that place Jehovah-jireh: as it is said to this day, In the mount of the LORD it shall be seen." It's a prophetic place-name; this is called a type, or a model, or a foreshadowing. Abraham is a type of the Father; Isaac is a type of the Son.

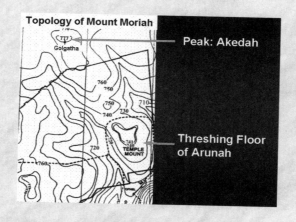

The bride finally joins the bridegroom at the well of Lahai-Roi, which means "the well of the living water." Back in Genesis 22, after Abraham substituted the ram, verse 19 says, "So Abraham returned unto his young men, and they rose up and went together to Beersheba; and Abraham dwelt at Beersheba." There is something strange about verse 19: Where is Isaac? The answer is, of course, that Isaac went along with them, but that's not what the text says. The text says that Abraham returned to his young men and they rose up and went together to Beersheba. If you study the text carefully, you'll find that Isaac is edited out of the record for two chapters, until 24:62, where he is joined with his bride by the well of Lahai-Roi. It would appear that the Holy Spirit has nudged the text here to make it fit the model.

ESAU AND JACOB

When Rebecca was giving birth to the twins who were struggling within the womb, the Lord said to her, "Two nations are in thy womb, and two manner of people shall be separated from thy bowels; and the one people shall be stronger than the other people; and the elder shall serve the younger." Before they were born, Jacob, who was second, was promised the birthright. His mother knew that, but they resorted to chicanery to get it anyway.

Esau, of course, was the firstborn; he was very red and very hairy. Esau was an outdoorsman and came home one day starving. Jacob was a mother's boy and apparently cooked great porridge. Esau exchanged his birthright for a mess of porridge, which tells the reader the birthright wasn't important to him. Jacob not only purchased the birthright from Esau, but he lied to get the formal blessing from his father, Isaac. Isaac had poor eyesight. Jacob's mother coached him to disguise himself so he would feel and smell like Esau. And he went through this whole charade to get Isaac to bless him—to confirm the birthright. After that, when Esau came home for the blessing, he was too late since Jacob had already received it. That caused enmity between Jacob and Esau, and Rebecca advised Jacob to run for his life.

Jacob went to the region where his mother was raised to get away from Esau. Laban was in charge there, and though he was a relative, Jacob was cheated by him again and again. Jacob worked for Laban for seven years to marry his daughter, Rachel. After the seven years of labor, on the wedding night Laban switched Rachel for his eldest daughter, Leah. And God gave Jacob a lesson on the rights of the firstborn. When he woke up and realized what had happened to him, it was too late. So he offered to work another seven years for the bride he wanted. He loved Rachel more than life itself.

Twelve sons—the twelve tribes of Israel—and at least one daughter were born to Jacob and his wives and their two handmaids. He finally returned to the land in chapter 31. In chapter 33, when he wrestled with an angel and was crippled for the rest of his life, his name was changed from Jacob to Israel.

In the rest of the Scriptures, sometimes he is called "Jacob" and sometimes "Israel." Rarely is the phrase used, "the God of Abraham, Isaac, and Israel;" it says, "Abraham, Isaac, and Jacob." When Jacob was in the flesh, he was called "Jacob." When he was walking in the Spirit, he was "Israel." Jacob loved the Lord, yet he was also a conniver. He cheated and got cheated time and again.

When he finally had to meet Esau, he created a ploy to keep from being murdered, and yet, Esau welcomed him. Esau founded the nation Edom, which later became an enemy of Israel, the nation.

In chapter 34, Dinah, a sister of the twelve brothers, was wronged by the men of Shechem, who wanted to marry the daughters of Jacob. Levi and Simeon, in an attempt to lure them, said, "You may marry them, but you must be circumcised first." But on the third day after circumcision, when the men were still in pain, Levi and Simeon killed them all. They avenged Dinah, but they did it so brutally that they forfeited their position in the lineage of rights.

After all this, Jacob returned to Bethel, and Rachel died giving birth to Benjamin.

THE TWELVE TRIBES OF ISRAEL

The following is a brief outline of the descendents of Abraham and how they became the Twelve Tribes of Israel.

Abraham and Sarah, in their old age and according to the promise, had Isaac—named and announced before he was born.

Isaac married Rebecca and they had twins: Esau and Jacob. Jacob purchased the birthright and got it blessed.

Jacob had two wives, Leah and Rachel. But Leah, not Rachel (whom he loved) had Reuben, the firstborn. Then she had Simeon, then Levi, then Judah. By this time, Rachel had had it! To be barren was an embarrassment, even a curse. So Rachel resorted to a common practice in their culture: she gave her handmaiden, Bilhah, to Jacob as a concubine, and Bilhah bore Dan and Naphtali.

In response, Leah also gave her handmaid, Zilpah, to Jacob. Zilpah bore Gad and Asher. Finally, Rachel, whom Jacob loved, bore her firstborn, Joseph.

Leah then bore Issachar and Zebulun.

Rachel finally bore Benjamin. Benjamin was much younger than Joseph but had a special relationship with him because of their mother.

The Descendants of Abraham

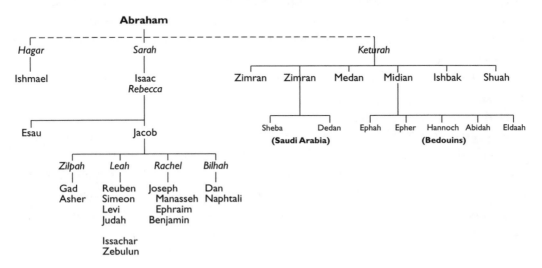

When Joseph went to Egypt, he married a Gentile and had two children by her, Manasseh and Ephraim. When the whole family gathered in Egypt, Jacob adopted Manasseh and Ephraim as his own. In fact, when he blessed them, he crossed his hands, which upset Joseph since he expected Manasseh, the firstborn, to get the better of the two blessings. Jacob, by the Holy Spirit, knew what he was doing. Ephraim got the better blessing of the two.

These constitute the Twelve Tribes. If you count, you'll find thirteen names, but Joseph can be broken into two. Manasseh and Ephraim together can be called "the tribe of Joseph." (There are twenty different listings of the tribes in the Scripture. Each one is slightly different.) If the tribes are involved in a military operation for which Levi was exempt, you still can get twelve by splitting the tribe of Joseph into two: Manasseh and Ephraim. So you have an alphabet of thirteen; you can always get twelve even if one is omitted for some reason.

There were problems in the succession. Reuben was the firstborn, the natural heir, but he had an illicit relationship with his father's concubine. Simeon and Levi brutally killed the men of Shechem. Judah would be the next in line, but Joseph was favored as the firstborn from Rachel, Jacob's favorite. There are many examples of bypassing the firstborn: Seth and Cain; Shem and Japheth; Isaac and Ishmael; Jacob and Esau; Judah and Joseph (each a successor to Reuben); Moses was younger than Aaron; David was younger than all his brothers.

The Career of Joseph

There are lists in our commentaries of over one hundred ways that the career of Joseph was a parallel, or a "type," of Jesus Christ. He was the firstborn of Rachel, therefore, he was favored by Jacob, who gave him the famed coat of many colors. (The word may also mean "a seamless" robe.)

When Joseph was young, he had some dreams which he foolishly revealed to his family. In one dream, there were twelve sheaves, and eleven of them bowed down to his sheave. His brothers didn't like that. In another dream with twelve stars and the sun and moon, eleven stars and the sun and moon bowed down to his particular star. Even Jacob his father was upset about that, saying, "You mean your mother and I will also bow down?" He interpreted the dream for us, that the sun and moon represented Jacob and his wife, and this will be helpful when we get to Revelation 12.

Joseph in Egypt

Because of the popularity of the young upstart, the brothers captured him and sold him into slavery. They took his coat, put some lamb's blood on it, and took it back to Jacob, causing Jacob to believe that Joseph was dead. In a sense, they deceived Jacob the same way Jacob had deceived his father, Isaac. You see retribution in every turn of his life. The conniver is being out-connived.

Joseph was taken to Egypt as a slave and served in Potiphar's house. Potiphar's wife tried to seduce him, but he refused her advances and fled. Insulted, she spread the story that he had attacked her, and Potiphar threw him in prison. (I believe Potiphar knew she was lying because he would have killed Joseph otherwise.) Imprisoned for many years, Joseph was confused but faithful, and he exhibited a skill God had given him to interpret dreams. A butler and a baker imprisoned with him each had dreams having to do with three days. The butler dreamt about wine; the baker dreamt about bread. Joseph interpreted the dreams and told the butler that in three days he would be freed, and in three days the baker would be killed. And they were.

The Mazzeroth

It is interesting that the twelve constellations of the Zodiac (Mazzeroth, in Hebrew) are identified with each of the Twelve Tribes. And the twelve signs of the Zodiac in their pre-Babylonian labels spell out the whole Gospel story.

There are traditions among the Persians and others that Adam and Enoch and others taught their children God's plan of redemption by stories associated with these twelve clusters of stars. It starts with Virgo, the Virgin Birth, and ends up with Leo, the Lion of the Tribe of Judah. Each of the twelve constellations is also associated with a tribe. This was all corrupted in Genesis 11 with the Tower of Babel, so the names we know today are derived from pagan religions that originated from Babylon. But in Revelation 12 the woman clothed with twelve stars is Israel. How do we know? We know because Jacob himself interpreted it here.

Joseph had implored the butler to remember him when he was freed from the prison, but he didn't. He forgot all about Joseph for several years . . . until Pharaoh had a dream. Pharaoh had two dreams: in one, there were seven fat cows, followed by seven lean cows. In another, seven rich, plump heads of grain were followed by seven thin, scrawny heads of grain. These dreams greatly troubled him. At this moment the Pharaoh's butler remembered that Joseph, with whom he was in prison, could interpret dreams.

Joseph revealed to Pharaoh that there would be seven fat years followed by seven years of famine. He recommended that Pharaoh appoint someone to take advantage of the seven good years by storing twenty percent of the excess each year to survive the coming seven lean years.

Pharaoh was impressed with his skill, but he also recognized that God favored this young man and so he made him the prime minister of Egypt, in effect. At this time a famine had overcome the land where Joseph's family lived. They were starving, but they heard things were good in Egypt. So Jacob commissioned the young men to go to Egypt—except for

Benjamin, the youngest—to buy grain. When the brothers arrived in Egypt, they met and had to deal with Joseph, but so many years had passed that they didn't recognize their brother in Egyptian regalia running the world.

Joseph asked about their family, and they alluded to the fact that they had a younger brother at home. To get his brothers to bring back Benjamin, Joseph kept Simeon as a hostage and sent the rest of them back. Further, they had paid for their grain, but Joseph secretly had the money put back in each grain sack. He accused them of being spies and sent them back to get Benjamin to prove they were not. After they left, they discovered they still had their money.

They told Jacob the whole story and he became distraught because now he had lost another son. Simeon languished in prison for a long time, and finally they ran out of grain and had to go back. Joseph toyed with the brothers for a while, then finally revealed himself. Can you imagine that scene with Joseph and his brothers who had sold him into slavery? He now ran the world, yet he still loved them. He shed tears of joy: "You meant it for evil but God meant it for good."

> *Joseph toyed with the brothers for a while, then finally revealed himself. Can you imagine that scene with Joseph and his brothers who had sold him into slavery?*

Jacob and the family, actually a total of seventy people, then moved to Egypt. This was where the family became a nation. They were in Egypt for over four hundred years. For about thirty years they lived comfortably, but then a pharaoh came into power who did not know Joseph and who put the Israelites into bondage, which leads us to the book of Exodus.

You really need to read the story of Joseph. It's one of the most colorful, readable, and moving episodes in the Scripture.

The Twelve Tribes were complete because Joseph's two sons were adopted by Jacob. From these thirteen names come every list of the Twelve Tribes in the Scripture.

In Genesis 49, old Jacob prophesied over each of the twelve sons, and each prophecy was a very enigmatic riddle. In one of them, concerning the tribe of Judah, Jacob said, "the scepter shall not depart from Judah, nor a lawgiver from between his feet until Shiloh comes, and to him shall be the obedience of the people." The word "Shiloh" is recognized by rabbinical authorities as referring to the coming Messiah.

Why do I mention this? In about A.D. 7 a Roman procurator, Caponius, removed the legal powers of the Sanhedrin (the Ruling body of the Jewish people at that time), including capital punishment. That's why the Sanhedrin had to go to Pilate when they wanted Christ to be executed. But interestingly, the Babylonian Talmud records that the Sanhedrin put on sackcloth and ashes and walked around the walls of Jerusalem weeping, "Woe unto us for the scepter is departed from Judah, and the Messiah has not come." They actually thought that the Word of God had been broken! They recognized Genesis 49:10 as a prophecy that the scepter would not depart until the Messiah came, and they wept because they had lost the scepter (power).

Little did they know that while they were marching around Jerusalem in sackcloth, up in the town of Nazareth, at a little carpenter's shop, was a young boy named Jesus, the very Messiah they had been waiting for.

We've spent some time on Genesis because it's so foundational to the rest of Scripture. In Romans 8:30, Paul makes the statement that Jesus would be the firstborn of many brethren: "Moreover whom he did predestinate, them he also called: and whom he called, them he also justified: and whom he justified, them he also glorified." We suspect that, in Paul's mind, was exactly the portion of Scripture we've been studying. Abraham was predestined for his role in God's plan. He says, "In Isaac is thy seed called." And Isaac's son was Jacob. If God can justify Jacob, He can justify any of us.

These four steps Paul had on his mind—predestined, called, justified, and glorified—were exemplified in the lives of the patriarchs Abraham, Isaac, Jacob, and Joseph.

Hour 5

EXODUS–DEUTERONOMY

EXODUS IN HEBREW means "the outgoing." They entered Egypt as a family; they emerged from Egypt as a nation. It's hard to imagine a more amazing national spectacle in all of human history. An entire race sheds their generations-long shackles of servitude, migrates to a new country, and emerges into a new corporate life.

There are three main subjects in the book of Exodus. The first eighteen chapters recount the plagues and the institution of the Passover, the exodus from Egypt, and the crossing of the Red Sea. Chapters 19–24 describe the giving of the Law at Sinai, the Ten Commandments, and the Mosaic Covenant. Chapters 25–40 deal with the Tabernacle and also highlight the Priesthood.

The Exodus was necessary for two reasons: Israel's expansion in Egypt, and Israel's oppression in Egypt. The Exodus was anticipated in Moses' preparation: raised in the court of Pharaoh, he then spent forty years in Midian where the Israelites subsequently would spend forty years in their wanderings before entering the Promised Land.

The Scripture tells us that a pharaoh came to power who did not know Joseph. Furthermore, he was not an Egyptian. In Acts 7:18, when Stephen is giving his presentation before the Sanhedrin, he speaks of "another king who knew not Joseph." The word "another" in Greek is *heteros* (not *allos*), meaning "of a different kind." Isaiah 52:4 tells us that the pharaoh of the oppression was an Assyrian. He became insecure and threatened as this race of Hebrews multiplied and became powerful, so he enslaved them.

The oppression of the nation of Israel brings us to the advent of Moses—probably the most remarkable man who has ever lived, next to Christ. He stands out in the pre-Christian world. He was born during, but delivered from, government-ordained genocide. Moses would take a race of slaves and mold them into a powerful nation that altered the course of all history.

THE BURNING BUSH

While Moses was shepherding in Midian, he noticed a bush on a hill, burning but not consumed. Rabbinic tradition says it was an acacia bush, the thorn bush of the desert. The thorn bush is Levitically suggestive of sin; the curse of Adam was characterized by thorns. Those thorns that Jesus bore on his brow were not just the painful thorns, physically, but emblematic of the curse that God had placed upon mankind from Adam's fall. So here we have a thorn bush burning but not consumed. To the rabbinical mind, that's grace or mercy—sin being judged, but not consumed. Grace always attracts; judgment repels. It was a symbol of grace that fascinated Moses. The bush was burning but was not consumed.

God identified Himself in this encounter and gave Moses a mission: to free the people of Israel. Moses pressed him, "When I approach Pharaoh, what name shall I use?" God said, "*I am that I am.*" In John 8:58, Jesus lays claim to being that person, the voice of the burning bush. In chapter 4 of Exodus, God told Moses not only that he was going to go, he was going to pronounce God's judgment with ten plagues, and Pharaoh would not yield until the last plague, the death of the firstborn. These plagues were not just to harass Pharaoh, but were against all the gods of Egypt. In Exodus 12:12 God says, " . . . against all the gods of Egypt I will execute judgment."

THE TEN PLAGUES

First, water was turned to blood. Many gods in Egypt were associated with the Nile, a principal resource of economy in Egypt.

Second, frogs covered the land; one of the Egyptian gods was in the form of a frog.

Third, the dust of the land became sand flies, translated "lice" in most Bibles.

Fourth was the plague of swarms, which, apparently, were the scarabs (the word is very similar).

Fifth, a murrain (or disease) killed the Egyptian livestock, but not those of the Israelites. Many of these animals were considered gods in the Egyptian pantheon.

Sixth, the plague of boils. Moses sprinkled ashes (which were supposed to be for blessings) into the air and sores broke out on the Egyptians.

Seventh, hail and fire together fell from the sky.

Eighth, the land was swarmed with locusts, which ate everything the hail and fire had left.

Ninth, thick darkness came upon the Egyptians (but not the Israelites) for three days. Even Josephus, the historian, recorded that it wasn't just that the sun was blocked, but the darkness could actually be felt.

These plagues were humiliating to the whole culture since they worshiped the very entities that God used to plague them.

The tenth plague, the climactic one, was the death of the Egyptian firstborn of both people and animals. This attacked Pharaoh's own dynasty. And, of course, it was the final blow that caused Pharaoh to let Israel go.

The night of the last plague was when Passover was instituted. The Jews were to splatter lamb's blood on each side of their doors so the death angel would "pass over," or pass by, their home. Note they were covered by blood, not by their race. If you were an Egyptian visiting a Jewish home that had the blood on the door you were spared; if you were a Jew without the blood, you were not. The Passover delivered them from bondage and symbolized fellowship. It restructured their calendar so that this month began the year, and it is memorialized as a feast in every observant Jewish home to this very day. The Passover was also prophetic: John the Baptist, twice, introduced Jesus publicly, saying, "Behold the Lamb of God who taketh away the sin of the world." Passover has two roles: a commemorative role, commemorating the deliverance from Egypt, and a prophetic role, describing the deliverance of the entire world from the bondage of sin.

Ancient Egypt was a type, or model, of the world. It represented material wealth and power. It was ruled by a despotic prince who, as the prince of this world (a title of Satan), has committed it to fleshly wisdom and false religion. Egypt is our world today—different vocabulary, same issues. Egypt was organized on the basis of force, ambition, and pleasure, just like our culture today. Egypt persecuted the people of God and was overthrown by divine judgment, just as today's world is destined to be.

Even after Pharaoh let the Hebrews leave the country, he changed his mind and went after them. Again, Satan put it into his heart to wipe them out. Israel finally found itself cornered against the sea. The *Shekinah*, appearing as a pillar of fire by night and a cloud by day, was present all through the wilderness wanderings. But here it was acting as a rear guard, separating Israel from the Egyptians until the Red Sea parted and Israel could cross. Once the Israelites crossed to the other side, the *Shekinah* left and the Egyptians tried to follow and were drowned.

The deliverance from Egypt is used as a benchmark of God's power throughout the Bible. You'll find the prophets, centuries later, speaking for God and pointing to this very deliverance. One example, Micah 7:15, says, "According to the days of thy coming out of the land of Egypt, will I show unto him marvelous things." In other words, it is an example of God's power. It comes up again and again in the psalms and writings of the prophets.

The deliverance was a measurement standard of several things: of judgment because of the plagues; of grace because of the blood covering; of might because of the Red Sea crossing; of guidance because of the *Shekinah* which is the Holy Spirit; of provision because of the water, manna, and quails; of faithfulness because it all derives from God's commitment in the Abrahamic Covenant; of condescension because of the Tabernacle.

Our exodus in Christ is also paralleled here. The emancipation from bondage was physical for them; it is spiritual for us. They were delivered by the shedding of lambs' blood; we are delivered by Christ's blood. The exodus was national; faith in Jesus is universal: "whosoever believeth."

THE LAW IS GIVEN

The big event that occurs at Sinai is the giving of the Law. Exodus 19-20 deal with the Commandments, which are the moral law. The terms are obedience, the parties are the nation, the covenant relationship is with God, and the altar is the provision for repair. God knew they would break the Law, so He provided an altar for sacrifice.

Here are the Ten Commandments:

　1. Thou shalt have no other gods before Me.

2. Thou shalt not worship any graven image.

3. Thou shalt not take the name of the Lord thy God in vain.

4. Remember the Sabbath Day to keep it holy.

5. Honor thy father and thy mother.

6. Thou shalt not murder.

7. Thou shalt not commit adultery.

8. Thou shalt not steal.

9. Thou shalt not bear false witness.

10. Thou shalt not covet.

Chapters 21 and 22 deal with social issues, rights, and practices of the community. The ordinances concerning the Sabbaths, the feasts, and other religious ordinances are in chapters 23 and 24.

THE WHY OF THE LAW

Why was the Law given? This is widely misunderstood. The first reason is to provide a standard of righteousness. How do you know right from wrong? By looking at God's standard, not relativism—God makes the rules, which were given to expose and identify sin.

The Law was also given to reveal the divine holiness. One thing that will become clear as we go through our survey of the Scripture is that the Gospel supersedes the Law. The commandments of God were fulfilled by Jesus Christ on our behalf. We can have His fulfillment of the Law appropriated to us through faith. That's what the New Testament is all about. Romans 10:4 says, "For Christ is the end of the Law for righteousness to every one that believeth." That changes the basis of our relationship with God, since we can't be perfect (and you have to be perfect if you are going to be in His presence).

The ordinances given, now superseded in Christ, are fascinating. We're in a new dispensation: not in the dispensation of the Law, but in what some call the Dispensation of Grace, where we replace the outward command of the Law with the inward power of the Holy Spirit. Instead of the condemning ethic of the Law, we experience the transforming dynamic of the Holy Spirit. Many don't understand the New Testament, especially the epistles, because they don't understand the problem they are resolving.

Our whole challenge is to walk, not after the flesh, but after the Spirit. Romans 8:3-4 says,

"For what the law could not do, in that it was weak through the flesh, God sending his own Son in the likeness of sinful flesh, and for sin, condemned sin in the flesh: that the righteousness of the law might be fulfilled in us, who walk not after the flesh, but after the Spirit."

THE TABERNACLE

One of the most important accounts in the Book of Exodus is of the constructing of the Tabernacle, sometimes known as the House of Blood. In addition to the two tablets of the Law, God gave Moses a very specific set of instructions for a portable sanctuary. More space is devoted in the Scriptures to the description of the Tabernacle than any other single subject, except Christ Himself. We're going to look at the structure, the furniture, the priesthood, and the offerings. If we had the space, we would see that every detail points to Jesus Christ.

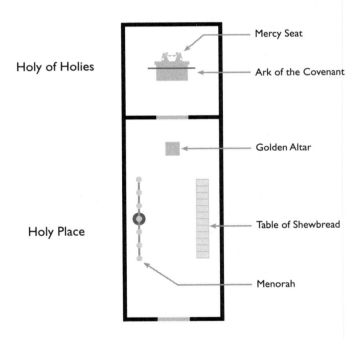

For example, brass was the material available to them and could sustain fire, therefore brass symbolized fire or judgment. Gold represented kingship or deity. Silver represented blood (the redemption coin of the Temple was silver—remember Judas when he said he betrayed innocent blood and threw the *silver* coin on the temple floor). The Tabernacle was about 75 feet wide and 150 feet long and was surrounded by a white linen fence about

7.5 feet high. The first thing seen when approached, was white—righteousness, in a sense. There was only one entrance, on the east side. The first thing you encountered upon entering was the brazen altar, the Altar of Sacrifice. The next thing was the laver—a huge, brass washbasin. In Solomon's Temple, it was about 15 feet in radius and 7.5 feet deep (the exact size is not specified in the Tabernacle). The laver was where the priests washed in preparation for their various duties. And then they could enter the Tabernacle proper—a building made of acacia wood planks covered with gold and placed vertically. The base of these gold planks rested on silver sockets. The entire Tabernacle rested on silver (rested on the Blood, as it were).

When first entering the Tabernacle proper, the priests entered a room that was roughly 15 feet by 30 feet called the Holy Place. It was separated from the inner sanctum, the Holy of Holies, which was an exact cube: 15 feet square. Here stood a seven-branched lamp-stand—the *menorah*. Across from it was the Table of Showbread: twelve loaves that were changed every Sabbath. In front of the veil of the Holy of Holies was a golden altar, also called the Altar of Incense. Then in the Holy of Holies was the Ark of the Covenant, a cof-fin-like structure that held the Ten Commandments and some other things. On top of the Ark was the Mercy Seat (the word means "propitiation"). It was solid gold with two cheru-bim over it. God described Himself as "He that dwells between the cherubim." And when this was all assembled, God, in the form of the *Shekinah* Glory, entered and hovered over the Mercy Seat. So, in a very literal sense, God was represented in the midst of His people.

All together, there were seven pieces of furniture in the Tabernacle, and each of these was linked to Jesus Christ.

John opened his Gospel by saying, "The Word was made flesh, and tabernacled among us." The Gospel of John was built around seven miracles which gave rise to seven discourses and seven "I am" statements. Jesus said, "I am the door, anyone who tries to get in other than by me is a thief and a robber." There was only *one* entrance to the Tabernacle; one way to the throne of God. Jesus said, "I am the light of the world"—the only light in the Holy Place was the light of the *menorah*.

In fact, Jesus said, "I am the vine, ye are the branches"—the one plus the six that make up the seven symbolic references. The Table of Showbread pointed to Jesus who would later say, "I am the bread of life." The Altar of Incense represented the prayers to the Throne, and Jesus "ever liveth to make intercession for us."[1] He is our intercessor and our High Priest. And He is our sin-bearer. He's also the propitiation ("Mercy Seat") for our sins. So He is identified with each one of these seven articles.

The first covering on this strange building was a tapestry of embroidered linen. From the inside looking up, the ceiling was embroidered with cherubim in gold, purple, blue, and scarlet. It was gorgeous. On top of that was goat's hair. Suddenly it was not as attractive, but it spoke of the sin bearer. On top of that were rams' skins died red, speaking of the substitutionary ram. And over the rest of this are porpoise skins, or badger skins, depending on the translation.[2]

"The Word was made flesh and tabernacled among us..."

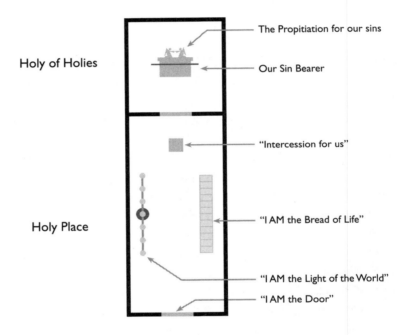

Holy of Holies — The Propitiation for our sins

— Our Sin Bearer

"Intercession for us"

Holy Place — "I AM the Bread of Life"

— "I AM the Light of the World"

— "I AM the Door"

Approaching the Tabernacle, "it had no beauty that you would desire it,"[3] until entering, then came the breathtaking beauty. The entire structure was replete with symbolism. Even the outer area, the inner court, and the Holy Place were symbolic: the outer area represents the body, the inner court the soul, and the Tabernacle itself, the Spirit.

LEVITICUS, OR THE LAW OF THE NATION

Exodus sets the stage for Leviticus, the Law of the Nation. Leviticus is not a book to just read; it is a book to study. It contains the requirements for fellowship, namely holiness (the precepts of His Law, the standards, the conduct) and the penalties for violating those requirements. It also presents the grounds for fellowship—the sacrifices that will be necessary when the other requirements are missed. Of course, all these sacrifices are symbolic, pointing to some aspect of the ultimate Sacrifice which took place on a wooden cross, erected in Judea. Every detail anticipates Christ's completed work on the Cross.

The Levitical offerings are too numerous to go through, but there was a group of voluntary offerings called "sweet savor offerings"—a burnt offering, a meal offering, and a peace offering. The compulsory offerings are for you and me—a sin offering and a trespass offering.

The writings in Leviticus also stress the requirement for Israel to stay separate, not to commingle with the nations, as a preparation for the coming Messiah.

Rabbi Samson Raphael Hirsch pointed out, "The Jew's catechism is his calendar."[4] The Jewish calendar, which is seven-fold or heptadic in its structure, is mentioned frequently in Leviticus. Modern calendars are built on weeks containing seven days. We are familiar with the seventh day as being Saturday, the Sabbath. The Jewish calendar also has a week of weeks, the Hog Shevot or Feast of Weeks; a week of months, the religious year from Nisan to Tishri; and a week of years. Six years they plow the land; the seventh it lies fallow.

Following the seventh week of years is the Jubilee Year—the "time of the restitution of all things"—when all land is reverted back to its original owners, all slaves are set free, and all debts are forgiven. When the Jews sold land, it was actually a lease on its use. Peter, in his second sermon in Acts 3:21, speaks of the Second Coming of Jesus Christ as "the time of the restitution of all things."

The Jewish calendar revolved around the Seven Feasts of Israel. There are three feasts in the first month of their year, the month of Nisan: Passover, the Feast of Unleavened Bread, and the Feast of First Fruits. There were four feasts in the seventh month, the last month of their religious year: the Fall Feasts: the Feast of Trumpets, the Day of Atonement, *Yom Kippur*, and Feast of Tabernacles. Each of these was commemorative, but also prophetic. Paul said they were all "a shadow of things to come."[5]

The first three feasts in the spring were prophetic of Christ's first coming; the last three feasts were prophetic of His Second Coming. There was a very interesting feast between these: the Feast of Weeks. It was the only feast in the entire Old Testament where leavened bread was ordained. It had a Gentile dimension to it and was the day the Church was instituted.[6]

During the Passover celebration, the lambs were examined on the tenth of Nisan, which was the same day that Jesus presented Himself, riding the donkey into Jerusalem. The Passover lamb was not to have a bone broken, and a Roman soldier at the Cross violated his orders by *not* breaking the legs of Jesus, our Passover, and unknowingly fulfilled Old Testament prophecy.[7]

At the Feast of Unleavened Bread there was also a prophetic aspect. Leaven is always a symbol for sin because it corrupts by puffing up, just as pride is always the source of sin. There were three *matzohs* in this Feast. One was broken and hidden between the other two, which represented Joseph, the baker, and the wine steward. Then there were four cups, symbolizing the delivering, the blessing, and the taking out. The third cup ordained the Lord's Supper, which was an unfinished feast. The final, fourth cup will be taken by Christ when we are all together at the Marriage Supper of the Lamb.

Next was the Feast of First Fruits. According to Leviticus, it should be "the morrow after Sabbath after Passover." (Passover could be any day of the week, depending on the year.) One morning long ago, when this was being celebrated at the Temple and the smoke from the offerings was going up to the sky early in that morning, some women were discovering an empty tomb and *our* first fruits—Jesus Christ.

> *Yom Kippur was and still is a day of national repentance, the most solemn day in the Jewish calendar.*

Between the three spring feasts and the three fall feasts was the Feast of *Shevout*, or Feast of Pentecost, fifty days after the Feast of First Fruits. This was the only time leavened bread was used and it was prophetic of the birth of the Church: Acts 2 is about the Feast of Pentecost, or the Feast of *Shevout*. (A tradition among Jewish rabbis says that Enoch was born on Shivot and that he was translated, or raptured, on his birthday prior to the judgment of the Flood. This raises a most provocative speculation: Is Enoch a type of the Church? Will the Jewish clock restart on the same feast day that it was stopped? We will explore that question in a later chapter.)

The Feast of Trumpets, the religious celebration, happened the same day as *Rosh Hashanah*, the civil new year, both on the first of Tishri. The Feast of Trumpets was followed by *Yomim Nurim*, the Days of Affliction, which then lead to *Yom Kippur*, the Day of Atonement.

Yom Kippur was and still is a day of national repentance, the most solemn day in the Jewish calendar. It was the only day that the High Priest was allowed to enter the Holy of Holies, and then only with great ceremonial preparation. This was the special occasion when he would bring the sins of the people before the Mercy Seat. Also on this day the priests would take two goats, sacrifice one and, after using the blood to symbolically lay the sins of the people on the live goat, they would turn it loose in the wilderness. The idea is of putting the sins on another—a substitution.

The climactic feast was the Feast of Booths, the Feast of Tabernacles, *Sukkot*. This was when the Jews would spend a week occupying temporary dwelling in their backyards to remind them of the wilderness wanderings. At the Feast of Booths they would leave these temporary dwellings and return to their permanent dwellings. It was all predictive of the climax of the Kingdom.

NUMBERS: THE WILDERNESS WANDERINGS

In Hebrew, *Be-midbar* means "in the wilderness," which is the real name of this book. The Greek translators called it *Arithmoi*, and in Latin it was *Numeri*, because the translators focused on the two census takings at the beginning and the end of the wanderings. But it's basically about "the wilderness wanderings."

Numbers picks up where Exodus left off. And it's really a book about arrested progress. It should, in a sense, never have happened. It took only forty hours to get Israel out of Egypt—the Passover. But it took forty years to get Egypt out of Israel. At Kadesh-Barnea, after forty days, Moses sent out twelve spies to spy out the new land. Ten of them came back terrified, and for good reason. They said they saw the *Nephilim*, the giant "fallen ones." These were the hybrids that were the products of mischievous angels commingling with women.

Numbers 13:33 records, "and we were in our own sight as grasshoppers, and so we were in their sight." Goliath was also one of those. He was nine feet tall. They had reason to be scared. And yet, it was also a lapse of faith. Two of the twelve spies, Joshua and Caleb, had a different attitude. They said, "This land is rich, it's full, it's marvelous. Let us go up at once and possess it for we are well able to overcome it." By their own strength? Of course not. By faith! God had said, "Go take it."

When God is on our side, our enemy is out numbered.

Unfortunately, the people rallied around the ten spies with their bad report. "And all the children of Israel murmured against Moses and against Aaron." And the whole congregation said to them (14:2), "Would God that we had died in the land of Egypt!" or "would God we had died in this wilderness!" That was a big mistake. God was listening and heard their murmuring and gave them their desires.

God threatened to wipe them out, but Moses interceded, "If you wipe them out, what will the Egyptians think? They survived all the plagues, and now you're going to wipe them out?"[8] His arguments are fascinating.

God knows what He is going to do, and says to the nation, "Your carcasses shall fall in this wilderness and all that were numbered of you, according to your whole number, from twenty years old and upward, which have murmured against me are going to die. You guys said you wished you'd die; now you will. Your children are going to grow up and take the land. Moses was gone for forty days you're going to be in the wilderness for forty years, until this unfaithful generation dies off!"[9]

Only two in the entire group, Joshua and Caleb, survived to go into the Promised Land. Joshua was the military leader who took over after Moses. Caleb was his sidekick. Together, these two rout the most powerful group of nations on the earth at that time.

Why did all the things happen during those forty years? The Scripture tells us it was for an example. These things happened to them for *our* admonition. Paul makes a point in 1 Corinthians 10 that everything written then is for our application. Every one of the events in Numbers has a lesson for us. And that's why it is so important to study this book in detail.

The word for *example* is *tupos* in Greek, which is "a figure, an image, a pattern, a pre-figuring." That's where we get the term "type," or model. Engineers speak of a prototype, which is from the same root. Types are common in the Bible, where some event, some object, some situation is a lesson, in advance, of what's coming. *Manna* is a type; the brazen serpent is a type; the water from the rock is a type. We're going to examine these three.

MANNA

God provided a daily provision of manna. Here were several million people wandering in the desert. Have you ever thought about how to feed them? It was a logistical nightmare! But God provided manna, a miracle bread from Heaven. It was provided only on six days of each week, with a double portion on the sixth to prevent it from having to be gathered on the Sabbath Day.

THE BRAZEN SERPENT

Moses had to put up with the Israelites' gripes and complaints all through these forty years. And it's funny to hear him talk to God: "I didn't ask for this job; You gave it to me!" In response to their murmuring, God sent fiery serpents that killed anyone they bit. Moses prayed, and God agreed to provide a remedy, but notice the strange remedy He chose. Moses was instructed to place a brass serpent on a cross-shaped pole and put it up on a high hill. Everyone who looked at the cross would be spared. Why this remedy? Jesus explained it to Nicodemus in John 3: "As Moses lifted the serpent in the wilderness; even so must the Son of Man be lifted up on a cross." And everyone who looks to it will be spared. This is a prelude to the most famous verse in the Bible: John 3:16.

It's a strange symbol, the brass serpent. Brass means "judged." Serpent means "sin." Jesus is exemplified or symbolized by a brass serpent? Yes. Scripture says He was "made sin" for us.[10] Sin was judged on that cross.

THE WATERS AT MIRABAH

At Rephidim, the Israelites needed water. God told Moses to take the staff and strike the rock and the rock would bring forth water (Exodus 17). Many years later, at Mirabah, again they needed water. This time God told Moses to *speak* to the rock and it would give water. But Moses was frustrated and upset with his people, and instead of speaking, he *struck* the rock. Water came, but Moses had misrepresented God because he let the people think that God was angry with them. Moses' penalty for disobedience was that he could not enter the Promised Land.

Moses spent forty years in Egypt in preparation for this leadership position, then forty years on the backside of the desert being prepared spiritually. He experienced the incredible drama of the Passover and the Red Sea crossing. Then he shepherded this complaining, grouchy, grumpy bunch through forty years of hardship in the wilderness. But God told him that he would see the land from the top of the mountain when they entered, but he would not be able to go in. What had he done that was so bad?

Paul tells us in 1 Corinthians 10:4 that the rock was Christ (speaking idiomatically). There were two episodes with the rock: in the first one, the rock was smitten and they benefited with living water; the second rock was not supposed to be smitten. If Moses had done what God told him, these rock incidents *would have modeled the first and second comings of Jesus Christ.* But because he blew it, he blew the model.

But God wasn't finished with Moses yet. He was denied entry into the Promised Land, but we'll see more of him when we get to the Gospels and the Book of Revelation. We see him again on the Mount of Transfiguration with Jesus talking about the Second Coming. I believe he will also be one of the Two Witnesses who show up in Revelation 11.

There is one other interesting thing in Numbers 2. The twelve tribes were told to group into four camps. Each tribe had a standard and symbol. Judah, Isaachar, and Zebulin were to rally around the standard of Judah. They collectively represented 186,400 people.

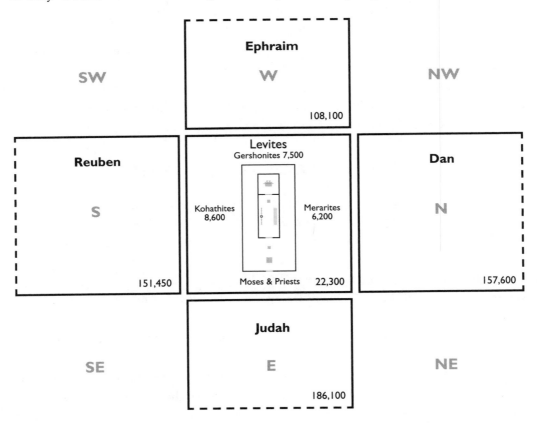

Reuben, Simeon, and Gad collectively represented about 151,000 people. Ephraim, Manasseh, and Benjamin collectively represented 108,100 people. Dan, Asher, and Naphtali 157,600 people. Judah's standard was the Lion of the Tribe of Judah. Reuben was a man. Ephraim was the ox. Dan, the eagle. These four symbols are also the four faces of the cherubim around the throne of God in Isaiah 6 and Ezekiel 1 and 10 and Revelation 4. The center of the camp was the Tabernacle surrounded by the Levites. Of the Levites, the Kohathites numbered about 8,600, the Gershonites 7,500, and the Mirarites about 6,200. Moses and the priests were on the east side, the Kohathites on the south, the Mirarites on the north, and the Gershonites on the west.

Judah had to camp east of the Tabernacle. Reuben was the camp to the south. Ephraim

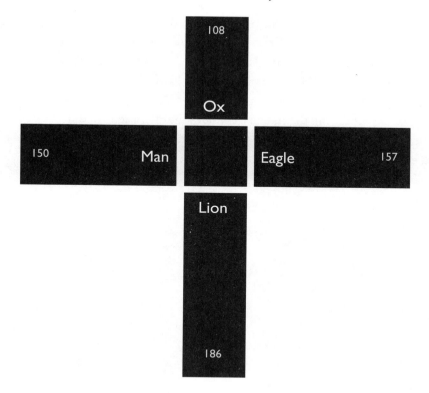

and Dan camped to the north and west. By calculating the space needed by each camp around the tabernacle, we find that the camp of Israel was in the shape of a cross.

DEUTERONOMY, THE SECOND LAW

Deuteronomy is the bridge between the first four books that are outside the land, and the next seven books which are inside the land. Jesus quoted from this book more than any other book. The song of Moses is here as well as the death of Moses.

Jesus quotes the *Sh'ma*, the Great Commandment (Deuteronomy 6:4-9): "Hear, O Israel, the LORD our God is one LORD: and thou shalt love the LORD thy God with all thine heart, and with all thine soul, and with all thine might." (Incidentally, Jews will quote the *Sh'ma* as a reference for their belief in one God. The word for *one* in Deuteronomy 6:4 is *echad* and is a compound unity, a collective sense. It implies plurality in unity, like in "one cluster of grapes." In contrast is *yacheed,* which is absolute unity, and it is never used of Jehovah. The word *Jehovah* here appears three times, which is also suggestive.)

One of the main things to learn from Numbers and Deuteronomy is the danger of compromise. Gad, Reuben, and half of the tribe of Manasseh petitioned Moses to stay on the east side of the Jordan, since the land looked very rich. Moses went to the Lord in prayer about it, and then agreed. It was a compromise, just like Lot and Abram when they split up. Lot picked the part he thought was best.

They did their part during the military conquest but then returned to this region of the Golan Heights. It was the first region to fall to idolatry. It was the first region to go into captivity, and even today it remains the vulnerable buffer between Israel and Syria.

JOSHUA, JUDGES, AND RUTH

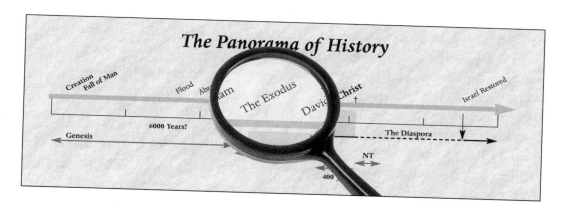

THE BOOK OF JOSHUA is an exciting book of military conquest. Joshua was the successor to Moses. The first five chapters are about entering the Promised Land.

God had miraculously preserved the Israelites through the wilderness wanderings by providing manna and quail. When Joshua led them across the Jordan, the manna stopped. They were now in the land. At Gilgal, he had all the males circumcised. For forty years while wandering in the wilderness, they had failed to observe the rite of circumcision which God had ordained for all the descendants of Abraham.

Chapters 6-12 are about overcoming the land. Canaan would be a battleground. There were some very powerful nations there. The Amorites were the biggest and most powerful, and their capital was Jericho.

Chapters 13-24 discuss the occupation of the land; the victory of faith.

CROSSING THE JORDAN

The first step was to enter the land. They crossed the Jordan on dry ground, a miracle comparable to the crossing of the Red Sea. The Jordan was not quite as formidable, but it was still a miracle. However, the water did not recede until the priests put their foot in it. It took faith to take that step. The step of obedience always precedes revelation. That pattern is evident all through the Scripture.

When they crossed the Jordan, Joshua had the people make two monuments of twelve stones each, one stone for each of the Twelve Tribes. One pile was placed in the Jordan and one placed on its banks. This monument of twelve stones is interesting. In the Gospel of John, when John the Baptist was baptizing in the Jordan, verse 1:28 says, "These things were done in Bethabara beyond the Jordan where John was baptizing." *Bethabara* means "the house of passage." Bethabara was where Joshua had crossed, fifteen hundred years earlier. John the Baptist was saying to the Jews, "[You say] we have Abraham to our father; for I say unto you, that God is able of these stones to raise up children unto Abraham" (Matt. 3:9). When he said that, he was probably able to point to the very twelve stones that Joshua had erected when they crossed the Jordan.

After they were circumcised at Gilgal, a strange visitor appeared. Joshua encountered a warrior with his sword drawn. And Joshua challenged him like a sentinel: "Are you for us or for our enemies?" The visitor replied, "I am the captain of the Lord's host." The English word, *captain*, makes us think of a field-grade rank. The term here is a senior rank; *"commander* of the Lord's host" might be a better way to translate it. Then he said, "Take off your shoes, you are on holy ground." Joshua remembered that phrase from Mount Sinai when God said it to Moses.

Angels do not allow themselves to be worshiped. This one commanded worship. Who was this visitor? It had to be God. Most scholars recognize him as a pre-incarnate presence of Jesus Christ. That raises a question: Who really fought the Battle of Jericho? It wasn't Joshua; it was the Captain of the Lord's Host.

Jericho, *Bet Yerah*, means "the house of the moon god." I think that's very interesting because today Jericho is the capital of the Palestinian Liberation Organization, the head of the Islamic interests in the region, which is, of course, the worship of the moon god. It is on every mosque throughout the world today.

The first thing Joshua did, even before they crossed the Jordan, was send two spies to spy out the land. They were in the mountains for three days; then in Jericho, they were hidden and sheltered by Rahab. Her house was on the wall, very strategically placed.

Since all that the "spies" accomplished was to get Rahab saved, you could translate the term "witnesses."

What was the battle plan for Jericho, the capital and stronghold of the Amorite nation? Can you visualize Joshua's staff meeting? "What's the plan, Boss?" "We're going to march around the city, once a day, for six days. Then we're going to march around seven times on the seventh day." "Gee, Joshua, I thought on the seventh day we rest." "The seventh time, we're going to blow trumpets and shout, and the wall is going to fall down." "Really?" "And, by the way, we're going to take no spoil. No accursed thing will be taken."

Each day for six days the people marched around Jericho. On the seventh day, they marched seven times around, and on the seventh time they blew trumpets and shouted, and down came the walls! They killed all the inhabitants except for Rahab and her family because she had sheltered the spies.

The Israelites felt so confident about this they didn't take seriously enough the next conquest, a smaller town in the mountains called Ai. They had confidence in themselves so they underestimated the enemy. They thought about three thousand men would be enough, but they got clobbered. Only thirty-six men were lost, but it was the largest loss they had encountered in the entire seven-year campaign for the land.

Joshua prayed to God. "And the LORD said unto Joshua, Get thee up; wherefore liest thou thus upon thy face?" (Joshua 7:10). To paraphrase, "Why are you asking me? The problem is in the camp; cast lots and find out what the problem is." So they cast lots by tribe, then by family, and finally found that a man named Achan had smuggled some forbidden loot out of Jericho. He had violated God's order. That's why they got clobbered. It wasn't a question of military strength; it was that they were not walking the talk. One man caused the failure of the nation at Ai. So they took him, his wives, his children, all of his goods, and they stoned them to death and burned their possessions. After stoning Achan, his family, and destroying his belongings, they attacked Ai again. This time, with God's instruction, they took thirty thousand men and wiped out the city. This was another demonstration that God means what He says and says what He means.

THE LONGEST DAY

The Gibeonites heard how Joshua had destroyed Jericho and Ai, and they deceived Joshua and Israel into making league with them. They lived in a great city, Gibeon, and five of their opponents' kings had aligned themselves under a leader who called himself Adonai-Zedek, the king of Jerusalem. Adonai-Zedek means "the Lord of righteousness." The kings joined with him and conspired to take Gibeon, but Israel honored the treaty and fought with the Gibeonites, clobbering Adonai-Zedek and his forces. The kings hid in a cave and were dealt with subsequently. This battle completed the southern strategy. From here on, they still had a lot to do, but it was mostly just mopping up.

These enemy kings were defeated by some rather dramatic techniques that are not in most people's arsenal. For one, a meteor shower slaughtered more of the enemy than did Israel's soldiers. Second, in order to complete the rout, the Lord actually lengthened the day.

In Joshua 10:12, Joshua commanded the sun to "stand still." Now, that is not just a figure of speech. The sun, and the moon in the Valley of Ajalon, actually extended the day about the space of one whole day to give them enough time to wipe out their enemies. This gives many people a problem. "Did the world really stop rotating? That doesn't make sense. What about inertia, tides, floods . . . ?" Stopping the world—even for a little bit—would seem to create more problems than we can imagine. But, there is another possibility: a change in the *precession* of the earth would also lengthen an apparent day.

Most ancient calendars were based on 360-day years. Yet all ancient calendars seem to change about 701 B.C. Something caused the calendars to be revised. The Romans added five and one-fourth days, in effect, but Hezekiah added a whole month to the

> *Most ancient calendars were based on 360-day years. Yet all ancient calendars seem to change about 701 B.C. Something caused the calendars to be revised.*

Jewish calendar: seven times in a nineteen-year period, a rather weird formula. The rabbis speculate as to why he did it that way, but they don't explain why he had to change it in the first place.

We also know that Mars was worshiped by the ancient cultures. We live in the space age; we're probably more enlightened about space and the stars than most cultures. But could *you* go outside tonight and point out the planet Mars? Not likely, unless you are an astronomer, because it doesn't affect your life. You don't need to know where Mars is. The ancient cultures not only knew; they were *terrified* of Mars. The word "Mars" is still in our vernacular: martial arts, the god of war, and so forth.

Some scientists have suggested that Earth and Mars were originally on resonant orbits, and had a near pass-by with each other on at least seven occasions in the past. Earth would revolve around the sun every 360 days, Mars every 720 days. Orbital models have indicated that near pass-bys would occur about every 108 years and would account for all kinds of catastrophic events recorded in history. Every 108 years in the ancient world brought the possibility of walls coming down, major earthquakes, surging tides, and other events caused by Mars. People worshiped Mars because they were terrified of it. Energy transfers, that occurred every time it passed nearby, eventually stabilized about 701 B.C.

On October 25, 1404 B.C., Mars may have been on one of those pass-bys at only about 70,000 miles away (that's close!). At that proximity, it would rise over the horizon and appear fifty times the size of the moon. There would be severe earthquakes and land tides. And there was a polar shift of about five degrees, which made the days longer. Meteors followed two to three hours later, falling at about 30,000 miles per hour. A third of a million men were in the battle at Beth-Horon.

Mars Near Pass-Bys?

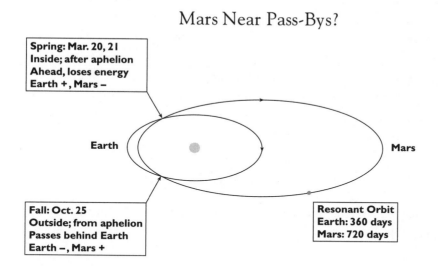

Spring: Mar. 20, 21
Inside; after aphelion
Ahead, loses energy
Earth +, Mars –

Earth

Mars

Fall: Oct. 25
Outside; from aphelion
Passes behind Earth
Earth –, Mars +

Resonant Orbit
Earth: 360 days
Mars: 720 days

Other folklore and legends record similar events. In China, Emanuel Vilakovsky uncovered the legend of the long night, which happened at about this same period of time.

Is this correct? I don't know. I present it because it is a very interesting possibility. If it serves no other purpose, it helps us not to dismiss out-of-hand the Biblical record that sounds, at first, so preposterous.

JOSHUA AND THE NEW TESTAMENT

There are many parallels between the Book of Joshua and Ephesians. Both books deal with victorious Christian living. Joshua deals with Israel; Ephesians, the Church. Joshua deals with Israel entering and possessing the Promised Land; Ephesians, the promises for the Church. Joshua, our earthly inheritance; Ephesians, our heavenly inheritance. Joshua is in Abraham and we are in Christ.

Each of these books is opened by a divinely appointed leader. In each are striking, divine revelations. Each has a scene of warfare and conflict. Joshua is a military book; so is Ephesians.

What you will not find in commentaries is the apparent parallel between the Book of Joshua and the Book of Revelation. The Book of Joshua is an Old Testament book with the name of Jesus on it. That should get your attention right away; it's not accidental. Each book is about a military commander dispossessing usurpers. In Revelation the decimal point is moved over; it's the whole planet Earth that is at issue. In each one there is a seven-year campaign against seven of an original ten nations. The first thing Joshua does is send in two witnesses, which is the same thing Jesus does in Revelation 11. There are seven trumpet events in each book. The enemies were confederated under a leader in Jerusalem: in Joshua it was Adonai-Zedek; in Revelation there is the "antichrist" in chapter 13. He and his forces are ultimately defeated by hailstones and fire from heaven. In each case we have signs in the sun and the moon. In the end, the kings hide in caves (in Revelation the kings hide in caves and plead, "Rocks fall on us . . . hide us from the wrath of the Lamb.")[1] The parallels between the books are striking and instructive.

THE LAND DIVIDED

After the campaign in Joshua, the land was divided among the Twelve Tribes. The Tribes were allocated their portion by casting lots.

THE CITIES OF REFUGE

The Levites are not mentioned because they did not inherit land; their inheritance was God Himself. They were awarded forty-eight cities, six of which were designated "cities of refuge." If you were an Israelite, you wanted to know where these were, because if you accidentally killed someone, you had to get to a city of refuge before his next of kin ("the

Avenger of Blood") got his hands on you. When you got to a city of refuge, you had to convince the town council at the gate that you were only guilty of manslaughter, not premeditated murder. If they granted you asylum, you were safe from the Avenger of Blood as long as you remained in the city. If you left the city, you were fair game; the victim's next of kin could kill you. This arrangement remained until the High Priest (in Jerusalem) died, and you were then free to go anywhere.

When you read this in the Torah, you might think it is just an ancient tribal custom, but I am convinced that every detail in the Scripture points to Jesus Christ. How can this weird, tribal procedure point to Jesus Christ? Consider this: was the crucifixion of Christ premeditated or was it manslaughter? From God's point of view it was premeditated. He planned it by His pre-determinate council.[2] From our point of view, however, can we claim manslaughter? What did Jesus say at the Cross? "Father, forgive them for they know not what they do." So we can plead manslaughter. He is our city of refuge. We're secured against the Avenger of Blood as long as we're abiding in Him as our City of Refuge. How secure are you in Christ? Completely secure. Who is our High Priest? Jesus Christ. When did He die? At the Cross. So the Avenger of Blood can't touch us.

THE BOOK OF JUDGES

The Book of Judges covers about 450 years following the conquest of Canaan. There are four segments of approximately five hundred years each in the nation's history: from the birth of Abram to the death of Joseph; from the death of Joseph to the Exodus; from the Exodus to the monarchy; and from the monarchy to the exile.

The Book of Judges is not a record of real leadership. The word *Judges* is slightly misleading. It does not mean a judge who holds court in the traditional sense; it really means "leaders." And these were occasional leaders. They were not any kind of a succession of governors but were raised up to deliver Israel from specific problems.

The book was probably written by Samuel prior to the accession of David. It pretty much makes the case that they needed a leader, a king, to get their act together. The main phrase in the Book of Judges is an indictment: "Everyone did what was right in their own eyes." And by the time you finish the Book of Judges, you will recognize that phrase as a present and terrifying possibility today. This phrase describes just how messed up their society was. Similarly, today everyone is doing what they think is right in their eyes.

Another generation rose up after Joshua, unwilling to help each other. The Israelites were living among idolaters and became contaminated with their false religions. The surrounding nations then exploited their degeneracy and subjugated them. Israelites inter-married with the pagan religions which led them to idolatry and apostasy from the true God, the Living God, who had delivered them from Egypt. The Book of Judges records God's occasional interventions interrupting their sordid slide into failure. The lessons He put them through were not accidents; they were punishments brought on by Jehovah; God was trying to teach them that privileges are not a license to sin. And God changes not.

A pattern emerges in each of these episodes: sinning, then suffering because of that sin, finally repenting (at least to some extent), and then God raising up a deliverer to get them out of it. But the sordid tale repeats and repeats.

There are six servitudes. Othniel delivers them from Mesopotamia (they were in servitude eight years); then they serve the Moabites for eighteen years and are delivered by Ehud; then Deborah and Barach deliver them after a twenty-year servitude; Gideon delivers them from the Midianites; Jephtaph from the Amonites; Samson from the Philistines. The Israelites were under some sort of servitude for 111 years.

One sordid episode in the Book of Judges you should be aware of is the story of the Levite and his concubine. This story is sort of an addendum to the book. A certain Levite's bride/concubine had left him and gone back home, so, wanting to repair his marriage, the Levite traveled some distance to pick her up. On their way back home, they stopped in Gibeah, a Benjamite city, and were unable to find suitable lodging. They decided to sleep in the street, but an old man begged them not do that for reasons reminiscent of Sodom and Gomorrah. The old man took them home to lodge for the night. The men of the town banged on the old man's door, demanding the (male) guest come out. The Levite gave them his concubine, and overnight she was raped until she died. He was crushed and upset so he cut her into twelve parts and mailed the parts to the Twelve Tribes. The tribes were outraged at the injustice and went to the Benjamites to find out who did this. The Benjamites made the mistake of stonewalling them so they attacked the Benjamites and almost eliminated the tribe of Benjamin—only six hundred were left after the attack. The other tribes realized they didn't want to wipe out the entire tribe of Benjamin, so they helped the survivors get brides. It's interesting that the first king of Israel is from the tribe of Benjamin.

RUTH

Let's make a more positive conclusion to this "hour" and look at what has to be the most charming little book in the entire Bible. In fact, the Book of Ruth is often studied for its elegance in university courses in literature.

In many respects Ruth is the ultimate love story. It's a love story on several levels. It's a love story because Ruth falls in love with Boaz—that's the main plot line. But overlaying that is the ultimate love story, a love story written in blood on a wooden cross, erected in Judea two thousand years ago.

Ruth is one of the most significant books in the Old Testament for the Church. And it's interesting that the book traditionally is read by rabbis on the Feast of Pentecost, the very feast day upon which the Church was born. It explains, like no other book in the Scripture, the role and mission of the Kinsman Redeemer. I believe this book is an essential prerequisite to understanding the Book of Revelation. Before you study Revelation 5, you need to understand the Book of Ruth.

Chapter 1 is "Love's Resolve," where Ruth cleaves to Naomi. Chapter 2 is "Love's Response," Ruth's gleaning. Chapter 3 is "Love's Request," a very pivotal threshing floor scene. Chapter 4 is "Love's Reward," the redemption of both the land for Naomi and a bride for Boaz.

Chapter 1: "In the days the judges ruled," famine drove a family to Moab. Elimelech (which means "God is my king") and his wife Naomi ("pleasant") lived in Bethlehem. Because of a serious famine they moved to Moab along with their two sons, Mahlon ("unhealthy") and Chilion ("puny"). The sons marry, but within ten years all the men are dead (Mahlon, Chilion, and Elimelech), leaving Naomi destitute.

During those ten years things began looking better back in Bethlehem, so Naomi decided to go back home. She released the two daughters-in-law from any obligations to her and encouraged them to find new husbands since they were young. She urged the daughters-in-law not to follow her. Orpah ultimately decided to stay with her people, but Ruth (which means "desirable") remained with Naomi. In fact, her commitment is one of the most famous passages in the Bible. Ruth said, "Entreat me not to leave thee, or to return from following after thee: for whither thou goest, I will go:

> *The Law of Gleaning was a form of welfare. If you owned a field, your reapers could go through the field once, and only once. Whatever they missed was left for the widows, the destitute, orphans, etc.*

and where thou lodgest, I will lodge: thy people shall be my people, and thy God my God: where thou diest, will I die, and there will I be buried: the Lord do so to me, and more also, if ought but death part thee and me" (1:16-17). She said this to her widowed mother-in-law. It was impressive; she was a very impressive person.

In chapter 2, Ruth is gleaning. One of the values of the book is that to understand it, you have to do a little homework about the Law of Gleaning and the Law of the Levirate Marriage. The Law of Gleaning was a form of welfare. If you owned a field, your reapers could go through the field once, and only once. Whatever they missed was left for widows, the destitute, orphans, etc. In her gleaning, Ruth happened upon the field of Boaz (which means, "in him is strength"), one of the wealthiest landowners in the area. He was probably the primary leader among the men at the gate. He was introduced to Ruth by an unnamed servant. She obviously caught his eye because he instructed his supervisors not to let the young men touch her, and he gave her protection. He also instructed them to drop handfuls of grain on purpose.

It so happened that Boaz was a kinsman for Naomi's family, which is why this is so important to us. The Law of Redemption said when someone sold their property, they actually sold only the rights to the property, not the title (the title belonged to God). If you died, a kinsman of your family could go and pay the money to redeem the land. Naomi had sold her property ten years before. Now they were back, but since she was destitute and couldn't buy it back, a kinsman of hers would have the right to purchase that land from whomever was using it (the Law of Redemption is in Leviticus 25). There is also a Law of the Levirate Marriage. If you were a widow without issue, you could ask your nearest kinsman to raise up issue with you. He didn't have to, but if he did, it would continue the line (see Deuteronomy 25).

Chapter 3 is the interesting opportunity. Naomi understood all of this background. When she realized that Ruth had happened upon the field of Boaz, she saw an opportunity because Ruth could put the bite on him to solve everybody's problem. He could get Naomi back the land she had forfeited years ago and give Ruth a new life. So Naomi instructed Ruth on what to do.

That night the men worked the threshing floor. A threshing floor was a parcel of ground, typically on a saddleback, where there was a prevailing breeze. They took the grain, threshed it and threw it in the air. If they did it properly, the wheat would fall nearby and the chaff would fall further down wind, making two piles. The first pile was bagged and prepared for market; the second was burned as trash to get rid of vermin. But all this could not be completed in one night. The landowner and his key people typically slept by the grain.

Naomi told Ruth to watch where Boaz was sleeping, and when it became dark, to lie at his feet. So Ruth quietly lay down and slept at his feet. When he woke up, he realized a woman was there. Ruth said, "Put your skirt over me." This is often misunderstood by those not familiar with the ancient customs.

The hem was a symbol of authority similar to putting a badge of honor on a sleeve or stripes on a uniform. In that culture, stature and authority was represented in the hem of the garment. (That's why the woman who had the issue of blood in the New Testament felt that if she could just touch the hem of Christ's garment, she could be healed. God says of Israel, "I will put my skirt over you," meaning He puts His protection on Israel.)

There was no improper behavior implied in this episode; she was asking him to take her as a Levirate bride and put the authority of his house over her. He was flattered because he was much older and because he had learned a lot about her; she had a good reputation. He wanted to do this, but there was a problem: "There is a nearer kinsman than I," he said, "But relax, we'll see how the matter will fall." Then he gave Ruth six measures of barley to take home as a code to Naomi that he would not rest until the matter was resolved. That brings us to the climax of chapter 4, the redemption itself.

Boaz was at the gate, which is like the city council, and told the nearer kinsman that Naomi had a piece of land to sell and needed a redeemer. The nearer kinsman said that it was no problem. But Boaz said, "By the way, the man who does this also has to take Ruth to bride." But the nearer kinsman replied, "I can't do that; it'll ruin my inheritance."

The nearer kinsman took off one shoe and gave it to Boaz, a symbol of him yielding the opportunity or the obligation. So Boaz purchased the land for Naomi and purchased Ruth as his bride. And that's the term he used: he "purchased a bride."

When Ruth gave birth to a child there was a big celebration, and someone gave what you and I might mistake as a toast: Ruth 4:12 reads, "And let thy house be like the house of Pharez, whom Tamar bare unto Judah, of the seed which the Lord shall give thee of this young woman."

Wait a minute! Tamar got pregnant by posing as a prostitute and tricking her father-in-law into bearing issue because her husband had died and she wasn't given a substitute.[3] So, the offspring, Pharez, was illegitimate, and thus was ineligible for inheritance for ten generations.[4] Let's take a look at those ten generations: Pharez begat Hezron, who begat Ram, who begat Amminadab, who begat Nahshan, who begat Salman, who begat Boaz, who begat Obed, who begat Jesse, who begat David. This prediction occurs as early as the time of the Judges, long before Samuel and others.

Now let's look at the Book of Ruth from the perspective of a *goel*, a kinsman redeemer. What are the requirements for a kinsman redeemer? 1) He has to be a kinsman; 2) he must be able to perform; 3) he must be willing; and 4) he must assume *all* of the obligations. God has a *goel* for you and me. He has to be a kinsman of Adam; He must be able to perform. Revelation 5 is about the Seventh Sealed book, the Title Deed of the Earth. No man was found to claim that Deed. It had to be a man. John sobbed convulsively because no man was found to redeem the earth. But wait! There is one who has prevailed to open the book and loose the seals thereof. "Behold, the Lion of the tribe of Judah, the Root of David, hath prevailed to open the book." And that unfolds in the story of Ruth. It has to be a kinsman; he has to be able; he has to be willing; he must assume all the obligations; and indeed, He has. "It is finished," He proclaimed.

Now, Boaz is the Lord of the harvest and he is also the kinsman redeemer. So Boaz is a type or foreshadowing of Jesus Christ. Naomi typifies Israel. She was out of the land; through his redemption, she was brought back into the land. Ruth was the Gentile bride, a type of the Church.

In order for Ruth to be joined to Naomi, Naomi had to be exiled from her land. The nearer kinsman couldn't take Ruth; it was against the law for an Israelite to marry a Moabite. But what the law could not do, grace did. Incidentally, Ruth did not replace Naomi. They are different; they are distinctive. Israel and the Church are distinctive; different origins, different missions. Ruth learned the laws of Israel through Naomi, a Jew. We Gentiles learn the ways of God by understanding the Jewish Scriptures. We worship a Jewish King in a Church composed of Jewish leaders using a Jewish Bible as our authority. In the threshing floor scene, no matter how much Boaz loved Ruth, he had to respond to her move. And Boaz took it upon himself to be her advocate; he was her intercessor. He confronted the nearer kinsman.

You and I are also beneficiaries of a similar love story that was written in blood on a wooden cross, erected in Judea almost two thousand years ago. Have you asked your Redeemer to be your *Goel*?

Hour 7

SAMUEL, KINGS, AND CHRONICLES THE RISE AND FALL OF THE MONARCHY

1 SAMUEL

SAMUEL IS REGARDED by many as the last of the judges. In the Old Testament his influence was exceeded only by Moses. He also was the leader of the order of the prophets. Samuel placed Israel's first king on the throne, and he also anointed David.

The Philistines on the coast were the main threat during this period. They oppressed Israel for forty years and, in fact, on one occasion even stole the Ark of the Covenant. That

77

little episode did not turn out so well for them, though. The Philistines had five primary cities, and each time they moved the Ark to a city, plagues of mice and hemorrhoids arose, until finally they concluded they would have to return the Ark. They couldn't return it without putting offerings inside it, so they put in five golden mice and five golden hemorrhoids! (Yes, the Bible has some rather hilarious episodes if you're paying attention!)

The Philistines were defeated under Samuel's leadership, but they were a major nemesis for Saul. His biggest failure was his inability to deal with the Philistines. They were ultimately subdued by David.

As Samuel got older, the people began clamoring for a king. That in itself was not bad; God had declared they would have a king as early as the days of Abraham. But they wanted a king for the wrong reasons—they wanted a king to go out and fight their enemies. This was a tragic viewpoint because God had been fighting for them; when they were in fellowship, they won, and when they were out of fellowship, they got clobbered. But they had failed to understand that God was giving them the victories. God told Samuel not to be dismayed: "And the LORD said unto Samuel, Hearken unto the voice of the people in all that they say unto thee: for they have not rejected thee, but they have rejected me, that I should not reign over them" (1 Samuel 8:7).

After Saul was installed as king, an interesting episode took place with the Philistines and their champion, Goliath. He was nine feet tall and a professional soldier all his life, a fighter from his youth. David, while still a boy, was sent on an errand by his father and encountered the standoff between the armies of the Philistines and the Israelites. Goliath was proposing a one-on-one decisive fight. But no one wanted to battle with the giant, understandably, even though Saul would be expected to. So David stepped up to the task. He didn't put on armor since he was so small, and he picked up five stones as he crossed the brook. With a sling he nailed Goliath between the eyes with his first shot. When Goliath fell, David took Goliath's own sword and sliced off his head. That sword later became a trophy in David's tent.

(Why did David pick up *five* stones? Because Goliath was from a family of five; David wanted to be ready for the other four!)

This episode gave David some public recognition as a deliverer of Israel. He ultimately became a chief among Saul's soldiers and became very close friends with Saul's son, Jonathan. Their friendship flourished despite the eventual tensions between Saul and David.

Saul showed early promise: a Benjamite from Gibea, he was physically striking and was also, in many ways, modest, direct, and generous, particularly in the early years. However, Saul fell into the trap many of us do when given some authority and responsibility—irreverent presumption, willfulness, and impatience. Many times he was disobedient and deceitful,

The Davidic Covenant

One of the most important passages in the entire Old Testament is in 2 Samuel 7 because it affects all that follows in the Scriptures and all that follows in the history of mankind. In 2 Samuel 7, we have the Davidic Covenant, a divine confirmation of a throne in Israel and the perpetuity of the Davidic Dynasty. God indicates that David's dynasty will endure forever.

Israel had some very bad kings and a few good kings in its history, but God always preserved the thread because of His commitment to David. The fact that the Davidic Covenant is unconditional is a critical point. I regret to report that most churches today fail to understand the significance of the Davidic Covenant. That covenant was confirmed to Mary by Gabriel: that Jesus is destined to sit on David's throne[1]—a political throne on the planet earth. Many people try to spiritualize this, making it symbolic, all which, in effect, makes God a liar. If you look through the passages, it's clear that God is very crisp, very precise, and very deliberate. One of His remarks is, "Would I lie to David?" It's clear what David understood. The Messianic implications of the covenant are incredible because the successor to David's throne is none other than Jesus Christ—the Root of David.

such as when he was told to wipe out the Amalekites. Instead of killing everyone and everything as God had instructed him, he saved some of the livestock and spared the king of the Amalekites, Agag (whose descendant will be a sinister guy by the name of Haman, whom we will encounter later in the Book of Esther). Samuel expressed the Lord's anger at Saul, and later killed Agag himself.

2 SAMUEL

David is introduced in 1 Samuel, but 2 Samuel covers his forty-year reign. Here we have his triumphs. He was king of Judah first at Hebron. For seven years, the rest of the tribes didn't receive him. He ultimately became king of all Israel and moved his capital to Jerusalem. We also have his troubles. David made some huge mistakes from which his family and the nation never recovered.

David was accepted over all Israel as a king for three major reasons—his human kinship; his proven merit in battle; and the recognition that the Lord had established him as captain over Israel. David's acceptance by the people is a sermon in itself because Christ's right of kingship over our lives is based on the same three things: His human kinship; His proven merit; and the Divine Warrant. But we will see in David's life—and throughout the Scripture—the fight between self will and God's leading. We should ask ourselves, "Is the government of our life on His shoulders?"

2 SAMUEL 7

Verse 11: And as since the time that I commanded judges to be over my people Israel, and have caused thee to rest from all thine enemies. Also the LORD telleth thee that he will make thee an house.

Verse 12: And when thy days be fulfilled, and thou shalt sleep with thy fathers, I will set up thy seed after thee, which shall proceed out of thy bowels, and I will establish his kingdom.

Verse 13: He shall build an house for my name, and I will establish the throne of his kingdom for ever.

Verse 14: I will be his father, and he shall be my son. If he commit iniquity, I will chasten him with the rod of men, and with the stripes of the children of men:

Verse 15: But my mercy shall not depart away from him, as I took it from Saul, whom I put away before thee.

Verse 16: And thine house and thy kingdom shall be established for ever before thee: thy throne shall be established for ever.

Several times here we have the kingdom, house, and throne all distinctly specified. *Forever* occurs, in effect, three times. The perpetuity is confirmed in Psalm 89:29, "His seed also will I make to endure forever, and his throne as the days of heaven," and in verses 35-37:

Once have I sworn by my holiness that I will not lie unto David. His seed shall endure forever, and his throne as the sun before me. It shall be established for ever as the moon, and as a faithful witness in heaven. Selah.

You can't wash that away. It's very real, very explicit—God will not mislead us. There is a similar passage in Acts 2:30, "Therefore being a prophet, and knowing that God had sworn with an oath to him, that of the fruit of his loins, according to the flesh, he would raise up Christ to sit on his throne."

It's the climax of the Davidic Covenant. So we have three key points: the Divine Confirmation of the Throne of Israel; the perpetuity of the Davidic Dynasty; and the Messianic implications. The New Testament opens referencing this: Matthew 1:1 speaks of "the Son of David, the Son of Abraham." At the end of the New Testament, Revelation 5:5 says the one who is qualified to take the seven-sealed book is from the Lion of the Tribe of Judah, the Root of David. These are very critical links.

These predictions are the continuation of the Scarlet Thread that began in Genesis 3:15 with the seed of the woman through whom the Redeemer would come. Genesis 22 confirmed that from Abraham would come "the nation." In Genesis 49, it was clearly confirmed that through Jacob "the scepter shall not depart from Judah." After 2 Samuel 7, Isaiah will continue the thread by predicting the Virgin Birth.

David's sins were not mere stumbles; they were the result of a process.

David did well at first. His zenith was glorious. He was a victorious warrior, a very clever general who ultimately subdued the Philistines to the west, the Syrians to the north, the Ammonites and Moabites to the east, and the Edomites and Amalekites to the south. The Scripture says he administered justice to all the people. He also organized the priesthood, which had grown quite large by then. At the same time, he was a profound poet and songwriter—most of the Psalms are his work.

But there was a turning point. People who know little else about David know about David and Bathsheba. First there was adultery and then, to cover up his sin, David arranged for Uriah—Bathsheba's husband and one of the mighty men of David—to be killed in battle.

We must recognize that these sins were not mere stumbles; they were the result of a process. David was enjoying his prosperity and ease. He was not with his fighting men any longer, but at the palace when these things transpired. He had begun a life of self-indulgence. Deuteronomy 17 prohibited kings from accumulating wives, yet David did. But the other side of this is David's repentance and remorse, which is sincere and committed and gives rise to the masterpiece known as Psalm 51.

Because of his repentant attitude and his commitment, God says something about David that is not said of anyone else in Scripture: God speaks of David as "a man after God's own heart."[2] But although he had remorse and contrition, that did not obliterate the consequences of what he did. The sword never departed from his house: incest, fratricide, intrigues, rebellion, and ultimately civil war derived from this act. Among other things, one of David's big ambitions was to build the Temple, and God told him since he was a man of war that his son Solomon would build it. David accepted that, but he prepaid most of the expenses. David's success provided much of the wealth that made the Temple possible.

But God said to David, "The sword shall never depart from thine house" (2 Samuel 12:10). His first son by Bathsheba died. He also lost his moral authority. Amnon, one of his sons, raped David's daughter, Tamar. Absalom, another son, then killed Amnon. Absalom led a rebellion against David, primarily counseled and encouraged by David's trusted counselor, Ahithophel. (Why did Ahithophel consistently conspire with David's own son to take over the kingdom? Ahithophel was Bathsheba's grandfather.) When the counsel was not heeded and Absalom did not win, Ahithophel committed suicide. Eventually, Adonijah seized the kingship from Solomon, so the whole Davidic household was a disaster.

1 KINGS

The first Book of Kings could be called "discontinuance through disobedience." Solomon was made king after David and also reigned forty years. The first eleven chapters deal with his reign.

Solomon acceded to the throne between the ages of twelve and fifteen. Adonijah attempted to preempt the throne but his attempts were thwarted. David, on his deathbed, instructed Solomon to "clean house." There were a number of overdue punishments. For one, Joab murdered Abner and was never punished. David recognized that unless those things were resolved, they would come back to haunt his son Solomon.

The Temple represents the zenith of Israel's glory and is a major topic in both the books of Kings and Chronicles. The design of the Temple, even though Solomon built it, was given by God to David.

To build the Temple, Solomon pulled together a 183,000-person work force: thirty thousand men who worked ten thousand at a time for a month and were off for two months to go home; seventy thousand carriers; eighty thousand hewers in the mountains; and about thirty-three hundred supervisors.

The basic design of the Temple was patterned after the Tabernacle except that it was twice as big—every dimension was doubled. Instead of a single *Menorah*, there were ten lampstands. Instead of one Table of Showbread, there were twelve.

There were also some things added. First of all, in front of a region we'll call the porch, there were two gigantic bronze pillars with names: Jachin ("in his counsel") and Boaz ("in his strength"). There were storerooms for the personal effects of the priests (they were also where the priests hid their personal idols). All these features turn out to be spiritually relevant.

What is the significance of the Porch, and the Inner Court and Outer Court? To properly understand the architecture, we need to understand what the New Testament says: "You are the Temple of God." In fact, it mentions that seven times. Furthermore, the Great Commandment says we should love the Lord with all our heart, soul, strength, and mind. What do we mean by the "heart," "soul," "spirit," and "mind"? What do these words mean?

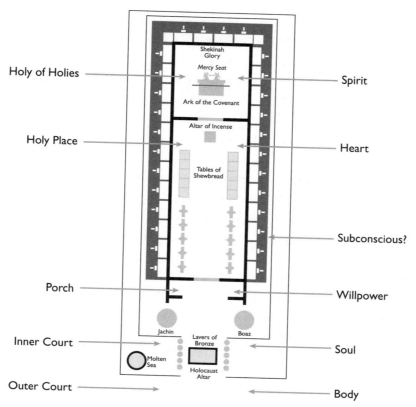

What is the difference between the heart and soul and spirit? Hebrews 4:12 says that only the Word of God can discern between the soul and the spirit.

The Temple architecture proves to be the key to understanding the architecture of our selves, our "software" (personality). You can't learn about a personality from X rays or MRIs or catscans. It's software, not hardware. How do you determine the architecture of the software? Only from the Designer's Manual.

Though we looked at the Tabernacle as being body, soul, and spirit, the Temple further refines it: the Outer Court seems to be relative to the body; the Inner Court, the soul; we have the heart in the Holy Place; the spirit in the Holy of Holies; the porch is the transition period. Everything outside the porch is bronze (the metal associated with fire). Everything inside the porch is gold. The porch is the transition point—we determine our lives by the decisions we make through our will power, through our volition, if you will, represented by the porch area.

THE SPLENDOR OF SOLOMON

Solomon was very brilliant even before he asked for wisdom, but he lacked moral vigor. He was very bright, but he wasn't decisive. He also became excessively self-indulgent. He presided over the peak of Israel's prosperity. The Queen of Sheba couldn't believe the stories she heard about Solomon so she actually traveled to meet with him. She's famous for saying, "The half of it was not told me." The splendor of the kingdom under Solomon was staggering, even by today's standards.

Solomon, however, even in all of his glory, is always an adverse reference point in the Scripture. Jesus said of the lilies, "Solomon, in all of his glory, was not arrayed as one of these." In other words, he's used as a very high point but not quite high enough. In a positive sense, Solomon may typify the millennial reign of Christ. There may also be a hidden negative in all of this because the only place the numerals 6-6-6 appear in the Bible—other than Revelation 13—is Solomon's salary. It's mentioned twice, related to the visit of the Queen of Sheba.

Solomon's reign was the zenith of the kingdom. The kingdom extended from the Mediterranean to the Euphrates River, from the Red Sea and Arabia to Lebanon, and all the tributary states were held in subjection. The Canaanites were peaceable subjects or useful servants. The immense treasures won by David were, however, supplemented with oppressive taxation. Solomon really laid it on them. His son, Rehoboam, would be foolish enough to make it even worse.

During this period a great body of literature emerged: in addition to the Torah, the teaching of Job, the history from Moses to Samuel, the theology of the Psalms, Solomon added the practical wisdom of the Proverbs, and mystical suggestions in some of the other passages like Song of Songs. Solomon is credited with over three thousand proverbs, over one thousand songs and many remarkable natural history insights that are studies in themselves.

But Solomon failed in spades also. Israel's kings were not to multiply wealth, horses, or wives, and Solomon did all three. He traded chariots and horses, which the Torah prohibited. He indulged seven hundred foreign wives and had approximately three hundred concubines. Many of the wives were political relationships, but they were from the very nations that he was warned against by Moses and the other counselors of the past. Among other things, his wives introduced false gods and false worship into the community. Solomon actually built temples to these false gods on the Temple Mount.

In the end, Solomon got sick and tired of his self-life and wrote Ecclesiastes, which concluded that all is vanity. He had access to every worldly thing, but found they don't satisfy.

Solomon's excesses led to apostasy. His heavy taxation turned the affection of the people away. He was led into idolatry by his wives. These failures gave his adversaries opportunities. Many people throughout the nation were upset with Solomon, and the tribal region of Ephraim became a center for the disaffected.

CIVIL WAR IN ISRAEL

God made it clear to Solomon in 1 Kings 11:11 that his kingship was finished:

Verse 11: Wherefore the LORD said unto Solomon, Forasmuch as this is done of thee, and thou hast not kept my covenant and my statutes, which I have commanded thee, I will surely rend the kingdom from thee, and will give it to thy servant.

Verse 12: Notwithstanding in thy days I will not do it for David thy father's sake: but I will rend it out of the hand of thy son.

Verse 13: Howbeit I will not rend away all the kingdom; but will give one tribe to thy son for David my servant's sake, and for Jerusalem's sake which I have chosen.

So Solomon, despite all the positives, got a failing grade. God was going to take the kingdom away—not from him but from his son, Rehoboam. And that was an accommodation, not to Solomon, but to David. The point was reiterated over and over, especially in Chronicles, that the accommodation was because of David.

When Rehoboam took over, his older and wiser advisors pleaded with him to lower the oppressive tax rate, but he listened to his young friends instead and arrogantly increased it.

That gave Jeroboam his opportunity. He led a rebellion, and he was smart enough to realize that Jerusalem, the religious center, would always tug at the hearts of the people. So it was just practical politics, from his point of view, to try to break Jerusalem's emotional hold on the people. To do that he set up several centers for idol worship: Dan in the north and Bethel in the south. And that nation split in two.

The northern kingdom under Jeroboam went into idolatry. They called themselves "The House of Israel" (depending on the context, "Israel" sometimes means the whole nation and sometimes only the Northern Kingdom). The northern capital was Samaria.

The Southern Kingdom, under Rehoboam, still maintained Jerusalem as its capital and was called "The House of Judah." It was the region for the Tribe of Judah, but don't confuse them. Also, both Benjamin and Simeon had been absorbed by then. It should also be recognized that the faithful from all tribes in the north migrated to the south where Temple worship was "politically correct."[3] (The myth of the "Ten Lost Tribes" will be discussed shortly.)

THE PROPHET'S MINISTRY TO THE NORTHERN KINGDOM

These were big problems, and God always raises a special person for special problems: in this case, Elijah. The New Testament speaks more of Elijah than any other Old Testament prophet. He actually appears twice in the New Testament: at the Transfiguration and, I believe, in Revelation as one of the Two Witnesses.

Among his many accomplishments, Elijah performed eight major miracles. The two to particularly notice are that he suspended rain for three and a half years,[4] and at the confrontation at Mount Carmel, he defeated the 450 priests of Baal.[5] In the opening of the next book, he does not die but gets translated directly into heaven.

2 KINGS

The Book of 2 Kings is probably among the most tragic national records ever written. The first ten chapters—to the death of Jehu, Israel's tenth king—are the annals of the rebellious Northern Kingdom. The next seven chapters are the annals of both kingdoms as they have strains between them. At this time some of the writing prophets show up: Jonah, Amos, and Hosea. Ultimately Assyria takes the Northern Kingdom into captivity—a captivity from which they, as a nation, never recover.

Chapters 18–25 are the annals of the Southern Kingdom. Many of the major and minor prophets wrote in this period: Obadiah, Joel, Micah, Nahum, Habakkuk, and Zephaniah as the minor prophets; Isaiah and Jeremiah as the major prophets. (The terms "major" and "minor" simply refer to the *size* of their writing, not their significance as prophets.) There is a substantial, prophetic focus on the Southern Kingdom. Babylonia takes Judah into captivity, but, unlike the Northern Kingdom, they eventually return to the land.

When Elijah is translated, Elisha, his understudy, receives Elijah's mantle. Elijah is one of the most fantastic prophets in the Scripture, and Elisha not only wants to follow in his footsteps, he wants a double portion—to be twice as good. Elijah did eight recorded major miracles; Elisha did sixteen. There are some interesting implications from this. The Scripture deliberately paints a parallel between Elijah and John the Baptist, who came in the spirit and power of Elijah. Elisha, while he was a very powerful prophet in his own right, had a very different style. He mixed with people; most of his acts were healing acts. His words were gentle. Almost all of his actions had to do with life rather than death. His motto could have been "the resurrection life." So some people see a parallel between Elisha and Christ.

The Northern Kingdom of Israel had nineteen kings who reigned for 250 years over seven different dynasties. They never returned from the Assyrian captivity. The Assyrians had a policy of transplanting their captives to other parts of the empire, to mix them so they would have no sense of identity and no sense of root. That is where the Samaritans came from—the "half Jews," as they are sometimes called.

The Southern Kingdom had twenty kings who reigned for 370 years, a century longer than the Northern Kingdom, but they had only one dynasty—the Davidic dynasty. With all of their problems, it was the line of David all the way through. They ultimately were taken captive to Babylon for seventy years, but they returned. When the prophets were scolding them, they always believed they were going to be restored.

In the Northern Kingdom, the kings went from bad to worse; it is a terrible chronicle. Hegel said, "The history of man teaches us that man learns nothing from history."[6] You would think that the Southern Kingdom, seeing the Northern Kingdom's predicament of going from bad to worse and then into captivity, would have gotten their act together, but Judah was not much better. Fortunately, there were a few good kings: Asa, Jehosophat, Azariah, Joaphin; Hezekiah and Josiah were singled out as good kings. Hezekiah reigned for twenty-nine years, Josiah, thirty-one. Unfortunately, Hezekiah's son, Manasseh, was the worst of the lot, and he reigned for fifty-five years. So it's a very dismal history. God ultimately used Nebuchadnezzar as his instrument of judgment to take them captive.

The Davidic dynasty is the main theme through all of this. David was the standard of measure for all the kings. Also, God, again and again, intervened to protect the Davidic line. After the death of Azaziah, Joash was going to be killed (they were trying to kill all the heirs to the throne), but he was preserved from the usurper's sword by Jehosheba, who hid the baby. His child was Hezekiah, who was miraculously preserved while under an Assyrian siege.

The captivity of Judah and the destruction of Jerusalem are emphatically ascribed to the sovereignty of Jehovah. So these things were not happenstance, but a result of God's intervention in their lives for His purposes.

A few quick comments on "The Ten Lost Tribes": it is a non-biblical myth. When Jeroboam started his rebellion, the Levites went down to Jerusalem as did others who were faithful to the God of the Torah.[7] So the tribes commingled. "Tribes" also refers to the regions assigned, not necessarily the people themselves. The faithful of all the Twelve Tribes migrated to the south; the idol worshipers of the south migrated to the north. All of these are freed by the Persians in 536 B.C. All Twelve Tribes are evident in the post-exile records of Ezra and Nehemiah and other Old Testament writings, as well as in the New Testament—in the epistles of James and Peter: "to all the twelve tribes."

> *The Davidic dynasty is the main theme through all of this. David was the standard of measure for all the kings. Also, God, again and again, intervened to protect the Davidic line.*

1 AND 2 CHRONICLES

The emphasis of 1 and 2 Chronicles is the Southern Kingdom and the preservation of the Davidic line. First Chronicles parallels 2 Samuel very closely, and 2 Chronicles parallels the Kings.

The first nine chapters in 1 Chronicles are a genealogy from Adam to Jacob, Jacob to David, and David to Zedekiah. The writer of the Chronicles, who is concerned with the nation and the monarchy, starts with Adam. The Holy Spirit is pointing out, in effect, that all mankind benefits, not just the Jews. The last twenty chapters chronicle David's reign in Jerusalem.

The second Book of Chronicles includes Solomon's forty-year reign, building the Temple and his glory, and then Judah's history of the exile, focusing on the second kingdom only—the division of the kingdom, the twenty kings of Judah and their deportation to Babylon.

Hour 8

JOB–SONG OF SONGS
THE POETICAL BOOKS

THE FIVE POETICAL BOOKS—Job, Psalms, Proverbs, Ecclesiastes, and the Song of Songs (or Song of Solomon)—are personal and experiential. The first of these is the Book of Job, the oldest book in the Bible. Many scholars believe that Job dates from about 2,000 B.C., probably earlier than the time of Abraham. Apparently it takes place very early in history in northern Arabia. Many analysts regard it as a literary masterpiece. In fact, Victor Hugo is quoted as saying it is the greatest masterpiece of the human mind.

THE BOOK OF JOB

In its very highly developed poetry, the book is about Job and the mystery of suffering. It is really a dramatic poem framed in an epic story. The first two chapters are the prologue where Satan went before the council of God and accused Job (the word *Satan* means "accuser"). It is important to realize that you and I are privy to a conversation between God and Satan that Job was not. Following the prologues are thirty-four chapters of dialogues with three of Job's "friends" and a fourth party, Elihu. After this extensive set of dialogues, God Himself spoke on behalf of Job. He started off with a science quiz and then climaxed with an epilogue.

The prologue starts with Job and his prosperity. He is recorded as the greatest of all men of the east. He was a very wealthy man—he had seven thousand sheep, three thousand camels, five hundred oxen, five hundred she-asses, and so forth. But remember, we have information that Job didn't—Satan challenged God, saying in effect, "No wonder Job worships You; he's got it made. He's got the wealth and health and the family, etc." So God allowed Satan to take the wealth away from Job. Satan slandered both Job and God.

After that, Satan went before God again and said, "Job still has his health." God allowed Satan to incrementally take away Job's life—his livelihood, family, and finally his health. In the prologue, God testified to Job's piety even in adversity. In fact, most of the book is about Job's piety and commitment, even in extreme circumstances.

We really learn a great deal from the first two chapters about an aspect of reality Job did not know. We learn that Satan is accountable to God. It's clear that Satan can't do anything without getting permission, and yet, it's also clear that Satan's thoughts are an open book to God. Many wonder, "If God is such a loving God, why does He allow sin and suffering?" Here we see that Satan is behind the evils that curse the earth. Something else we should remember—Satan is not omnipresent nor omniscient. Don't confuse the attributes of God with the limitations of Satan. Realize that he can't do anything to any of us without divine permission. We also learn through the Book of Job that God's eyes are always on His children.

The bulk of the book consists of dialogues with three friends who try to deal with Job. They tried to tell Job why he was suffering, and they were very eloquent. The first, Eliphaz, sounded good except he based his arguments on his own observation and experience, arguing that Job must be suffering as a result of sin in his life. But the early chapters of Job make it clear that he was upright.

His next "friend," Bildad, argued from tradition, basically saying that Job was a hypocrite. The third, Zophar, rested on orthodox dogma, also arguing that there must have been something in Job's life that had caused all of this. These three "friends" went through a triad of dialogues.

A fourth person showed up—a younger, spirit-filled man by the name of Elihu. There's a lot of speculation on the role of Elihu. When God answered for Job, He put down the first three counselors, but not Elihu. Elihu had a different approach; he was more of a brother or intercessor than a judge. He suggested in his dialogue that the suffering of Job may have a higher purpose. It may be moral, rather than penal. It may be aimed at restoring rather than requiting. It may be chastening rather than chastising. He really set the stage for the divine response, which is the last part of the book—a voice came out of the whirlwind where God Himself stepped in and answered Job's counselors.

First, God gave them a science quiz: "Where were you when I created the earth?" This quiz involved passages about the earth, the heavens, and living beings, and he dealt with twelve representative animals, two of which are dinosaurs. The behemoth represents land dinosaurs and leviathan typifies the sea types. Many scholars have tried to take what's said

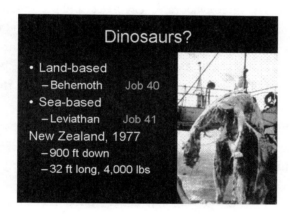

about these and apply them to animals we know about. But it's clear that doesn't fit. There's a tremendous amount of insight about dinosaurs in Job 40 and 41.

In the epilogue, God rebuked Job's three comforters and restored to Job double of all he had before. We can see from Job's counselors that Satan has many dangerous tools in the guise of piety, in the name of religious orthodoxy. Each of these "friends" seemed to make a lot of sense, and yet they were serving Satan's purpose. They were giving false comfort, and most importantly, untrue impressions of God. God made the point that Eliphaz, Bildad, and Zophar did not speak of Him the thing that was right. There is a profound lesson here: when you read something in the Bible, you need to discern where it's coming from, who is speaking, and under what circumstances. There are false doctrines expressed by someone but later rebutted. That's the danger of just extracting a verse from somewhere and trying to apply it. Context is critical.

At the end of the book, Job was restored. His inventory was doubled: he had fourteen thousand sheep, six thousand camels, one thousand yoke of oxen, and one thousand she-asses—literally double what he had before. What is interesting is that he received seven new sons and three daughters, the same number he had lost. Why weren't they doubled? There is a very profound insight there: the fact that his family died *didn't mean he had lost them.* He still had his family, and they would be reunited in eternity.

They are incidental to the story, but in these dialogues are some fascinating scientific insights. At least 15 scientific facts are suggested in the Book of Job, written in 2000 B.C., which were not "discovered" until recent centuries. One is the fact that the planet is uniquely designed for life—scientists call that the anthropic principle. All the ratios, elements, and laws of the universe are uniquely tuned to support life. Another is the hydrological cycle (the idea that water evaporates, circulates, and precipitates)—we take that for granted. How do clouds stay aloft? Water is heavier than air. How does the water stay in clouds? Air and wind have weight, but water weighs more than air. How are they supported? That's all described in Job. Also, Job 26 says, "He stretcheth out the north over empty space; He hangs the earth on nothing." Contrast that with the cosmology of the ancient Greeks or ancient Egyptians.

Job is a most rewarding book for the diligent student.

THE PSALMS: ISRAEL'S HYMNAL

The next book is the hymnal of the Nation Israel, the Book of Psalms. The Book of Psalms is poetry, but is laced with extremely strong theology. It is one of the contrasts you can't help but notice—the hymns of Israel and, I might add, the ancient hymns of the church are rich in theology, in contrast to the choruses we sing today. So much of contemporary Christianity is rich in some aspects, but vacuous in terms of theology.

The Hebrew term for the Psalms is *praises*. Fifty-five of these are addressed to the "Chief Musician." We get our name for the Book of Psalms from the Greek translation of the Old Testament *psalmoi,* "a poem to be sung with a stringed instrument"; and *psalter,* which is "a harp; a stringed instrument." Those are derivative terms from Greek, not Hebrew.

Hebrew poetry is different from how we think of poetry. We think of poems as having a rhyme (a parallelism of sound), or a rhythm (a parallelism of time; a meter). But Hebrew poetry has a different structure; it is designed conceptually rather than metrically. The parallelism is of ideas, not just sound. There are comparative pairings to illuminate, contrasting parallelisms for antithesis, and ones with completive syntheses. You often see the word *Selah* in your Bible. It's an untranslated Hebrew term. Many scholars assume it's an instruction for the singers. Others have concluded that it is not musical; *Selah* is to connect the thought—the subject matter—not the music. It connects the end of one strophe with the beginning of the next. It's sometimes synthetic, sometimes antithetic. It's concerned with truth, not tunes. *Selah* actually comes from two similar roots meaning "to praise, or lift up." It is a pause for the thought, not the instrument.

Of the 150 Psalms, seventy-three are attributed to David; twelve to Asaph, who was a musical director; twelve to the sons of Korah; one to Moses; and about fifty are anonymous.

Many scholars divide the Book of Psalms into five books, paralleling the five books of Moses. The Psalms from 1 to 41 are really about man, which some call the "Genesis package"; from 42 to 72 are about deliverance, "the exodus book"; from 73 to 89, the sanctuary is the predominant theme, "the Leviticus book"; from 90 to 106 are about unrest and wandering, "the Book of Numbers"; and the fifth's focus is on the Word of the Lord, the "Deuteronomy section." This is a very common way of organizing the Psalms, but it is certainly not the only way.

The fifteen Songs of the Degrees, or the Songs of Ascents, are traditionally thought to have been so named because the Temple had fifteen steps. But there could be another explanation. Hezekiah, one of the godliest of Judah's kings, wrote many Psalms and Proverbs. He restored the Temple worship and he also reorganized much of the documentation. In 2 Kings 20, he prayed to God and God extended his life for fifteen years. And to confirm it to Hezekiah, God told him to go out and look at Ahaz's sundial. God moved the shadow on the sundial back fifteen degrees as a confirmation to Hezekiah that he had fifteen years added to his life. This episode shows that the Psalms of Degrees may be about those events.

THE MESSIANIC PSALMS

The Book of Psalms, this hymnal of Israel, is quoted more than any other book in the Old Testament and constitutes irrefutable testimony to the divine inspiration of the Scriptures. In addition to being wonderful resources for praise and devotion, the psalms also are profoundly significant from an apologetic and prophetic point of view. Messianic allusions are sprinkled throughout the Psalms, but Psalms 2, 8, 16, 22, 23, 24, 40, 41, 45, 68, 69, 87, 89, 102, 110, and 118 are very clearly Messianic. They definitely deal with the coming of the Messiah.

More than even the Book of Isaiah, the Messianic Psalms speak about Christ's birth, His betrayal, His agony, His death, resurrection, ascension, His coming glory, and His world-wide reign. All of these are pictured in supernaturally inspired vividness.

The fact that the Messiah would be the Son of God is mentioned in Psalms 2, 45, 102, and elsewhere. The fact that He would also be the Son of Man is empha-sized in Psalm 8. That He would be the Son of David is elaborated on, especially in Psalm 139. His office as a prophet is in 22, 25, and 40; His office as a priest is in Psalm 110; His office as a king is in 2, 24, 72; the fact that He will speak in parables, calm the storm, be despised, rejected, mocked, whipped, and that He'd be derided are all portrayed vividly in the Psalms. The facts that He would be impaled on a cross, that He would be thirsty and given wine mixed with gall, that lots would be cast by His enemies for His garments, and yet, in all of this, not a bone would be broken, are detailed in the Psalms. The facts that He would rise from the dead and ascend into heaven, that He would sit at the right hand of God, that He is our high priest, that He will judge all the nations, that His reign will be eternal, that He is the Son of God, and also the Son of David; that people would sing "Hosanna" to Him, that He would be blessed forever, and that He will come in glory in the last days—all this is laid out in these incredible poems.

> *The Book of Psalms, this hymnal of Israel, is quoted more than any other book in the Old Testament.*

THE SHEPHERD PSALMS

Psalms 22-24 are the Shepherd Psalms. Psalm 22 is the Suffering Savior, which is parallel to the Good Shepherd passage in John 10. The Living Shepherd is in Psalm 23; "The Lord is my Shepherd," which is parallel to the Great Shepherd passage in Hebrews 13. The Exalted Sovereign is in Psalm 24, which Peter alludes to in his first letter, chapter 5, verse 4.

Let's take a look at Psalm 22. It opens with a declaration, "My God, my God, why hast thou forsaken me?" This, of course, was the fourth of the seven exclamations of Jesus from the Cross. Psalm 22 reads as if it were dictated as He hung on the Cross, yet it was written seven hundred years before crucifixion was even invented. The form of capital punishment in Israel was stoning, not crucifixion. David was inspired, supernaturally, to write this Psalm. Verses 7 and 8 read, "All they that see me laugh me to scorn: they shoot out the lip, they shake the head, saying, He trusted on the LORD that he would deliver him: let him deliver him, seeing he delighted in him." And that's virtually a quote of Matthew 27:43 when the crowd was making fun of Him while He hung on that cross.

Psalm 22 goes on about the Crucifixion: the voice of the Crucified One says in verses 14-18,

Verse 14: I am poured out like water, and all my bones are out of joint: my heart is like wax; it is melted in the midst of my bowels.

Verse 15: My strength is dried up like a potsherd; and my tongue cleaveth to my jaws; and thou hast brought me into the dust of death.

Verse 16: For dogs have compassed me: the assembly of the wicked have enclosed me: they pierced my hands and my feet.

Verse 17: I may tell all my bones: they look and stare upon me.

Verse 18: They part my garments among them, and cast lots upon my vesture.

This is astonishing when you realize that David was never in that kind of predicament, yet he was inspired to compose this hymn, this declaration. Psalm 23 is actually a declaration of God's adequacy in our lives. The Scripture presents seven compound titles of God, each describing God in terms of our needs: YHWH-jireh, the Lord will provide (Genesis 22); YHWH-rapha, the Lord that healeth (Exodus 15); YHWH-shalom, the Lord our Peace (Judges 6); YHWH-tsidkenu, the Lord our Righteousness (Jeremiah 23); YHWH-shammah, the Lord ever-present (Ezekiel 48); YHWH-nissi, the Lord our Banner (Exodus 17); and YHWH-raah, the Lord our Shepherd (Psalm 23). These describe God's seven-fold completeness for each of us. In Psalm 23, each of these seven compound titles is reflected behind each phrase. Hidden beneath the beauty of the poetry is profound theology, a comprehensive packaging of the Lord being complete in His adequacy for each of us.

Psalm 2 is another fascinating Psalm because it is a trilogue among three people: the Father, the Son, and the Holy Spirit. Just reading it through is interesting, but it really hits you between the eyes when you realize who's saying what to whom. The first one speaking, I believe, is the Holy Spirit, in verses 1-3: "Why do the heathen rage, and the people imagine a vain thing? The kings of the earth set themselves, and the rulers take counsel together, against the LORD, and against his anointed, saying, Let us break their bands asunder, and cast away their cords from us." Here is the Holy Spirit, almost chuckling at the futility of the kings of the earth, who have taken it upon themselves to go to war against God the Lord and His anointed. He concludes in verses 4 and 5: "He that sitteth in the heavens shall laugh: the Lord shall have them in derision. Then shall he speak unto them in his wrath, and vex them in his sore displeasure."

Then the Father speaks in verse 6: "Yet have I set my king upon my holy hill of Zion." This is yet future, obviously.

The Son speaks in verses 7–9: "I will declare the decree: the LORD hath said unto me, Thou art my Son; this day have I begotten thee. Ask of me, and I shall give thee the heathen for thine inheritance, and the uttermost parts of the earth for thy possession. Thou shalt break them with a rod of iron; thou shalt dash them in pieces like a potter's vessel."

Then the Holy Spirit turns and speaks to the kings of the earth in verses 10–12: "Be wise now therefore, O ye kings: be instructed, ye judges of the earth. Serve the LORD with fear, and rejoice with trembling. Kiss the Son, lest he be angry, and ye perish from the way, when his wrath is kindled but a little. Blessed are all they that put their trust in him."

Psalm 2 has little meaning until you realize who's talking to whom.

THE WISDOM OF THE NATION ISRAEL

The Book of Proverbs can be summarized as "prudence through precept." These brief instructional proverbs are intended to be memorized, just a few at a time. The word *proverb* means "a very terse maxim." You don't read through the Book of Proverbs—you take a little bit at a time. Proverbs is to our practical life what the Psalms is to our devotional life. Since there are thirty-one chapters, many will read the chapter that corresponds to that day on the calendar. This is very practical.

The Proverb does not argue, it assumes. It's not an apologetic device; it is a practical instruction device. Solomon wrote three thousand of these, though only a few are included in this book. Most of these, we believe, were arranged during the reign of Hezekiah, somewhat later.

The first nine chapters of Proverbs, "the extolling of wisdom," consist of fifteen sonnets (short poems devoted to one particular theme and then molded into some special form), and two of them are monologues.

After that there are about fourteen chapters of "maxims in joining prudence"—375 aphorisms and couplets and then sixteen epigrams.

After more maxims on prudence are the "thirteen sayings of Agur," the oracle of "Lemuel's mother," and the climax in Proverbs 31 is an acrostic on "the virtuous woman."

In Hebrew, each line of that starts with a different Hebrew letter, so it's a very skillfully designed acrostic.

There are many structural devices in Proverbs. A contrastive Proverb would be, "A fair woman without discretion is like a jewel of gold in a swine's snout." In a completive Proverb, the second line agrees with or amplifies the first line: "As cold waters to a thirsty soul, so is good news from a far country." The colorful expression is what helps capture the thought. An example of a comparative Proverb is, "The tongue of a nagging woman is a continual dripping in a very rainy day."

ECCLESIASTES: "ALL IS VANITY"

The next book, Ecclesiastes, is a widely misunderstood book. The Hebrew word for this book is *Koheleth,* the preacher, and it appears to be Solomon's sermon on the natural man's quest for the good life. Solomon had inconceivable wealth and power, and he was able to satisfy his every wish. But he ended up pretty cynical about it all. Solomon's authorship of Ecclesiastes is important because here's someone who really knew, who had really "been there." He speaks of the "old and foolish king" (must be himself), who's followed by a "poor and wise youth" (remember it was his scheming usurper, Jeroboam, who divided the empire after Solomon died). He speaks of a woman as "a seductress more bitter than death." (He apparently hadn't found one virtuous woman in one thousand.) In contrast to the Book of Proverbs, this is not a collection of scattered precepts, but a cumulative sermon with a climax.

Many people misunderstand Ecclesiastes because, while it penetrates the human condition, it looks beyond death. It seems pessimistic at first, but only if you stop at death. In fact, the main thrust of the book is that you need to look beyond, into the afterlife, to make sense out of anything. In other words, it is, in a sense, the cure for pessimism.

The conclusion in Ecclesiastes: all is vanity. It's bravely honest, rather than pessimistic. It sees beyond life's ironies and wearying repetition to the divine control and future restitutions.

The first two chapters are the quest by personal experiment—the preacher's own search for wisdom and pleasure. The next few chapters are the quest by general observation; these deal with the enigmas of human society. And the next few chapters are the quest by practical morality. The conclusion is that material things cannot satisfy the soul. The last few chapters are the quest reviewed and concluded. And it concludes that all is vanity.

The final significance is, "Let us hear the conclusion of the whole matter: Fear God, and keep his commandments: for this is the whole duty of man" (12:13). This is written by the

Ecclesiastes Deals with Ten Vanities

1. *The vanity of human wisdom: both the wise and foolish die.*
2. *Human labor: the worker is no better than the shirker in the end.*
3. *Human purpose: man proposes, but God disposes.*
4. *Human rivalry: success brings more envy than joy.*
5. *Human avarice: much feeds lust for the elusive more.*
6. *Human fame: brief, uncertain, and soon forgotten.*
7. *Human insatiety: money does not satisfy but only feeds other desires.*
8. *Human coveting: gain cannot be enjoyed despite desire.*
9. *Human frivolity: only camouflages the inevitable sad end.*
10. *Human awards: good and bad often get wrong deserts.*

exhausted man at the end, and he goes on (in verse 14), "For God shall bring every work into judgment, with every secret thing, whether it be good, or whether it be evil." It really sets the stage for the Book of Romans and is the opposite of pessimism. Romans 8:20,21 says, "For the creature was made subject to vanity, not willingly, but by reason of him who hath subjected the same in hope, because the creature itself also shall be delivered from the bondage of corruption into the glorious liberty of the children of God."

THE SONG OF SONGS, OR SONG OF SOLOMON

The Song of Songs' theme is "ultimate love." No Book of the entire Bible has given rise to more commentary or difference of opinion. Some think it is just an allegory, others that it is literal, and still some as a handbook for sensual lovemaking. This book has only 117 verses, yet it is the least studied, most emotionally controversial, and, in some respects, one of the most difficult books in the Bible.

There are over five hundred commentaries on the Song in the first seventeen hundred years of church history. It's been interpreted as an allegory, an extended type, a drama involving two or three main characters. Some say it's just a collection of Syrian wedding songs, and more. The Jewish tradition—in the Mishna, the Talmud and the Targum—views the book as an allegorical picture of the love of God for Israel. Early Church leaders, including Hippolatus, Origen, Jerome, Augustine, and others, consider it an allegory of Christ's love for His bride, the Church. Some see it as just a collection of seven Syrian idylls.

However, I think it is more accurate to see this as an opera. Solomon is the hero of the piece. Shulamit is the Cinderella. The word *Shulamit* is simply the feminine rendering of the Book of Solomon, so the characters are Mr. and Mrs. Solomon.

The story takes place in the mountain district of Ephraim. King Solomon had a vineyard; he let it out to an Ephraimite family as keepers. The husband and the father had apparently passed away, but there was a mother and at least two sons and daughters. The older daughter, Shulamit, is forced by her brothers to do the hard tasks, and she is denied the privileges a growing girl might have expected in a Jewish home.

"My mother's sons were angry with me" is one of her cries, which sounds like they were probably half-brothers. "Mine own vineyard have I not kept": she had no opportunity to look after herself. One day she discovered a handsome stranger, a shepherd, who viewed her as without blemish. The friendship ripened to affection and finally love; he promised to return and make her his bride. After his extended absence, the brothers were skeptical and thought she had been deceived by this stranger. She dreamed of him at night; she trusted him. One day a glorious cavalcade arrived. The attendants announced, "The king has sent for you," and in obedience she responded, as she looked in the face of the king. Guess who? It was the shepherd. She declared, "I am my beloved's, and his desire is toward me."

Great stuff. The rabbis wouldn't let anyone study the book until they were over thirty.

Hour 9

THE BOOK OF DANIEL

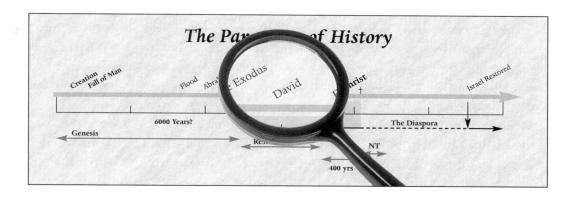

DANIEL HAD THE MOST incredible career imaginable; he was transported as a teenage captive to a pagan empire and became the primary confidante to the ruler of Babylon. When Babylonia was taken over by its enemies, he rose to the second or third position in the Persian Empire. There are only two people in the Bible other than Jesus Christ of which there is no evil spoken—Joseph and Daniel. Both were administrators and executives.

The book of Daniel is in two halves: the first six chapters are historical, which deal with the adventures and career of this remarkable man. The second six chapters are prophecy; in fact, among the most astonishing in the entire Bible. Daniel is the most authenticated book of the Old Testament. It has been attacked because of its remarkable prophecies, but to no avail.

Daniel and his three friends were deported as teenagers in the first of three sieges by

Nebuchadnezzar. Nebuchadnezzar took the most promising of his captives and put them through post-graduate school to serve at court. Daniel was among the most favored youth, and was probably from the royal line. But these four Jewish young men committed themselves to remain faithful to the God of Israel despite their enforced pagan environment.

One of the first things the pagans did was to rename the four. Daniel, which means "God is my judge" was renamed Belteshazzar, "prince of Baal"; Hananiah means "beloved of the Lord," and he was renamed "illumined by the sun-god," Shadrach; Mishael, which means "who is God?" was renamed Meshech, "who is like the moon-god"; Azariah, "the Lord is my help," was renamed Abednego, "servant of Nego" or "shining fire."

NEBUCHADNEZZAR'S PREDICAMENT

A young general, Nebuchadnezzar was very successful against Nineveh, and his great accomplishment was the defeat of Pharaoh Neco at the Battle of Carcemish. That defeat made Babylon ruler of the known world. On his way home he laid siege to Jerusalem. During that siege his father, Nabopalazar, died. When he arrived in Babylon to assume the throne, he realized that he also inherited his father's advisors in the court.

He had a very disturbing dream one night, and he decided to use it as a way to find out if these cronies could really perform. So he insisted that they interpret the dream without telling them what the dream was. When they pointed out that they couldn't do that, he said he was going to tear them limb from limb and make their houses a dunghill.

Daniel, who was included in that job category, asked for a chance at it, had a prayer meeting with his friends and then staged an incredible scene in the palace. All the cronies in the back row were watching. Daniel said he couldn't tell the king what his dream was either,

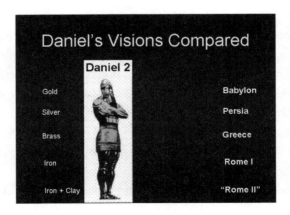

but there was a God in heaven that could. "And here's what your dream was and here's what it means." And that was the beginning of his incredible career in Babylonia.

Nebuchadnezzar had dreamed of a giant metal statue. It had a head of gold, arms and chest of silver, belly and thighs of brass, legs of iron, and the feet were iron mixed with clay. We know from Daniel's interpretation that the gold head represented Babylon. The silver represented an empire that would be succeeding them—the Persian Empire. The Persian Empire would be succeeded by the Greek Empire. That would be succeeded by Rome, but in two phases. But that wasn't the end of the dream: a stone cut without hands struck the image at the feet, disintegrating it, and the stone grew to become a mountain that filled the whole earth.

Daniel told Nebuchadnezzar the dream, which impressed him, and pointed out that the dream was about the end times. Then, from chapters 2 through 7, the language of the original shifts from Hebrew to Aramaic, the Gentile language of that day. And this is a window in the Scripture that is very unique. Generally the Bible talks about history—past, present, and future—through the lens of Israel. But here is one place in Scripture where we get a profile of all Gentile history, from Babylon to the end: Babylon is captured by the Persians, the Persians are conquered by the Greeks, the Greeks are conquered by the Romans. The Roman Empire disintegrated into separate elements about A.D. 476.

These chapters, 2–7, describe the "times of the Gentiles," which start with Nebuchadnezzar and end with a final world leader who will be dealt with by Jesus Christ at His Second Coming. Israel went into captivity, they will come out of captivity, they will be restored as a nation, but they will be persecuted until "The King of Kings" shows up.

You can imagine how the staff advisors felt, being upstaged by this young captive. To get back at Daniel, they talked Nebuchadnezzar into building an image of himself (probably like the one he saw in his dream, except all gold—sixty cubits high and six cubits wide). Everyone was required to bow down to the image, and if they didn't, they would be put into the fiery furnace. Daniel's three friends, of course, refused to do that. So they were thrown into a furnace heated to seven times its normal temperature, so hot it consumed the guards standing duty. When Nebuchadnezzar looked in the furnace, he saw not three, but four, people. And who was with them? "The Son of God." The only things that burned were the ropes that bound them.

DANIEL 4: NEBUCHADNEZZAR'S TESTIMONY

Nebuchadnezzar had another weird dream: a huge tree was cut down for seven years. Daniel interpreted and warned Nebuchadnezzar to repent of his pride. Exactly one year later, Nebuchadnezzar was stricken with a mental derangement that lasted for seven years. The tradition in the Talmud is that Daniel was his personal nurse during that period. But when Nebuchadnezzar recovered, he told his whole story in chapter 4. He acknowledged that the God of Daniel is the God of the universe and published his personal testimony throughout his entire world.

DANIEL 5: THE FALL OF BABYLON

By this time Nebuchadnezzar had died and Belshazzar, his grandson, was in charge. Babylon was under attack by the Persians but was thought to be impregnable. So Belshazzar, instead of preparing for a siege, threw a party and used all the Jewish Temple vessels they had taken seventy years earlier as party vessels. When the party was really rolling, they saw the fingers of a man's hand write on the wall. That shook them up. The experts couldn't decipher it. The queen mother was still alive, and she told Belshazzar that there was a man, Daniel, who was a specialist in this sort of phenomenon. So Daniel was called out of retirement to interpret.

Unknown to them, while all of this was going on, the Persian army had sealed off the Euphrates River, which both supplied and protected the city, slipped under the gates and was taking over the town. The Persians took Babylon without a battle.

Daniel told them that the writing said in Hebrew, *"mene, mene, tekel, upharsin."* Mene means "numbered; reckoned," which is like saying, "God hath numbered thy kingdom and finished it," or "your number is up," as we might translate it. The third word, *tekel,* means "weighed." The last word was *peres* (by its plural form, *upharsin*), and it means "broken; divided." The writing said, "Your kingdom is divided and given to the Medes and Persians." That night Babylon fell to the Persians and Belshazzar was killed.

DANIEL 6: THE REVOLT OF THE MAGI

Daniel, by that time, was about eighty-three years old and emerged very prominent in the Medo-Persian Empire. There was a hereditary priesthood among them called the Magi; a powerful sect of priestly magistrates, and Daniel was appointed to be the *Rab-mag,* their chief. (In fact, the word "magistrate" comes from this root.)

You can imagine how having this Jew appointed over this hereditary priesthood went over with the regulars. So they plotted and contrived to convince the king to put Daniel in the lion's den. The king himself was most relieved when, the next morning, they found

Daniel totally unharmed. He had been miraculously spared. The king then fed Daniel's accusers to the lions.

Daniel apparently established a cabal within this priesthood as conservators of a private prophecy that resulted in the fabled visit to the birth at Bethlehem over four centuries later.

DANIEL 7–10: THE PROPHECIES

In chapter 7, the aged Daniel was by the river in Babylon and saw in the night visions of a creature like a winged lion come out of the sea. He saw another, a bear raised on its side. Another was a leopard that moved so fast it didn't touch the ground. And the fourth was so awesome that he couldn't even think of an animal to compare it to; he called it "the great and terrible beast," which in a second phase has ten heads. In Daniel 2, we saw the empires of the world as man might see them: bright, shiny metals. In Daniel 7, we see the same series of empires as God would see them: a series of voracious beasts.

Both visions—the dream in chapter 2 and the visions of chapter 7—portray the same series of four empires, the fourth in two phases. This is why scholars have been anticipating a "revival" of the Roman Empire, and why there is such attention being given to the current emergence of a European Super State.

DANIEL 8: THE RAM AND THE GOAT

This vision was two years after the vision of chapter 7, but twelve years before the fall of Babylon in chapter 5. Bear in mind, these six chapters at the end of Daniel are like an appendix. So Daniel 8 actually was given between chapters 4 and 5.

In this vision, Daniel saw a ram and a goat, and the ram, which was very powerful, was defeated by the goat attacking him from the west. It was the Greek Empire against the Persian Empire. The notable horn of the goat breaks into four horns. There's also a little horn that has a very key role at the end. Daniel interpreted that a leader from the west (which turned out to be Alexander the Great) would subdue the Medo-Persian Empire. This is so vivid that when Alexander the Great entered Jerusalem, the High Priest showed him the writings of Daniel and he recognized his own career being prophesied and spared the city.

It's interesting that the notable horn breaks into four. When Alexander, on his deathbed, was asked who would get the empire, he said, "Give it to the strong." His four generals divided it: Cassander took Macedonia and Greece; Lysimacus took Thrace, Bithynia, and most of Asia Minor; Ptolemy took Egypt, Cyrene, and Arabia Petraea; Seleucus took Syria and all the lands east to India. Ptolemy and Seleucus are the ones we are concerned with in Biblical history; Israel was the buffer state between continual tensions between Ptolemy of Egypt and the Seleucid Empire. One of those leaders, portrayed as the "little horn," is Antiochus Epiphanes, whose desecration of the Temple led to the Macabbean revolt and its rededication is celebrated to this day as *Hanukkah*.

DANIEL 9:
THE MOST ASTONISHING PASSAGE IN THE BIBLE

I want to focus on what I think is the most fruitful, most beneficial, most astonishing passage in the Bible—the last four verses in Daniel 9. Jesus gave his disciples a confidential briefing on the end times, pointed them to this very passage, and attributed it to Daniel the Prophet. So anyone who believes in Jesus Christ has no problem with the authority of the book of Daniel.

The first nineteen verses of chapter 9 is Daniel's prayer. He realized from reading the prophecies of Jeremiah that the seventy years of captivity were almost over and so he prayed over the whole situation. The prayer is so intense that even in the translation you can feel him tremble. But he gets interrupted; this is known as the interrupted prayer in the Old Testament. Gabriel interrupts his prayer and gives him a four-verse prophecy that has no equal in the entire Scripture. Daniel 9:24-27:

Verse 24. Seventy weeks are determined upon thy people and upon thy holy city, to finish the transgression, and to make an end of sins, and to make reconciliation for iniquity, and to bring in everlasting righteousness, and to seal up the vision and prophecy, and to anoint the most Holy.

Verse 25. Know therefore and understand, that from the going forth of the commandment to restore and to build Jerusalem unto the Messiah the Prince shall be seven weeks, and threescore and two weeks: the street shall be built again, and the wall, even in troublous times.

Verse 26. And after threescore and two weeks shall Messiah be cut off, but not for himself: and the people of the prince that shall come shall destroy the city and the sanctuary; and the end thereof shall be with a flood, and unto the end of the war desolations are determined.

Verse 27. And he shall confirm the covenant with many for one week: and in the midst of the week he shall cause the sacrifice and the oblation to cease, and for the overspreading of abominations he shall make it desolate, even until the consummation, and that determined shall be poured upon the desolate.

These are the so-called "Seventy Weeks of Daniel." They are weeks of years. The first of the four verses is the scope of the whole prophecy. Then we will encounter sixty-nine weeks of years; and then an interval before the seventieth week. That's very important to understand. The last of the four verses is the final week of the "seventy weeks." The sixty-nine weeks end in verse 25. The verse 26, *between* 25 and 27, details events that occur after the sixty-ninth but before the seventieth week starts.

The first of these four verses (verse 24) is the scope of the entire passage. Of course, these events have not been completed yet. We have not finished transgressing; we have not made an end of sins; we have not brought in everlasting righteousness. The scope of this prophecy is still incomplete. Notice that the focus of this prophecy is specifically Jewish: "Seventy sevens are determined upon thy *people in the Holy City*."

Then Gabriel gave Daniel a mathematical prophecy: the sixty-nine weeks of verse 25. There is a starting point: the commandment to restore and rebuild Jerusalem. When Daniel was receiving this from Gabriel, he was in captivity in Babylon. Several hundred miles to the west, Jerusalem was in ruins, but he knew it would be rebuilt because of the prophecies in Jeremiah. Gabriel said in verse 25 that it shall be "seven weeks and threescore and two weeks."

From the commandment to restore and rebuild Jerusalem to the Messiah the King shall be sixty-nine weeks of years. The Bible clearly uses, both in Genesis and in Revelation, 360-day years. Sixty-nine weeks of 360-day years equals 173,880 days. When we get to Ezra and Nehemiah, we will learn that they went back to build the Temple in Ezra but got nowhere until Nehemiah was able to obtain the authority *to rebuild the city*. That authority was given by Artaxerxes Longimanus on March 14, 445 B.C. That is the trigger; but when was the Messiah presented as King?

There is a prophecy in Zechariah 9:9: "Rejoice greatly, O daughter of Zion; shout, O daughter of Jerusalem: behold, thy King cometh unto thee: he is just, and having salvation; lowly, and riding upon an ass, and upon a colt the foal of an ass." And that's exactly what Jesus did. He never allowed himself to be worshiped as a king except for the one day that he not only allowed it, He arranged it. He had the disciples get a donkey, and He rode from Bethany up over the Mount of Olives down through the Kidron Valley into Jerusalem, deliberately fulfilling Zechariah 9:9. In Luke 19, in what we call the Triumphal Entry account, the people sang Psalm 118, which is a Hallel Psalm proclaiming Him as the Messiah: "Blessed be the King that cometh in the name of the Lord: peace in heaven, and glory in the highest".[1] The Pharisees said, "Master, rebuke your disciples." Why did they say that? Because they recognized that the disciples were proclaiming Jesus as the *Meshach Nagid,* the

Messiah the King, and felt they were blaspheming! And Jesus declared, "I tell you that, if these should hold their peace, the stones would immediately cry out" (verse 40).

This event occurred on April 6, A.D. 32, which turns out to be 173,880 days from the decree authorizing the rebuilding of Jerusalem! The Angel Gabriel gave Daniel a prediction of the exact day the Messiah would present Himself as King to Jerusalem. What makes this particularly remarkable is that the Old Testament, including Daniel, was translated into Greek in the third century *before Christ was born.* This is one of the most astonishing verifications that Jesus Christ really was the Messiah of Israel.

When Jesus rode the donkey into Jerusalem, Luke 19:41 says, "When he was come near, he beheld the city, and wept over it." Why? He said, "If thou hadst known, even thou, at least *in this thy day,* the things which belong unto thy peace! but now they are hid from thine eyes" (verse 42, emphasis added). He held Jerusalem accountable to understand that this was the day that was scheduled in God's plan.

The Angel Gabriel gave Daniel a prediction of the exact day the Messiah would present Himself as King to Jerusalem.

Jesus further prophesied, "For the days shall come upon thee, that thine enemies shall cast a trench about thee, and compass thee round, and keep thee in on every side, and shall lay thee even with the ground, and thy children within thee; and they shall not leave in thee one stone upon another."[2] And thirty-eight years later Titus Vespasian, with the Fifth, Tenth, Twefth, and Fifteenth Roman Legions, laid siege to the city of Jerusalem. The Romans laid siege for about nine months in A.D. 70 and slaughtered over a million inhabitants. Titus had hoped to spare the Temple as a trophy but a torch was thrown through the window and the Temple caught fire, burning the wood interior and melting all the gold inside. He reluctantly had to command his troops to take it apart, stone by stone, to recover the gold. So this was very literally fulfilled.

The question is, *why* was Jerusalem destroyed? There are lots of good answers to that, but in the last part of Luke 19:44, Jesus said, "because thou knewest not the time of thy visitation." Jesus held them accountable to know the specifications of Gabriel's prophecy to Daniel in Daniel chapter 9.

Now we come to that verse that is the *interval,* Daniel 9:26: "And after threescore and two weeks shall Messiah be cut off, but not for himself: and the people of the prince that shall come shall destroy the city and the sanctuary; and the end thereof shall be with a flood, and unto the end of the war desolations are determined."

We've looked at verse 25 (the sixty-nine weeks, seven plus sixty-two); verse 27 is the seventieth week, yet future. Verse 26 is an interval at the end of the sixty-two weeks, which means after the sixty-nine, and yet prior to the seventieth. And in that interval, at least two events occur: the Messiah will be cut off (*karat,* executed) and the city and sanctuary will be destroyed. So if you're looking for a Messiah, you're looking for someone who presented himself on a donkey to Jerusalem prior to the destruction of Jerusalem in A.D. 70. (And we have a good candidate in mind!)

There is a final week of Daniel's prophecy: the so-called "Seventieth Week." "And he shall confirm the covenant with many for one week: and in the midst of the week he shall cause the sacrifice and the oblation to cease, and for the overspreading of abominations he shall make it desolate, even until the consummation, and that determined shall be poured upon the desolate."[3] This week is defined by a coming leader enforcing a covenant for seven years. But in the middle of seven years he will establish an idol in the Holy of Holies: this act is called the Abomination of Desolation. It will be a major political event.

The last half of that seven-year period is labeled by Jesus Christ as "The Great Tribulation." He was quoting from Daniel 12 in His briefing to His disciples. This is the most documented period of time in the entire Bible. It's spoken of in many places as a seven-year period, the two halves as three and a half years each; each half is also called forty-two months, or 1,260 days. Obviously it's very literal and very climactic because it ends with the Second Coming of Jesus Christ.

In a sense, Israel's timepiece has been stopped; it was stopped by Christ in Luke 19, expressly. That clock has one seven-year period left yet to be ticked off. And as we study the Scripture it would seem that there are more and more reasons to suspect that the seven-year period, the "Seventieth Week," is not far away.

Something else that is worth noting is that this "seventy-sevens" is the fourth 490-year period in Israel's history. It seems that if you take the calendar years and subtract the time Israel is out of favor, you always end up with a 490-year period. When we were in Genesis and Exodus, we looked at the period from Abraham to the Exodus, which was 505 years, until you subtract the fifteen years of Ishmael (as an implicit usurper), then you have 490 years. From Exodus to the Temple is 601 years. But the six servitudes in Judges added up to 111 years. Take the 111 from 601 and again you get 490 years. From the Temple to the Decree of Artaxerxes is 560 years, but if you subtract the seventy years of captivity you again get 490 years. The seventieth week adds the seven to the forty-three totaling, again, 490 years. When Jesus instructed His disciples to forgive "seventy times seven,"[4] it may have been more than a figure of speech: that was an apparent threshold in Israel's own history!

DANIEL 10-12

Daniel 10 is a very strange but provocative chapter. Daniel had fasted for twenty-one days, and at the end of the twenty-one days an angel appeared who apparently had been dispatched twenty-one days earlier, but for twenty-one days had been withstood by someone called, "the Prince of the Kingdom of Persia." This wasn't the literal king of Persia, but was a demonic presence of some kind. For twenty-one days he was fighting with him until Michael came to join him; Michael is called "the Chief Prince." The term "prince" here is a term for angels. He explained to Daniel that he was held up for these twenty-one days. He told him (paraphrase), "As soon as I give you these visions, I've got to go back and deal with the Prince of the Power of Greece." Before leaving, he gives Daniel the visions of Daniel 11 and 12, but this little glimpse into the spirit world helps us see that the events you and I encounter are the results of spiritual combat. It's also interesting that he will have to go back and battle the Prince of the Power of Greece: the Greek Empire was still two centuries away, and yet there was apparently spiritual combat going on.

Chapters 11 and 12 are rather complex. They included a detailed profile of the subsequent kings of both the Seleucid and the Ptolemaic dynasties that are fighting with each other over several centuries. It is so precise that the critics have tried to late-date Daniel to the first or second century B.C., which is nonsense since it was translated into Greek in the third century

B.C. The chapters also include a rather detailed series of glimpses regarding the final world ruler who will prevail until the end, interrupted by the Second Coming of Christ.

The Scriptures are prophetic. According to *the Encyclopedia of Biblical Prophecy* by J. Barton Payne,[5] there are 8,352 verses in the Bible making over 1,800 predictions on over 737 separate matters. The main theme of Bible prophecy is obviously the Messiah, but there are other themes, too. Israel is the subject of all kinds of major predictions. Israel's entire future is laid out in advance. The city of Babylon is a subject of some specific prophecies; Russia's invasion of the Middle East is a major topic we will see in Ezekiel. The rise of China as a superpower is in the Scripture, as well as the emergence of a European Super State. The movement toward an ecumenical religion at the Last Days, the trends toward a global government, and the rise of the occult are all predicted.

We believe we are being plunged into a period of time about which the Bible says more than it does about any other time in history, including the time Jesus walked the Shores of Galilee or climbed the Mountains of Judea. It is essential for you to challenge this preposterous statement by finding out what the Bible says about all these things and then carefully finding out what is actually going on. It's the ultimate adventure, indeed!

Ezra, Nehemiah, and the Inter-Testament period

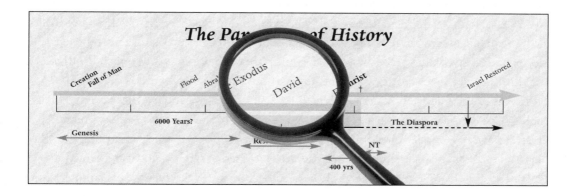

The Post-Exile Era

At this point in our reading, we are between the Exile of the Nation in Babylon and the Advent of our Lord Jesus Christ. As we continue our study, the Babylonian Empire will shortly be succeeded by the Persian Empire, which will be succeeded by the Greek Empire, which will be succeeded by the Roman Empire just prior to the Advent of Christ.

In about 270 B.C., the early part of the Greek Empire, the entire Old Testament was translated into Greek. The resulting document is called the Septuagint, and it is very valuable because it gives us a definitive copy of the Old Testament. And the fact that it was translated into Greek in 270 B.C. demonstrates that these writings are prophetic about the New Testament period.

In the previous hour, we discussed the accomplishments of Nebuchadnezzar, who became king of Babylonia after his father died. Nebuchadnezzar laid siege to Jerusalem at that time. He sacked the city of Jerusalem, appointed a vassal king, and took many from Judah into captivity (including Daniel and his three friends). That began the "Servitude of the Nation," which lasted seventy years to the exact day.

This vassal king ultimately rebelled. Some false prophets convinced him God would throw off the yoke of the Babylonians. Both Ezekiel and Daniel pleaded with the people not to rebel, insisting that Nebuchadnezzar was the hand of God, but the people didn't listen. A rebellion occurred.

Nebuchadnezzar laid siege to Jerusalem again, took more captives, and replaced the rebellious king with his uncle, Zedekiah. After a few years, Zedekiah also listened to the false prophets and began to believe he could throw off the yoke of Babylon. Jeremiah, who was in Babylon at the time, and Ezekiel, who was among those transported in the second siege, again pleaded with them not to do this because God had said that if they rebelled, the city of Jerusalem would be destroyed. Of course, they rebelled anyway, which brought on the third siege of Nebuchadnezzar. This time, as predicted, Jerusalem was destroyed.

The third siege and subsequent destruction began "the Desolations of Jerusalem." Many Bible helps presume that since both are predicted to be exactly seventy years, the "Desolations of Jerusalem" and the "Servitude of the Nation" are the same thing. But the Servitude started at the first siege when the nation ceased to be free, and the Desolations of Jerusalem started at the third siege. Sir Robert Anderson, in 1894, published his famous book entitled *Daniel's Seventy Weeks*,[1] and he recognized that these two periods were distinctively different, although overlapping. The Persian Empire arose after Cyrus conquered Babylon. The Decree of Cyrus released the nation. After seventy years, they were allowed to go back and rebuild the Temple. In fact, Cyrus even gave them financial incentives to do so. Later, Nehemiah was granted the authority from his boss, Artaxerxes Longimanus, to rebuild the city of Jerusalem. The decree of Artaxerxes triggered the Seventy Weeks of Daniel.

THE BOOK OF EZRA

Ezra was probably the author of 1 and 2 Chronicles, in addition to the book that bears his name. In fact, the last couple of verses of 2 Chronicles and the first few verses of Ezra are identical. Some scholars even believe that 1 and 2 Chronicles, Ezra, and Nehemiah originally were one book. Ezra is a very prominent person in Jewish history. He is credited with, among other things, establishing "the canon," the official version of the Old Testament.

The Book of Ezra covers the return from captivity to rebuild the Temple up to the decree of Artaxerxes, the event covered at the beginning of the Book of Nehemiah. Nehemiah chapter 2 deals with the Decree of Artaxerxes to build the city-state. Haggai was the main prophet in the days of Ezra, and Zechariah was the prophet in the days of Nehemiah.

THE RISE OF CYRUS THE GREAT

Cyrus the Great, formally known as Cyrus the Second, established the Medo-Persian Empire. His father was Cambius the First, king of Anshan (or East Elam, the Biblical term for what we would call Persia). His mother was Mandane, the daughter of Astyages, the king of Media. Bible scholars speak of the Medo-Persian Empire because Cyrus was half Mede, half Persian, and united the two groups to establish the empire. After his father died he assumed the throne, but in 550 B.C. he attacked his grandfather, the very corrupt Astyages. The king had wronged the Median general, Harpagus, who then facilitated the capture of Ectabana, capital of the Persian Empire, without a battle. That was Cyrus's pattern at Babylon eleven years later. Cyrus welded these two peoples—the Medes and the Persians—into a unified nation and a world empire that lasted for two hundred years.

Cyrus had a very sharp general named Ugbaru. On October 12, 539 B.C., Ugbaru captured Babylon without a fight. We read about this when we reviewed Daniel. According to Herodotus, the Greek historian known as "The Father of All History," "The Persians were successful at diverting the River Euphrates into a canal up river so that the water level dropped to the height of the middle of a man's thigh, which rendered the flood defenses

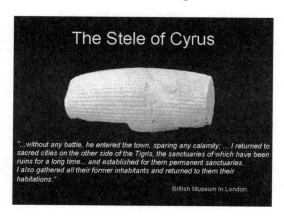

The Stele of Cyrus

"...without any battle, he entered the town, sparing any calamity; ... I returned to sacred cities on the other side of the Tigris, the sanctuaries of which have been ruins for a long time... and established for them permanent sanctuaries. I also gathered all their former inhabitants and returned to them their habitations."

British Museum in London.

useless and enabled the invaders to march through the riverbed under the gates by night."[2] It was so uneventful that for three days many people didn't know that it had been taken over. The Temple services weren't even interrupted.

The London Museum has on display the Stele of Cyrus, which is a record of him bragging to the world. Some of the words on this are, "Without any battle he entered town sparing any calamity. I returned two sacred cities on the other side of the Tigris, the sanctuaries of which have been ruins for a long time, and established them for permanent sanctuaries. I also gathered all their former inhabitants and returned to them their habitations."[3]

Let's visualize the scene. Cyrus's general had successfully conquered a city which all the experts in that day thought to be impregnable. So Cyrus, a few days later, made his grand entrance into Babylon. When he entered the city, an old man named Daniel presented him with an ancient scroll of Isaiah, which contained a personal letter addressed to Cyrus, by name. It described his career and his history. But, of course, Isaiah died 150 years before Cyrus was born. The letter said, "That saith to the deep, Be dry, and I will dry up thy rivers [Cyrus might have responded, "What a coincidence; that's how we got in here".] that saith of Cyrus ["Hey, there's my name!"], He is my shepherd, and shall perform all my pleasure: even saying to Jerusalem, Thou shalt be built; and to the temple, Thy foundation shall be laid."[3] Cyrus was different from all the previous conquerors. Instead of making them slaves, Cyrus would be their shepherd; he took care of them and helped them rebuild their Temple.

Isaiah continued, "Thus saith the Lord to his anointed, to Cyrus, whose right hand I have holden, to subdue nations before him; and I will loose the loins of kings, to open before him the two leaved gates; and the gates shall not be shut."[4] Cyrus subdued forty-six nations.

"And I will loose the loins of kings" is one of the funniest fulfillments of prophecy in Scripture. You may recall the incident from Daniel 5 when Belshazzar was shook up about the handwriting on the wall. The King James Version is so quaint, saying, "his knees smote one against the other and his loins were loosed." That embarrassment about Belshazzar apparently became common knowledge, and here it is alluded to a century and a half earlier.

Isaiah continued,

I will go before thee, and make the crooked places straight: I will break in pieces the gates of brass, and cut in sunder the bars of iron: and I will give thee the treasures of darkness, and hidden riches of secret places, that thou mayest know that I, the Lord, which call thee by thy name, am the God of Israel. For Jacob my servant's sake, and Israel mine elect, I have even called thee by thy name: I have surnamed thee, though thou hast not known me. I am the Lord, and there is none else, there is no God beside me: I girded thee, though thou hast not known me.[5]

Can you imagine Cyrus reading this letter written over a century before he was born? What was Cyrus' response to all of this? Obviously, he was duly impressed. He freed the captives and gave them financial incentives to return to their homeland and rebuild their Temple. His decree is in Ezra:

> Thus saith Cyrus king of Persia, The LORD God of heaven hath given me all the kingdoms of the earth; and he hath charged me to build him an house at Jerusalem, which is in Judah. Who is there among you of all his people? his God be with him, and let him go up to Jerusalem, which is in Judah, and build the house of the LORD God of Israel (he is the God), which is in Jerusalem.[6]

The focus of the decree was the Temple, the House of God. In A.D. 536, 49,697 people returned under the leadership of Zerubbabel and about eighty years later a smaller group returned under the leadership of Ezra: less than 50,000 out of the whole nation. But they did not have the authority to build the wall and protect themselves as a city-state, the basic political unit in that era. That comes with the Book of Nehemiah. Nehemiah chapter 2 deals with the Decree of Artaxerxes to build the city-state.

TWO IMPORTANT PERSIAN KINGS

Following Cyrus, we will focus on just two of the many kings of the Persian Empire: Xerxes the First (known as Ahasuerus in Esther), and Artaxerxes the First (or Artaxerxes Longimanus), who will be very critical because he gave the authority to Nehemiah to rebuild the city wall.

Xerxes the First was characterized by passionate extremes: he had gigantic ideas but a very imperious temper. He's famous for several exploits: he built a canal through the Isthmus of Athos for his fleet; he built a bridge over the Hellespont, which was destroyed by a tempest just after completion. Xerxes was so blindly enraged by that, he commanded three hundred strokes of a scourge inflicted on the sea and threw a pair of fetters into the Hellespont as a way of expressing himself; he also had the builders of the bridge beheaded. There was also a man by the name of Pitheus the Lidian, whose contribution to the bridge expedition was about five and a half million dollars by today's standards. Xerxes was so impressed with his loyalty that he gave him the money back plus a very handsome gift. But when Pitheus requested that just one of his sons be spared from military service, Xerxes ordered the son cut into pieces and had his army march between the pieces. When you understand more of Xerxes' character you will understand more the Book of Esther. He was the kind of king who would dethrone his queen for not immodestly exposing herself at a party on the one hand; he's also one who would, on a whim, order all the Jews in the empire (which extended from Ethiopia to India) exterminated.

THE BOOK OF ESTHER

The Book of Esther is a fascinating drama. Xerxes (or Ahasuerus) hosted a gigantic banquet with his queen, Vashti, who was apparently very beautiful. He requested that she expose herself immodestly to the guests, and she refused. As punishment, Ahasuerus dethroned her. A nationwide search was launched for a replacement for Vashti, and Esther, an orphaned Jewish girl raised by her cousin, Mordecai, was ultimately selected. A Jewish girl was now the queen of the Persian Empire. Mordecai warned her not to reveal her Jewish background.

An incident occurred that seems trivial to the basic plot of the story, but turned out to be very important later. Mordecai, who had a position in the palace, discovered a plot against the king, and he tipped Esther off. She told the king and the assailants were caught and killed. But Mordecai was not rewarded. This is an example of how God's timing is perfect. God had something in mind that was so fantastic it would seem contrived as if it was fiction. But it's a matter of history.

Haman's hatred was so intense that he plotted to wipe out all the Jews . . . Mordecai found out about the plan and prevailed upon Esther to intercede.

Many have failed to appreciate who Mordecai was or his background. Way back in 2 Samuel, David decided against killing Shimei, who was cursing him. Shimei was a descendant of King Saul. David said that if God had called him to curse David, then let him curse. And because David showed grace, Shimei's descendants include Mordecai. So Mordecai is literally a product of the grace of David.

Haman, the villain of this episode, was a big shot—one of the insiders of the Kingdom. He was born because Saul failed to follow God's instructions in 1 Samuel. Haman hated the Jews in general, but he hated Mordecai in particular because Mordecai refused to do obeisance to him. When Haman was promoted and Mordecai refused to bow down to him, his hatred became an obsession.

Haman's hatred was so intense that he plotted to wipe out all the Jews. Haman convinced the king that the Jews were enemies of the state and should be exterminated. Mordecai found out about the plan and prevailed upon Esther to intercede. He made it clear that if Haman was left to his devices, he would wipe out, not just Mordecai, but the entire Jewish population in the Persian Empire.

He finally convinced Esther to intercede, and his argument to her is one you will hear echoed many times throughout Scripture: "Thou art come to the kingdom for such a time as this." He saw the hand of God, that Esther was the queen for the very purpose of thwarting Haman's satanic plan.

The problem was that the Persians were ruled by very strict laws that couldn't be reversed, even by a capricious king. And part of royal protocol was if you entered the king's throne room without having been summoned, you were subject to death. What Mordecai was asking Esther to do was highly dangerous. She had not been summoned by the king for over a month and suspected she might be out of favor. But she ultimately yielded to Mordecai's instructions and declared, "If I perish, I perish."

The critical moment came when she entered the inner court. When the king saw her, he extended the scepter (meaning she was accepted). For some reason, rather than tell the king the problem immediately, she simply invited the king and Haman to a banquet. This deferral of the opportunity really set the stage for some other things because Haman was ecstatic—he was invited to a banquet with the king! In celebration, he prepared gallows to hang his enemy, Mordecai. (The actual language really implies that he was to be impaled or crucified, not to be hung with a rope as is commonly assumed.)

After the banquet, Esther invited them to yet another banquet. The deferral was used by God in some fascinating ways. That night, the king couldn't sleep, so he decided to read the chronicles of what had transpired in the empire. He discovered something very troubling; he read that Mordecai had exposed a plot against the king's life. The would-be assassins were executed, but there was a bureaucratic blunder in that Mordecai was never rewarded.

The next morning Haman was excited because he was going to get Mordecai. He arrived at the palace early. The king called him in to ask his advice, and Haman felt very important. The king said to Haman, "What would you do for someone that the king really wanted to honor?" Haman presumed, *Naturally he's talking about me.* So he recommended, "You should take off your crown and let him wear it for a day, and give him your robe, and put him on your best horse, and parade him through the whole town to let the people know that you

The Roman Empire

The Roman Empire began taking shape in 63 B.C. when Pompey conquered Judea. Herod Antipater, who was an Edomite, was appointed ruler. A rival group east of Rome called the Parthians (derived from remnants of the extinct Persian Empire) had grown strong enough to conquer Judea in 40 B.C. The Romans regained it in 37 B.C. In fact, when Herod the Great was appointed as the king of Judea, he stayed in Rome because it was too dangerous to be in Judea. In 31 B.C. Octavian defeated Mark Anthony at the Battle of Actium, and that established Rome as an Empire.

Octavian (who called himself Augustus) took a census in about 2 B.C., which caused Mary and Joseph to go to Bethlehem. When the Magi (the priest magistrates of the Parthian Empire) arrived in Jerusalem with a military escort, Herod was very nervous. For all he knew, his buffer state, Judea, was only very tenuously held by Rome. That is why he was nervous, because they had come with an armed guard to find out about this new "King of the Jews." Their inquiry included a serious put-down since he was a non-Jewish appointee.

Something interesting happened about A.D. 7: Caponius was appointed procurator, and he removed the legal powers of the Sanhedrin so they could no longer administer capital punishment. The Babylonian Talmud records that the Sanhedrin went around Jerusalem wailing, "Woe unto us, for the scepter has departed from Judah and the Messiah has not come!" They were relying on a prophecy of Jacob which said, "The scepter will not depart from Judah until the Messiah comes . . ."[7] They actually believed that the Word of God had been broken. What they didn't know, as we mentioned in Hour 4, was that at that time there was a young man growing up in a carpenter's shop up in Nazareth . . .

really honor him." The king exclaimed, "Good idea! I want you to do that for Mordecai!" (Can you imagine Haman's chagrin?!)

The stage was now set for the second banquet. Haman began to realize that the tables were turning. At this banquet, the king asked Esther, "What is on your heart? What is your request? I'll give you up to half the kingdom . . . " She answered, "Only that mine and my people's lives are spared." And, of course, the king was shocked. As Esther explained the situation, the king was so astonished that he had to leave the room to compose himself. His anger grew as he considered the fact that he had been the pawn of Haman's deceits. While he was out of the room, Haman panicked. He knew his moments were numbered. He pled with Esther for his life and fell on the couch she was reclining on just as the king returned. He misconstrued (perhaps deliberately) what was happening: "You would attack the queen, also?" He ordered Haman hanged (or impaled) on the very gallows he had designed the previous night for Mordecai.

Haman's estate was given to Esther and assigned to Mordecai for his supervision. They couldn't reverse the order to exterminate all the Jews because of peculiarities of Persian law, but the king gave Mordecai his signet as the authority to enact any orders necessary. So they authorized the Jews to defend themselves. In all 127 provinces, from India to Ethiopia, the magistrates and the government helped the Jews defend themselves. This very famous event in Jewish history is celebrated as the Feast of Purim. (The word *purim* means "lots," as it was by drawing lots that the specific day to kill the Jews was decided.) The Book of Esther is always read during this feast.

THE GREEK EMPIRE AND ANTIOCHUS EPIPHANES

An event happened during the Greek Empire that you won't find detailed in your Bible, but the New Testament takes pains to point to it—an event which involved Antiochus Epiphanes. The Greek Empire was ushered in when Alexander the Great conquered the Persians in 332 B.C. When Alexander died he was succeeded by his four generals. Each of the generals assumed leadership over specific regions. Ptolemy and Seleucus held territory on either side of Israel, and Seleucus was later succeeded by Antiochus Epiphanes. He is the "little horn" of Daniel 8.

Antiochus the Fourth called himself Epiphanes, which means "illustrious." The children of the street called him Epimanes, which means "the madman." He hated the Jews. He made Torah reading a capital crime. Then he slaughtered a sow on the altar in Jerusalem. He didn't stop there: he erected an idol to Zeus in the Holy of Holies in the Temple. Putting an idol in the most sacred spot on earth—in Jerusalem, in the Temple, in the Holy of Holies—was called the Abomination of Desolation.

This desecration led to the Macabbean Revolt. Mattathias was a patriotic priest with five sons. His son Judas was a military genius, and they actually succeeded in throwing off the yoke of the Greek (Seleucid) Empire. It took them three years, but when they finally did it (on Antiochus Epiphane's birthday, the day he chose to desecrate the Temple), they destroyed the elements he used to defile the Temple, made new ones and rededicated the Temple on the 25th of Kislev in 165 B.C. The Jews celebrate the event every year as *Hanukkah.*[8]

Jesus spoke of an "Abomination of Desolation" as a future event in His briefing to His disciples on His Second Coming.[9] He was pointing out that it will happen again and when it does, a whole series of events will follow.

ISAIAH, JEREMIAH, AND EZEKIEL

OUR EXPLORATION of the prophets continues with the other "Major" prophets—men who wrote down history *before* it happened. These amazing passages constitute the most unassailable demonstrations that the origin of the Biblical messages are from outside the dimension of time itself.

ISAIAH

Isaiah is "the Messianic Prophet." He is quoted in the New Testament more than any other prophet. One of the greatest discoveries, the Dead Sea Scrolls, brought to light a complete scroll of Isaiah—about 24 feet long—dated around 200 B.C. In that scroll, only about nine letters are different from the Masoretic text we use today, even though the Masoretic is around eleven hundred years younger. That is an awesome testimony to the rigor, discipline and commitment of the scribes who hand-copied the Scriptures.

The Book of Isaiah is so rich and full that it's difficult to summarize, but the principal messages include, first of all, judgment on the Southern Kingdom for sin and lack of loyalty to God. Isaiah not only hammered on the coming judgment, he also focused on the restoration, in spite of the fact that they refused to repent. They would be judged, but not wiped out like the Northern Kingdom. They would be restored.

Most of the books we have looked at are historical narratives. When the prophets wrote, though, they were using a telescoping perspective, like a zoom lens with dynamic focal length. They would prophesy about something that would not be far away, and then, in the same breath, talk about something that would happen centuries later. That also resulted in double references, like an echo in advance. For instance, Daniel wrote of a particular king, but he was also referring to events in the final days. The prophets also often threw out little nuggets of extra insight that revealed new treasures.

In chapter 6, Isaiah had a breathtaking vision of the Throne of God. He was terrified, which was the typical response to such a vision. In the vision, God commissioned Isaiah to prophesy to His people.

THE VIRGIN BIRTH

Isaiah 7 details a plot against the throne. Rezin was the king of Syria (a Gentile), and Pekah was the king of the Northern Kingdom, the House of Israel. The Syrians and the Northern Kingdom mounted an expedition to depose Ahaz, the king of Judah. Ahaz was evil, but he was in the line of David. This was an attempt to make an end of the House of David. But fortunately God, in Isaiah 7:7, said, "It will not come to pass."

As part of this commitment that their plot would not succeed, Isaiah challenged King Ahaz:

Ask thee a sign of the LORD thy God; ask it either in the depth, or in the height above. But Ahaz said, I will not ask, neither will I tempt the LORD. And he said, Hear ye now, O house of David; Is it a small thing for you to weary men, but will ye weary my God also? Therefore the Lord himself shall give you a sign; Behold, a virgin shall conceive, and bear a son, and shall call his name Immanuel.[1]

Some skeptics quibble about the Hebrew word for *virgin* in verse 14. It is *alma* (and it's *ha alma* meaning "*the* virgin," not just any virgin), and some say that it can mean just a young maid. If that were the case, how would that be a sign? The context is clear that it means "virgin." In fact, in the Septuagint, three centuries before Christ was born, the Greeks used the term *parthenos,* which means clearly, specifically, and scientifically, "virgin." Greater Hebrew experts than the modern skeptics translated the word into a Greek word which is absolutely unambiguous.

In chapter 9, Isaiah specified again that from the House of David would ultimately come a supernatural king:

> For unto us a child is born, unto us a son is given [not synonymous]: and the government shall be upon his shoulder [hasn't happened yet]: and his name shall be called Wonderful, Counselor, The mighty God [A child? No. This is the Son who is given], The everlasting Father, The Prince of Peace. Of the increase of his government and peace there shall be no end, upon the throne of David,[2] and upon his kingdom, to order it, and to establish it with judgment and with justice from henceforth even for ever. The zeal of the LORD of hosts will perform this.[3]

ISAIAH 53

As we move to Isaiah 53, the best way to cover this incredible chapter is to actually read it. (Chapter 53 really should start three verses earlier at the end of chapter 52.) Here is the whole text from 52:13 through chapter 53:

> Behold, my servant shall deal prudently, he shall be exalted and extolled, and be very high. As many were astonished at thee; his visage was so marred more than any man, and his form more than the sons of men: So shall he sprinkle many nations; the kings shall shut their mouths at him: for that which had not been told them shall they see; and that which they had not heard shall they consider. Who hath believed our report? and to whom is the arm of the LORD revealed? For he shall grow up before him as a tender plant, and as a root out of a dry ground: he hath no form nor comeliness; and when we shall see him, there is no beauty that we should desire him. He is despised and rejected of men; a man of sorrows, and acquainted with grief: and we hid as it were our faces from him; he was despised, and we esteemed him not. Surely he hath borne our griefs, and carried our sorrows: yet we did esteem him stricken, smitten of God, and afflicted. But he was wounded for our transgressions, he was bruised for our iniquities: the chastisement of our peace was upon him; and with his stripes we are healed. All we like sheep have gone astray; we have turned every one to his own way; and the LORD hath laid on him the iniquity of us all. [Notice it's always He and us, He and us, like an antiphonal choir.]

He was oppressed, and he was afflicted, yet he opened not his mouth: he is brought as a lamb to the slaughter, and as a sheep before her shearers is dumb, so he opened not his mouth [He made no defense because He couldn't; He was in our shoes and we are guilty]. He was taken from prison and from judgment: and who shall declare his generation? for he was cut off out of the land of the living: for the transgression of my people was he stricken. And he made his grave with the wicked, and with the rich in his death; because he had done no violence, neither was any deceit in his mouth. Yet it pleased the LORD to bruise him; he hath put him to grief: when thou shalt make his soul an offering for sin, he shall see his seed, he shall prolong his days, and the pleasure of the LORD shall prosper in his hand. He shall see of the travail of his soul, and shall be satisfied: by his knowledge shall my righteous servant justify many; for he shall bear their iniquities. Therefore will I divide him a portion with the great, and he shall divide the spoil with the strong; because he hath poured out his soul unto death: and he was numbered with the transgressors; and he bare the sin of many, and made intercession for the transgressors.

Besides a clear presentation of atonement and judgment, behind the text are encrypted, in equidistant letter sequences: Yeshua's my name; Messiah; Nazarene; Galilee; Pharisee; Levites; Caiaphas; Annas; Passover; Moriah; the Cross; Pierce; the Atonement Lamb; etc. These, plus the names of everyone at the Cross—Peter; Matthew; John; Andrew; Philip; Thomas; two James's; Simon; Thaddeus; Matthias; and three Marys (one of which is cryptically linked with John); Salome—are all encrypted within the twelve verses of Isaiah 53.

MANDATE FOR MINISTRY

Jesus uses Isaiah as His mandate when He begin His ministry in Nazareth: "The Spirit of the Lord GOD is upon me; because the LORD hath anointed me to preach good tidings unto the meek; he hath sent me to bind up the brokenhearted, to proclaim liberty to the captives, and the opening of the prison to them that are bound; to proclaim the acceptable year of the LORD."[4]

Where Jesus *stopped* reading is significant. In the text of Isaiah there is a comma where he chose to finish (in verse 2). The part of the text Jesus did *not* include is, "and the day of vengeance of our God." He read the part of the mandate that He would fulfill in his first appearance. Yet to be fulfilled is, "the day of vengeance of our God," which will be at His Second Coming.

Deutero-Isaiah?

Many skeptics say that there are really two authors of Isaiah. They say the first thirty-nine chapters speak of the Day of the Lord, the judgments against Judah, Israel, the nations, and Jerusalem. Chapters 40 through 66 are from a different writer because the focus is on the Messiah—the One who is going to right all these wrongs.

The "higher" critics argue that because the two styles are so different, they must be from two different authors; this is called the Deutero-Isaiah theory. It's a myth and a fallacy. First of all, the change of style is because there is a change of subject, from God's Judgment to God's Remedy (the Messiah). The skeptics argue their point from the stylistic distinctives, but they do that because they have no grasp of the total design of the book. Their theory is refuted because the style, the images, the vocabulary, and grammatical constructions used throughout Isaiah are consistent.

Furthermore, we know from references in the Septuagint that Isaiah is one book. There are many ways to refute the skeptics, but there is one quote that should end the arguments. In John 12:38, Jesus quoted from Isaiah 53, "That the saying of Isaiah the prophet might be fulfilled, which he spake, Lord, who hath believed our report? and to whom hath the arm of the Lord been revealed?" Jesus is quoting the first verse from chapter 53 ("Isaiah Two"). In the next verse (John 12:40,41), Jesus says, "He hath blinded their eyes, and hardened their heart; that they should not see with their eyes, nor understand with their heart, and be converted, and I should heal them. These things said Isaiah, when he saw his glory, and spake of him."

That quote is from Isaiah 6. The first quote is from Isaiah 2 and the second from Isaiah 1. Between verses 38 and 40 of John 12, there is verse 39, which says, "Therefore they could not believe, because that Isaiah said again . . . " (emphasis added). Verse 38 refers to Isaiah the Prophet. Was Isaiah a prophet? Absolutely. How do I know? Jesus said so. If you believe in Jesus Christ, you have no problem with Isaiah. Jesus quotes from Isaiah 53 and from Isaiah 6 and between the two quotes He says, "Therefore they could not believe because that Isaiah . . . " Which Isaiah? The same Isaiah. Don't confuse disbelief and doubt. Doubt is healthy inquiry. Disbelief is a willful choice.

JEREMIAH

Jeremiah was probably one of the bravest, tender, and most pathetic figures in all of history. He was a patriot as well as a prophet, and he had the dismal task of proclaiming to his own people that they were headed for destruction.

The Weeping Prophet ministered for over forty years, approximately eighty years after Isaiah. In forty years, Jeremiah never once had a grateful response from anyone. One verse that captures Jeremiah's heart is Jeremiah 9:1: "Oh that my head were waters, and mine eyes a fountain of tears, that I might weep day and night for the slain of the daughter of my people!"

There was another "weeping prophet" who described the purpose of all history, "O Jerusalem, Jerusalem, thou that killest the prophets, and stonest them which are sent unto thee, how often would I have gathered thy children together, even as a hen gathereth her chickens under her wings, [but the tragedy of all history] and ye would not! Behold, your house is left unto you desolate. For I say unto you, Ye shall not see me henceforth, till ye shall say, Blessed is he that cometh in the name of the Lord [the triumph of all history]."

That was Jesus, in Matthew 23:37-39.

Every time you see the word *till*, it signals some major milestone for change. There is a key prerequisite to the Second Coming of Christ: they (the believing remnant of Israel) have to ask Him. They have to repent and the remnant has to ask Him.[5]

Jeremiah is an extensive catalog of prophecies, but the key theme is divine judgment in national life; the fact that God is *not* dead, but is very concerned and active in history; and the message from God to Jerusalem: "I will punish and I will restore."

A verse in Jeremiah (31:31) is the very passage from which the New Testament gets its name. He announces the New Covenant, where the Law will be written in their hearts, and it's from "New Covenant" that we get the term "New Testament."

It is somewhat incidental to his purpose, but Jeremiah specifies precisely the seventy-year captivity. In fact, when Daniel was in Babylon reading the prophecies of Jeremiah, he noticed the seventy years were almost over. (When people in the Bible read the Bible, they read it literally.)

THE BLOOD CURSE ON JECONIAH

Through Jeremiah, God also pronounced a blood curse on King Jeconiah. The kings were going from bad to worse, and Jeconiah and Zedekiah were bad news. God was so angry with Jeconiah that he said, "Thus saith the LORD, Write ye this man childless, a man that shall not prosper in his days: for no man of his seed shall prosper, sitting upon the throne of David, and ruling any more in Judah."[6] Do you realize what that's saying? There was now a blood curse pronounced on the royal line. Jeconiah and all his sons were cursed. I think the councils of Satan probably threw a party when they heard that. Satan had to believe that God had shot Himself in the foot because the Messiah had to come from the royal line, and now that very line had been cursed. But then I visualize God turning to His angels and saying, "Watch this one." (We'll examine this further when we get to the Book of Luke.)

THE DESTRUCTION OF BABYLON

Both Jeremiah and Isaiah detail the ultimate destruction of Babylon. Two extensive passages—Isaiah 13 and 14 and Jeremiah 50 and 51—are about their enemy, Babylon, being destroyed. When Isaiah wrote his passages, Babylon hadn't even risen yet. But it would rise and would be destroyed. Most scholars fumble this because they assume that when Cyrus the Persian conquered Babylon, it was destroyed (in 539 B.C.). Not true! They took it over without a battle. Two centuries later when Alexander conquered the Persians, he made Babylon his capital; in fact, he died there. Babylon wasn't destroyed; it atrophied. Even in the 1800s, it was occupied and is currently being rebuilt. Why is this so important? Because Isaiah and Jeremiah proclaim that once it is destroyed, it will never be inhabited again; in fact, they declared that even the building materials would never be reused.

Isaiah 13 and 14 and Jeremiah 50 and 51 claimed that Babylon would be destroyed like Sodom and Gomorrah, with fire from heaven. That has never happened. For that to happen, Babylon has yet to reemerge as a power of some kind. That's the problem we're going to have when we get to the Book of Revelation and the Mystery of Babylon (Revelation 17 and 18). It is clear from the passages in Isaiah and Jeremiah that the Babylon in question is on the banks of the Euphrates. It is the pride of the Chaldeans, not some kind of symbol for pagan Rome. We'll deal with that when we get to Revelation, but recognize that Isaiah and Jeremiah have much to say about this.

EZEKIEL

Daniel and Ezekiel were prophets of the captivity. Daniel was taken in the first siege. Ezekiel was the prophet taken in the second siege, one of the ten thousand captives taken by Nebuchadnezzar eleven years before the final overthrow of Jerusalem. He was a priest and a prophet just like Jeremiah. He prophesied from Babylon before Jerusalem was destroyed.

Ezekiel also wrote nine chapters on the millennium. There are so many details, it is almost like an architect's drawing. He was also commissioned by God to communicate His message in some very strange ways. He shut himself up in his home; he bound himself; he was struck dumb; he had to lie on his right and left sides for a total of 430 days; he deliberately ate bread prepared in an unclean manner; he shaved his head and beard, which was considered a shame in his particular calling. He did all this and more in addition to writing and preaching—all ways to make a point.

THE FOUR FACES

Ezekiel had two visions of the throne of God, in chapters 1 and 10. What distinguished his visions from Isaiah's vision were four strange "living creatures" called cherubim. They each had faces—one was the face of a lion, one was the face of an ox, one was the face of a man, one was the face of an eagle. But you may recall the camps of Israel, where four groups of three tribes each rallied around a standard. One was the Lion of the Tribe of Judah. The tribe of Ephraim had the ox; Reuben, the man; and Dan, the eagle. This is not very clear in the book of Numbers, but after reading Ezekiel or Isaiah, you see how these camps were forming a model of the Throne of God. The New Testament Gospels bring this out again. Matthew presents Jesus as the Lion of the Tribe of Judah, the *Meshiach Nagid*, Messiah the King. Mark presents Christ as the servant, the symbol of which is the ox. Luke is a doctor and presents Jesus as the Son of Man; and John, the Son of God. Many scholars in the early church recognized the peculiar parallel between the focus and design of the Gospels and the cherubim that Ezekiel saw in the camps of Judah. The fingerprint of God was behind all of this.

THE 430 DAYS

Another important point in Ezekiel is when he lay on one side and then the other side for a total of 430 days. God told him each day represented a year, so what he proclaimed to Israel was that they were going to be judged 430 years. The problem with this is it doesn't seem to fit anything in history. Scholars have tried to figure it out, but nothing really works. Only the seventy years of the Babylonian captivity are accounted for. Where are the remaining 360 years?

The answers begin in Leviticus 26, where you read in four different verses in that chapter (verses 18, 21, 24 and 28): "If ye will not yet for all this hearken unto me, then I will punish you seven times more for your sins." Some scholars say to themselves, "Gee, that's kind

The Origin of Satan

Another passage in Ezekiel 28 deserves some comment. In Isaiah 14, Isaiah addressed the origin of Satan. The famous "I wills" describe the origin of Satan's ambition. In Ezekiel 28, we find out that he was the anointed cherub that covers, which means he was a super-angel in charge of everything, and yet he rebelled. Revelation 12 contains a summary of his attempts to thwart God's plan of redemption.

of interesting. If you take seven times 360, that's 2,520 years." Some say this is approximately the number of years they've been in the Diaspora. My problem with that is I don't believe the words "God" and "approximate" should be in the same sentence. It either fits precisely or it doesn't.

No one that I'm aware of had applied what we learned from Sir Robert Anderson about the seventy weeks—that God deals in 360-day years. On a 360-day basis, 2,520 years is 2,483 years, 9 months, and 21 days on our calendar. So let's take another look at the situation. We talked about Babylon, the first, second, and third siege of Nebuchadnezzar and the Decree of Cyrus. The Servitude of the Nation started at the first siege, and the Desolations of Jerusalem started at the third siege, which ended with the Decree of Artaxerxes. What do we do with these 2,520 years? If you reckon the 2,520 years from the Servitude of the Nation, it comes out to be May 14, 1948, when Israel was restored as a nation, the day when David Ben Gurion, on international radio, using Ezekiel as his authority, announced that the name of the Jewish homeland was Israel. What a coincidence!

What happens if you begin the 2,520 years from the Desolations of Jerusalem? You come to the Restoration of Jerusalem on June 7, 1967, as a result of the Six-Day War. Again, what a coincidence!

THE RESTORATION OF ISRAEL

In chapter 37, Ezekiel related the famous vision of the Valley of Dry Bones, which he then interpreted as a vision of the restoration of Israel. These bones came together and came back to life—at first, flesh without the spirit. Later, breath was breathed into them. But notice it's two steps: flesh first, spirit later.

Isaiah, incidentally, made an interesting remark, speaking of the same thing. He said, "The Lord shall set His hand again the second time to recover the remnant of His people."[7] When was the first time? After Babylon, when Cyrus gave the decree to build the Temple. Isaiah was saying that when God would gather them the second time, it would be the last time. What's exciting about this, of course, is that it has been fulfilled in the first half of the twentieth century. From the nineteenth century on we have the move toward Zionism. On May 14, 1948, all the debates should have ended. Are these things literal? Is Israel going to be restored? Argue all you like until May 14, 1948. From that point on, throw the old books out unless they agree with what Isaiah is saying because Israel is there. They are in danger, but they are there.

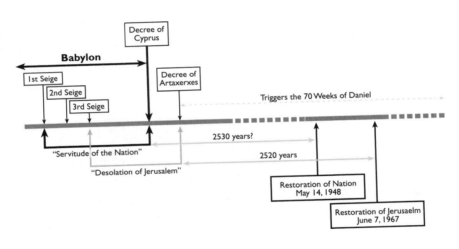

They are being restored, but many people who study Ezekiel 37 fail to read Ezekiel 36. Why is Israel to be restored?

Therefore say unto the house of Israel, Thus saith the Lord GOD; I do not this for your sakes, O house of Israel, but for mine holy name's sake, which ye have profaned among the heathen, whither ye went. And I will sanctify my great name, which was profaned among the heathen, which ye have profaned in the midst of them; and the heathen shall know that I am the LORD, saith the Lord GOD, when I shall be sanctified in you before their eyes. For I will take you from among the heathen, and gather you out of all countries, and will bring you into your own land.[8]

God is restoring Israel because His name is on the document. He said He was, that's why He's going to do it. Not because Israel deserves it or because of their foreign policy, but because He said He would.

The next nine chapters are about the millennial temple. There's a description of it that is so highly detailed most scholars realize that somehow it is very specific and very literal. What's interesting about it is that all nations will come to worship there, not just the Jews. Offerings and sacrifices will be resumed. And it will only be open on the Sabbath Day and on New Moons.

THE MAGOG INVASION

Ezekiel 38 and 39 describe an event that will occur after Israel is restored, but before the millennium is established. The Magog invasion is well known for two reasons. First, it describes the event in which God Himself will intervene to quell an ill-fated invasion of Israel by Magog and its allies. Second, it appears to describe the use of nuclear weapons, even though it was written over twenty-five hundred years ago!

To identify the various countries involved from their ancient tribal designations, you have to go back to Genesis 10, to the Table of Nations, to sort it all out. Who on earth are the Magog? Hesiod, a Greek didactic poet who wrote in eighth century B.C., described the Magogians by their Greek name, the Scythians. Heroditus, known as the "Father of

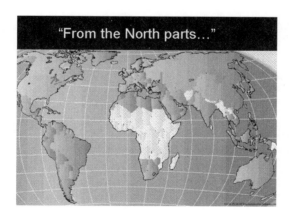

History," in the fifth century B.C. wrote extensively about the Scythians, who terrorized the southern steppes of Russia from the tenth century B.C. to the third century B.C.

Philo, Josephus, and other ancient writers clearly identify the Scythians as the descendants of Magog; they called the Great Wall of China the "ramparts of Gog and Magog." It was designed to keep the Magogians out. The passage in Ezekiel describes Magog as coming from the uttermost parts of the north. All you have to do is look on a globe, find Israel, and go north as far as you can and you come to Moscow. They are almost in the same longitude.

The allies of Magog are also well identified. Persia, of course, is Iran; Cush (translated "Ethiopia") settled south of the second cataract of the Nile, so it really speaks of Black Africa; Phut (translated "Libya") speaks of North Africa, and so on.

Why do we think the passage has nuclear weapons in view? Because after God intervenes, the leftover weapons, the Scripture tells us, provide all the energy needed in Israel for seven years. (The ancient commentators said it must be symbolic because nothing could burn for seven years, and we smile at that because we know today that nuclear energy can easily "burn" for seven years.) Also, Ezekiel even describes how they hire professionals to clear the battlefield. They wait for seven months before entering and then they clear for seven months. They bury what they find east of the Dead Sea; that is, downwind.

Ezekiel was still not finished: he said that if a traveler finds something that the professionals have missed, he is not to touch it, he is to mark the location, and let the professionals deal with it.[9] These are contemporary department of defense procedures for handling nuclear, chemical, or biological warfare materials.

The more one knows about the details of the Ezekiel text, and the more one is informed on the global geopolitical situation, the more it appears that this classic passage could happen any time.

Exciting times! "Film at eleven."

Hour 12

THE MINOR PROPHETS

The Panorama of History

Creation / Fall of Man — Flood — Abraham — Exodus — David — Christ — Israel Restored

6000 Years?

Genesis

The Diaspora

NT

400 yrs

THE TERM "MINOR" refers to their size, not their significance. The twelve Minor Prophets are typically dated from the end of the monarchy to about four hundred years before the New Testament period. They are Hosea, Joel, Amos, Obadiah, Jonah, Micah, Nahum, Habakkuk, Zephaniah, Haggai, Zechariah, and Malachi. The problem with this list is that it is not in any kind of sensible or chronological order.

- **Hosea** was a prophet who wrote to the Northern Kingdom during the reign of Jeroboam the Second.
- **Joel** prophesied to the Southern Kingdom—Judah—in the time of Amaziah.
- **Amos** was right after Hosea, roughly at the time of Zechariah, king of the Northern Kingdom.

- **Obadiah** was in the late part of the Southern Kingdom, but his prophecies were against Edom, the enemies of Judah.

- **Jonah** preached to Nineveh, a city on the rise, about the time of Jeroboam the second. Jonah was very anxious for the Ninevites *not* to repent because he knew from prophecies that Nineveh would eventually rise to destroy his entire nation. He was a patriot, strangely enough, a point many people miss.

- **Micah** was right after Isaiah, or almost contemporaneous with him, in the days of Ahaz.

- **Nahum** preached to Nineveh again, but this was at the end of their existence. They repented under Jonah and got an extra century, but later when Nahum preached they refused to repent and so were absorbed by Babylon as Babylon rose to power.

- **Habakkuk** was between Jeremiah and Obadiah in the Southern Kingdom.

- **Zephaniah** was a little earlier, roughly in the days of Manasseh, subsequent to Isaiah.

- After the Babylonian captivity were three post-exile prophets—**Haggai**, **Zechariah**, and **Malachi**—who close out the Old Testament.

- Following the post-exile are 400 "silent years," and then the New Testament.

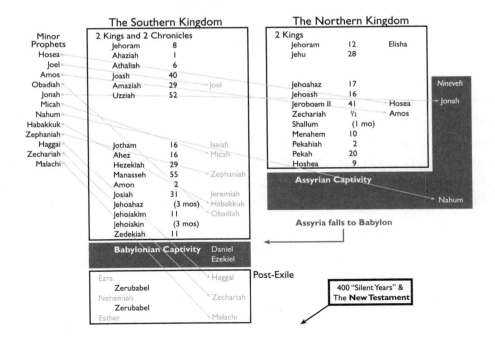

HOSEA

Hosea's burden was the apostasy of the Northern Kingdom. He was to the Northern Kingdom what Jeremiah would later be to the Southern Kingdom. He was concerned for their apostasy and their lack of loyalty to God.

The timespan from Jeroboam the Second to the Assyrian invasion was about fifty years. Jeroboam the Second was quite a character: he murdered his son, which ended the Jehu dynasty; Shallum slew Zechariah (he was there for only six months); Manahem killed Shallum and Pekah killed Pekahiah, the son of Manahem; then Hoshea slew Pekah. It was a slaughterhouse!

Jeroboam put golden calves at Bethel and Dan which ultimately led to nature worship, child sacrifices, and other evils.

The first three chapters of Hosea are a prologue where he was instructed to marry a harlot, and through her he had three children: Jezreel, Lo-Ruhamah, and Lo-Ammi. God told him what to name them because they would be prophetic models.

The reigning House of Israel had succeeded to the throne through what was called "the blood of Jezreel," since Jehu had ruthlessly massacred the house of Ahab and Jezebel earlier. Jezreel is on the plain of Esdrelon, and in the future, will also be known as Armageddon. Jezreel can mean "scattered" in a negative sense, or "sown" in a positive sense. In Jeremiah 31, God will scatter, but God will sow in Zechariah 10. Both terms are prophetic of Jezreel. The Valley of Jezreel is about ten miles in breadth—from the Mediterranean, near Mount Carmel, near the Jordan, from Galilee to the mountains of Ephraim. It's a huge valley. It was the great battlefield of Gideon in Judges 6. It became a symbol of national disgrace and defeat as it had been after Saul's death. It will also be the final climactic battlefield of the entire world at the Battle of Armageddon.

Another child, *Lo-Ruhamah*, meant "not loved," and *Lo-Ammi* meant "not my people" (*lo* in Hebrew means "not"). God told Hosea to name his children to show there would be a time that Israel would be set aside ("*not* His people"). But the good news is that they will be renamed later. "And I will say to them which were not my people, Thou art my people; and they shall say, Thou art my God."[1] But that's yet future.

No other prophet gave as complete an outline in the ways of God with His earthly people as did Hosea. God suffers when His people are unfaithful to Him. God cannot condone sin and yet will never cease to love His own. And consequently, He seeks to win back those who have forsaken Him.

Let's understand the situation Hosea was facing—Jeroboam's army had recovered all of the territory previously lost. They enjoyed unparalleled material prosperity. But from God's point of view, they had exchanged loyalty to their heritage for pagan worship. That disloyalty had caused widespread adultery, social injustice, violent crime, religious hypocrisy, political rebellion, selfish arrogance, and spiritual ingratitude. Does this sound familiar? Their situation is best summarized by Charles Dickens's famous opening line in *Tale of Two Cities*: "It was the best of times; it was the worst of times." They thought it was the best of times; but God said it was the worst of times.

Hosea had to tell them that although a loving God had provided their abundance and prosperity, their sin, disloyalty, and abandonment of Him would force Him to use their enemies as His instrument of judgment. And very shortly, they would be no more.

Hosea highlights three essentials: "Hear ye the word of the LORD ye children of Israel: for the LORD hath a controversy with the inhabitants of the land because there is no truth, nor mercy, nor knowledge of God in the land."[2]

Is there an American parallel here? Let's take a look at America as Hosea might see it—our country is prosperous; our people are buying their third and fourth cars; almost every home has a computer; it's hard to find anyone walking down the street without a cell phone; our fuel costs less than a bottle of drinking water—"It is the best of times." However, homosexuality is considered "an alternative lifestyle"; we murder babies that are socially inconvenient; we change marriage partners like a fashion statement; we have abandoned the sanctity of commitment in all our relationships. God rebuked Israel for their brutality, murder, and warfare; we've had Waco, Columbine High School, and more. New York City has recorded more crimes than Scotland, Wales, England, Ireland, Switzerland, Spain, Sweden, Netherlands, Norway, and Denmark combined!

> *God rebuked Israel for their brutality, murder, and warfare; we've had Waco, Columbine High School, and more.*

Our culture has clearly disconnected character from destiny. Our politics have condoned and covered up more murders than we dare list. Our entertainments celebrate fornication, adultery, violence, abhorrent sexual practices, and every imaginable form of evil. We have become the primary exporters of all that God abhors. Indeed, "It is the worst of times." Thomas Jefferson said, "I tremble for my country when I reflect that God is just; (and) that His justice cannot not sleep forever."

Hosea has some other interesting lessons for us. The Gospel of Matthew has an interesting quote when Joseph and Mary went down to Egypt and stayed until the death of Herod, "that it might be fulfilled which was spoken of the Lord by the prophet, saying, Out of Egypt have I called my son."[3] Matthew's quote is from Hosea when he says, "When Israel was a child, then I loved him, and called my son out of Egypt."[4] The context of Hosea's quote, however, is that of God calling the nation Israel out of Egypt in the Exodus. Yet Matthew's use of this quote is Messianic, not historical. This is an instructive example of a *Midrashic* principle: prophecy is pattern, not just prediction. (This will also show up frequently in Paul's writings and will be discussed in Hour 19.)

Another fascinating passage God gives us through Hosea is a critical prerequisite to the Second Coming: "I will go and return to my place, till they acknowledge their offence, and seek my face: in their affliction they will seek me early. Come, and let us return unto the LORD: for he hath torn, and he will heal us; he hath smitten, and he will bind us up. After two days will he revive us: in the third day he will raise us up, and we shall live in his sight."[5]

In order to return to His place, He must have left it! The word *till* indicates a prerequisite condition for His return to the earth: the acknowledgement of their (Israel's) offense and to petition His return.

When the Abomination of Desolation is installed in the Temple, Jesus commands them to flee into the mountains immediately, and the believing remnant will flee to a secure place (apparently Petra or Bosrah). From there they will petition His return. When the world's forces go against them, Jesus Himself will return to rescue His remnant.[6]

Hosea also gives another useful clue about Biblical interpretation. God said through Hosea, "I have also spoken by the prophets and I have multiplied visions, and used similitudes, by the ministry of the prophets."[7] The Scripture uses many rhetorical devices (i.e. allegories, analogies, metaphors, similes, similitudes, types); in fact, there are over two hundred different figures of speech in the Bible.[8]

JOEL

The theme found in Joel's writings is "Jehovah is God," and his main focus was "the Day of the Lord," and the end of the present age. Joel issued an alarm (an invasion by a plague of locusts), then an appeal: "Turn ye to me and I will restore."

The army of locusts in Joel came from the north. That's strange; locusts usually came from the south. He said they were *like* horsemen, *like* chariots, *like* men of war, and they had a king over them. The Bible declares that natural locusts have no king.[9] Why does Joel use this imagery for locusts? Because they were not necessarily natural insects; they were something else—probably a demon army. This will be significant for us in several other passages. We must also note that God promises that He will restore to Israel the years the locusts have eaten.

AMOS

Amos was different from the other prophets. He came from Tekoa, which is in the wilderness of Judea, about six miles south of Jerusalem, where David had sought refuge from Saul. He was a layman, a man of the fields; he wasn't a professional priest or prophet, but he was called to go up to Bethel, the center of calf worship. His theme to them was "the ultimate rule of David," strangely enough. His eight "burdens" were against Damascus, Gaza, Tyre, Edom, Ammon, Moab, Judah, and Israel. He delivered three sermons and had five visions.

The book of Amos gives us a fundamental insight in pointing out, "Surely the Lord GOD will do nothing, but he revealeth his secret unto his servants the prophets."[10] That would imply that everything that God is going to do is tucked away somewhere in the Scriptures.

But there's another mystery Amos resolves that may surprise many. There is a puzzle regarding Gog, who shows up so prominently in Ezekiel 38. From the context, Gog is clearly the leader of Magog in that famous prophecy. Who is he? Where is he from? It is unusual for a key figure to show up in the text without some background. There is a strange translation problem in Amos 7:1 which seems to shed some light on this mystery. From the Massoretic text, the English translation reads, "Thus hath the Lord GOD shewed unto me; and, behold, he formed grasshoppers in the beginning of the shooting up of the latter growth; and, lo, it was the latter growth after the king's mowings."[11] That seems to make no sense. The Masoretic text, from which this was translated, was written about A.D. 900. But the Septuagint translation into Greek was about twelve hundred years earlier and has a very different rendering: "The Lord hath shown me and behold a swarm of locusts were coming, and behold one of the young devastating locusts was Gog the King."[12]

When I first discovered this, Hal Lindsey and I dug into some of his background research materials. The locusts in Revelation 9 have a king—Apollyon or Abaddon[13]—but Proverbs 30:27 declares that locusts have no king. So these locusts are not natural insects; they are demon locusts. If that's the case, then Gog, who is the king of the locusts, is apparently a demon king. And so the Gog of "Gog and Magog" is a demon.

OBADIAH

Obadiah is a little book from the Southern Kingdom about the destruction of Edom. The Edomites were a fierce, proud, profane people. They were the enemy of Israel and they always had an active alliance with whomever was against Israel. In Obadiah, they were judged, and the sentence was poetic justice.

Edom had indulged in treachery; Edom would perish through treachery. Edom had seized a chance to rob Judah, but Edom would be robbed. Edom had indulged in violence; Edom would perish by slaughter. Edom sought the utter destruction of Israel; Edom would be utterly destroyed. Edom had sought to dispossess Jerusalem; Edom would be possessed by the remnant.

JONAH

Jonah's four chapters could be named, "The Storm," "The Fish," "The City," and "The Lord." We often call Jonah the Reluctant Prophet. The book was a warning to Nineveh in the later years of Joash.

Nineveh was the world capital covering 350 square miles. The walls were over one hundred feet high with fifteen hundred towers two hundred feet high; chariots could race three abreast on top. The population was over a million. The Assyrians ruled the world for several hundred years.

But why was Jonah so reluctant to preach to Nineveh? Because he didn't want them to repent; they were the enemy of Israel. Jonah had read in Isaiah 7 that Nineveh was going to be the instrument of God's judgment. He saw Hosea's prophecy in chapters 9, 10, and 11 where God was going to use the Assyrians to judge Israel. He didn't want Nineveh spared; he wanted them wiped out. But that wasn't God's calling.

Nineveh was forty days from destruction, and Jonah was sent to preach there. Even God's mercy apparently had definitive limits.

Jonah was not excited about the assignment until God explained it to him a little more clearly. When he finally got there, his message was not market-researched. He went through town saying, "Forty days and you get yours!" Then one of the greatest miracles of the Old Testament happened—not the fish episode, but the repentance within forty days of everyone from the king down to the peasants. Notice that when that king repented, he did it on speculation, thinking that maybe if they repented, God might change His mind.

Indeed, they were spared another century. Later Nahum would be dispatched to again preach and they failed to repent and fell to Babylon who was on the rise at that time.

MICAH

Micah is a charming little book. An eminent judgment is declared: the Assyrians are going to strike Egypt. They will march through Micah's neighborhood on the way to Judah. An ultimate blessing is promised, however. The incarnation of Christ is referred to in Micah 5:2, a passage that leads the Magi to Bethlehem. The star just brought them to Herod, but Micah takes them to Bethlehem. The key truth is that there is an eternal ruler yet to come: "But thou, Bethlehem Ephratah, though thou be little among the thousands of Judah, yet out of thee shall he come forth unto me that is to be ruler in Israel; whose goings forth have been from of old, from everlasting."[14] That last phrase—"whose goings forth have been from of old, from everlasting"—shows that He was preexistent; He was incarnated in Bethlehem, but He was preexistent from before time began.

Another oft-quoted passage from Micah summarizes what God requires: "He hath shewed thee, O man, what is good; and what doth the LORD require of thee, but to do justly, and to love mercy, and to walk humbly with thy God?"[15] That says it all!

NAHUM

A century after Jonah, Nahum, a prophet from Galilee, predicted the doom of Nineveh, the world's greatest city at that time. He came from Capernaum, which means "the village of Nahum." (This city will later become the base of operations during the Galilean ministry of Jesus Christ.) His message was "Jehovah will not acquit the wicked." It objectifies for all peoples for all time the way God deals with the Gentile nations: God will forgive repented sin, but He will not condone persistent sin.

Nineveh's doom was declared, described, and deserved, and the decisive test of the prediction was its fulfillment.

HABAKKUK

Habakkuk had a real problem: he didn't understand the ostensible silence, inactivity and apparent unconcern of God. Have you ever had that problem? In Habakkuk's case, why would God use a people far more wicked than Judah as His instrument of judgment?

A key verse in Habakkuk, the verse that motivated the Reformation, was, "The just shall live by his faith."[16] Martin Luther had become obsessed with his sinfulness. He went through all the medieval church rituals to deal with his sin and was still dissatisfied. A monk pointed out this verse to him, and it became the banner verse of the Reformation.

In the New Testament, the Book of Romans quotes this verse,[17] and the whole Book of Romans answers the question, "*Who* are the just?" The Book of Galatians focuses on, "How shall the just then *live?*"[18] The Epistle to the Hebrews further emphasizes, "The just shall live by *faith*."[19] These three epistles are, thus, a trilogy on this key verse in Habukkuk (and this is one of the reasons I believe that Paul was the writer of the unsigned Epistle to the Hebrews).

ZEPHANIAH

Obadiah, Nahum, and Habakkuk were really preaching against Israel's enemies: Obadiah to Edom; Nahum to Assyria; Habakkuk to Babylon. But Zephaniah preached about the wrath coming upon Judah. Then he spoke of the wrath coming upon all nations, both east and west: Philistia, Moab, and Ammon; and then south and north: Ethiopia and Assyria; then after the wrath, healing. Then he predicted the conversion of the Gentile nations and the restoration of the covenant people.

It's just a little verse, but Zephaniah also predicted that when Israel would be regathered in the land, they would return to pure Hebrew as a language. "Experts" on language said that would never happen since no dead language had ever been restored, but in Israel today, the people speak Hebrew—Zephaniah could walk down the street in Tel Aviv today and read a menu.

HAGGAI

Haggai's message was to arouse in chapter 1, to support in chapter 2, and then to confirm and assure. His prophetic problem was that prophecy in his day had become a sort of narcotic. It had given way to hopelessness, fatalism, and inevitability. People had read prophetic writings, and since everything was foreordained, "let's just kick back." Does that sound like us? There's a big danger in allowing awareness of and, our interest in, Bible prophecy to make us complacent. Remember what Daniel did when he realized the Babylonian captivity was up? He prayed for it! That's what Jesus instructed us to do in the Lord's Prayer: "Thy Kingdom come."

If we believe the Lord Jesus is coming back soon that should be a reason to get with it, witnessing to friends and loved ones and coworkers. Everybody in Haggai's day had become very fatalistic and indifferent.

ZECHARIAH

The first eight chapters of Zechariah are about the Temple being rebuilt, and then he focuses on the Second Coming. For instance, he declared, "His feet shall stand in that day upon the mount of Olives, which is before Jerusalem on the east, and the mount of Olives shall cleave in the midst thereof toward the east and toward the west, and there shall be a very great valley; and half of the mountain shall remove toward the north, and half of it toward the south."[20] There's a fault in that mountain just waiting for the pressure of a particular foot.

There's another fascinating and oft-quoted verse: "And I will pour upon the house of David, and upon the inhabitants of Jerusalem, the spirit of grace and of supplications: and they shall look upon me whom they have pierced, and they shall mourn for him, as one mourneth for his only son, and shall be in bitterness for him, as one that is in bitterness for his firstborn."[21] In the phrase, "they shall look upon me whom they have pierced," there are two untranslated letters, an *aleph* and a *tau,* the Hebrew equivalents of the Greek *alpha* and *omega*. This is the way it could be read: "And they shall look upon me, the *aleph* and the *tau* (or *alpha* and *omega*), whom they have pierced," or to put it another way, "the Beginning and the End, the A and the Z, whom they have pierced."

MALACHI

Malachi is the final message to a disobedient people. Malachi has many purposes, but nothing more important than to announce a dare God gives you. Jesus warned us in Matthew that we should never put God to a test, but there is an exception, and it is here in Malachi 3. Here the God of the universe puts Himself in a box and gives you the solution to every financial problem: "Bring ye all the tithes into the storehouse, that there may be meat in mine house, and prove me now herewith, saith the LORD of hosts, if I will not open you the windows of heaven, and pour you out a blessing, that there shall not be room enough to receive it."[22] Now there's a challenge! Tithing is not just for the Old Testament. The first tenth belongs to the Lord—you're not giving Him anything He doesn't already own. But here's an opportunity to put God to the test—even today!

CONCLUSION OF THE OLD TESTAMENT

After Malachi is the four-hundred-year period known as "The Silent Years"—the years between the testaments. There are four hundred years of silence until an angel visits a priest in the Temple by the name of Zechariah, which brings us to John the Baptist. (The Old Testament period doesn't really end with Malachi; it ends with John the Baptist.[23] That will be critical to understand when we get to the New Testament.)

The Old Testament closes with unexplained ceremonies, unachieved purposes, unappeased longings, and unfulfilled prophecies. What are the sacrificial rituals all about? To this day, on Passover, the rabbis wonder why they mix the wine with warm water. The answer, of course, is found at the Cross: The Passover Lamb had His heart broken, and out of His side came blood and water as predicted in the Passover ritual.[24]

Many covenants in the Old Testament are not complete. Where is the Messiah on the Throne of David? And the poetry books are full of unappeased longings for Zion, for David's Throne, for the peace of Jerusalem, and of the world.

And, of course, there are all kinds of unfulfilled prophecies. Three hundred prophecies were fulfilled at Jesus' first coming. For every one of those there are at least seven prophecies of His Second Coming.

What are the answers to these questions? Jesus invited all to, "Search the scriptures; for in them ye think ye have eternal life: and they are they which testify of me."[25] The Old Testament is the record of a nation; the New Testament is the record of a man, and that's what the Bible is really all about!

Hour 13

HOW SURE CAN WE BE?

ACCORDING TO J. BARTON PAYNE'S *Encyclopedia of Biblical Prophecy,* the Bible contains at least 8,362 predictive verses, and 1,817 specific predictions on over 737 different matters. Other scholars might catalog them a little differently, but clearly most of the Bible is prophetic.

William Thompson, who later was known as Lord Kelvin, one of the great men of science, is famous for pointing out that until we measure a thing, we really know very little about it. It's one thing to point out a little verse here and how it is fulfilled there; but it can prove so much more meaningful if we can do that in a way that is a little more quantitative, more systematic, more measurable. In order to do that, we're going to examine a number of prophecies in the Old Testament.

There is one fact about the Old Testament we can verify from any encyclopedia: The

Hebrew Scriptures, those which we call the Old Testament, were translated into Greek by 270 B.C. This process was started about 285 B.C., when Ptolemy Philadelphus II funded seventy scholars to translate the Hebrew Scriptures into Greek. This is extremely important because it is a matter of history that these Scriptures were in wide circulation three centuries before the gospel period. In fact, most of the quotations from the Old Testament in the New Testament are from this Greek translation, known as the Septuagint (a word meaning "seventy"). In other words, it is a matter of secular record that the Old Testament was in black and white, tangible form three centuries before Jesus was preaching in Israel.

These Scriptures—in print and circulated well before the time of Christ—contain more than three hundred prophecies detailing the coming Messiah; and all of them were fulfilled in the first century A.D. Let's consider some examples; say, just the ones that are quoted in the New Testament as being fulfilled by Jesus:

- He was to be of David's family—2 Samuel 7:12-13; Matthew 1:1.
- He would be born of a virgin—Isaiah 7:14; Matthew 1:23.
- He would be born in Bethlehem—Micah 5:2; Matthew 2:6.
- He would sojourn in Egypt—Hosea 11:1; Matthew 2:15.
- He would minister in Galilee and in Nazareth—Isaiah 9:1-2; Matthew 4:12-17.
- He would be announced in advance by an Elijah-type herald—Isaiah 40:3-5; Malachi 3:1; Mark 1:2-3.
- He would occasion the massacre of Bethlehem's children—Jeremiah 31:15; Matthew 2:18.
- His mission would include the Gentiles—Isaiah 42:6; Luke 2:32.
- His ministry would be one of healing—Isaiah 35:5-6; Matthew 12:10-14; Mark 7:32-35; 10:51.
- He would teach through the use of parables—Ezekiel 20:49; Matthew 13:3.
- He would be disbelieved and rejected by the religious rulers of that period—Psalm 118:22; Matthew 21:12-13.
- He would make a triumphal entry into Jerusalem—Zechariah 9:9; Matthew 21:6-9.
- He would be betrayed for thirty pieces of silver—Zechariah 11:12; Matthew 26:15.
- He would be smitten like a shepherd and His sheep scattered—Zechariah 13:7; Matthew 26:31.

- He would be given vinegar and gall, and they would cast lots for His garments—Psalm 22:18; 69:21: Matthew 27:34; John 19:23-24.

- He would be pierced—Zechariah 12:10; John 19:34.

- Not a bone of His would be broken—Exodus 12:46; Psalm 34:20; John 19:33, 36.

- He would die among criminals—Isaiah 53:12; Mark 15:28.

- He would be buried by a rich man—Isaiah 53:9; Matthew 27:57-60.

- He would rise from the dead on the third day—Psalm 16:10; Jonah 1:17; Luke 24:6-7.

- His resurrection would be followed by the destruction of Jerusalem—Daniel 9:26; Matthew 24:2.

There are many more; but these give us a sampling of the kinds of prophecies that were specifically fulfilled in Christ. And for the purposes of this review, we are going to examine eight of the simplest prophecies concerning the coming of Messiah; but we are going to try to quantify them—estimating their probabilities—as we go.

EIGHT SPECIFIC PROPHECIES

(1) "But thou, Bethlehem Ephrathah, though thou be little among the thousands of Judah, yet out of thee shall he come forth unto me that is to be ruler in Israel; whose goings forth have been from of old, from everlasting" (Micah 5:2). This first one is familiar to most of us. There are many amazing things hidden in this verse—not just that Messiah will come from Bethlehem, but that He preexisted from eternity past. However, the point we want to extract here is simply that the Messiah clearly would be born in Bethlehem.

Therefore we might ask, "What was the probability of somebody being born in Bethlehem over the past two thousand years?" We can take a look at the world and start zeroing in on the Middle East, then Israel, then the Jerusalem region, then south of Jerusalem into Bethlehem (which has remained pretty much unchanged in population throughout history). So what is the probability that somebody we might meet over a period of two thousand years would have been born in Bethlehem?

Using round numbers and staying conservative, let's assume that the population of Bethlehem is less than ten thousand. Let's assume that the average world population at any point in time over the past two thousand years is something in the region of a billion people. So the probability that someone picked at random would be from Bethlehem is something in the region of one chance in 100,000. And that's a generous estimate.

(2) "Rejoice greatly, O daughter of Zion; shout, O daughter of Jerusalem: behold, thy King cometh unto thee: he is just, and having salvation; lowly, and riding upon an ass, and upon a colt the foal of an ass" (Zechariah 9:9). This second example is a well-known prophecy and famous verse because Jesus deliberately fulfilled it in the triumphal entry. However, the question here is, "How many people throughout history have presented themselves as king in Jerusalem, riding on a donkey?" I really have no idea; but if we said less than one in a hundred, that would be more than safe. So we'll take that figure: less than one in a hundred people have presented themselves as a king in Jerusalem, riding on a donkey.

(3) "If ye think good, give me my price; and if not, forbear. So they weighed for my price thirty pieces of silver" (Zechariah 11:12). Let's consider this little phrase from God in Zechariah. Most of us are aware of the fact that this is the precise amount that Jesus was betrayed for by Judas Iscariot. The question, then, is, "How many people throughout history have been betrayed for precisely thirty pieces of silver?" I don't happen to know of any others, but if we say less than one in a thousand, we would be well within the limits of reason.

(4) "And the LORD said unto me, Cast it unto the potter: a goodly price that I was prised at of them. And I took the thirty pieces of silver, and cast them to the potter in the house of the LORD" (Zechariah 11:13). This verse immediately follows the previous prophecy, and it gives additional details which we will treat separately. In the New Testament, we read, "Then Judas, which had betrayed him, when he saw that he was condemned, repented himself, and brought again the thirty pieces of silver to the chief priests and elders, saying, I have sinned in that I have betrayed the innocent blood. And they said, What is that to us? see thou to that. And he cast down the pieces of silver in the temple, and departed, and went and hanged himself."[1]

The thirty pieces of silver Judas had been paid ended up on the Temple floor. What happens next is that "the chief priests took the silver pieces, and said, It is not lawful for to put them into the treasury, because it is the price of blood. And they took counsel, and bought with them the potter's field, to bury strangers in."[2] The priests couldn't put that type of money into the treasury, because that would violate the law. But they decided they could use the cash to prepay some expenses. If a stranger died in Jerusalem, the Temple was responsible to take care of the funeral and burial arrangements. And since there happened to be a potter's field that was being offered at a bargain price at the time, they took the cash and bought the field as a place in which to bury strangers.

Notice the details in Zechariah 11:13. The price is thirty pieces of silver; the transaction takes place in the house of the Lord, the Temple; and the potter who owns the field ends up with the money. What is the probability that all of these details would be fulfilled by chance? I could say one in a million and probably support it, but certainly the chances would not be better than one in 100,000.

(5) "And one shall say unto him, What are these wounds in thine hands? Then he shall answer, Those with which I was wounded in the house of my friends" (Zechariah 13:6). The next prophecy we want to look at is a verse I can remember coming across as a teenager; but as I tried to memorize it, I kept stumbling. The more I looked at it, the less sense it made. The more I thought about it, the more I had to admit that Jesus's crucifixion did not seem to fit this verse's description of Him being "wounded in the house of my friends."

But then I reread John 20, which describes Jesus appearing to His disciples after His resurrection. Of course, on this first evening Thomas wasn't with them, and when he was told later that Jesus had appeared to the others, he said, "Except I shall see in his hands the print of the nails, and put my finger into the print of the nails, and thrust my hand into his side, I will not believe."[3]

Thomas would not be convinced unless he saw for himself. But then the narrative continues: "And after eight days again his disciples were within, and Thomas with them: then came Jesus, the doors being shut, and stood in the midst, and said, Peace be unto you. Then saith he to Thomas, Reach hither thy finger, and behold my hands; and reach hither thy hand, and thrust it into my side: and be not faithless, but believing. And Thomas answered and said unto him, My Lord and my God. Jesus saith unto him, Thomas, because thou hast seen me, thou hast believed: blessed are they that have not seen, and yet have believed."[4]

Suddenly I realized that the verse in Zechariah 13 which states, "What are these wounds in thine hands? Then he shall answer, Those with which I was wounded in the house of my friends," doesn't refer to the wounds Jesus received from the nails; it refers to the wounds of Thomas's unbelief.

Regardless, if we just take from Zechariah 13:6 the fact that Jesus was wounded in His hands, how many people in the world during the past two thousand years have been wounded in their hands? If we say less than one in a thousand, we would be making a generous allowance.

(6) "He was oppressed, and he was afflicted, yet he opened not his mouth: he is brought as a lamb to the slaughter, and as a sheep before her shearers is dumb, so he openeth not his mouth" (Isaiah 53:7). How many prisoners accused of a capital crime make no defense even though they are innocent? I suspect if we scan the court records of history, we could find someone, maybe even a few, who were accused of a capital crime, facing the death penalty, and yet made no defense. But if we say conservatively that certainly less than one in a thousand have done so, again it would be more than generous.

(7) "And he made his grave with the wicked, and with the rich in his death; because he had done no violence, neither was any deceit in his mouth" (Isaiah 53:9). This is a strange apparent contradiction. His grave is with the wicked, and yet He is with the rich in his death. So based on that we might ask, how many people have died among the wicked, but were buried among the rich? Again, we can say less than one in a thousand and be well within reason.

(8) "For dogs have compassed me: the assembly of the wicked have inclosed me: they pierced my hands and my feet" (Psalm 22:16). Finally let's take one more, this time from Psalms. This reads as though it was dictated in the first person singular as Jesus hung on the cross, even though it was written eight hundred years earlier. Let's pick just one of the phrases there: "they pierced my hands and feet." What makes this remarkable is that it was penned by David seven hundred years before crucifixion was invented! Remember that in Israel the form of capital punishment was stoning, not crucifixion. Crucifixion was invented by the Persians about 90 B.C. and was adopted heavily by the Romans. But here, eight hundred years before the fact, all of Psalm 22 graphically portrays crucifixion. In fact, there have been articles in the American Medical Association Journal based on Psalm 22 analyzing the medical cause of death by crucifixion.[5]

So then, how many people taken at random have died by having their hands and feet pierced in crucifixion? A lot of people probably have, but if I propose that less than one in ten thousand people have been killed by a crucifixion-like method, that would be generous.

COMPOSITE PROBABILITIES

What we've done is briefly review eight prophecies concerning Jesus and offer very cautious estimates concerning the probability of each one. The question now is this: What is the probability that one particular person could fulfill *all eight* of these simultaneously? To do this properly, we need to have a feeling for what is called "composite probabilities."

Probabilities

If a population has 60% male and 40% female, what is the probability that one taken at random is female?

| M M M M M M M M M M |
| M M M M M M M M M M |
| M M M M M M M M M M |
| M M M M M M M M M M |
| M M M M M M M M M M |
| M M M M M M M M M M |

| F F F F F F F F F F |
| F F F F F F F F F F |
| F F F F F F F F F F |
| F F F F F F F F F F |

40%, or p = 0.4

To illustrate, let's assume we have a room of one hundred people; 60 percent of the people in the room are male, and 40 percent of the people are female. If one was blind-folded and was to pick just one person out of the crowd at random, what then is the probability that one would pick a female? If the people were uniformly mixed together, the probability is 40 percent that one would have picked a female.

Probabilities

R R R R R R	L L L L
R R R R R R	L L L L
R R R R R R	L L L L
R R R R R R	L L L L
R R R R R R	L L L L
R R R R R R	L L L L
R R R R R R	L L L L
R R R R R R	L L L L
R R R R R R	L L L L

If a population is 60% right-handed and 40% left-handed, what is the probability that one taken at random is left-handed?

40%, or p = 0.4

Let's take another characteristic of this crowd. If 60 percent of those one hundred people are right-handed, and 40 percent are left-handed, and if those attributes are uniformly

Composite Probabilities

What is the probability of selecting a left-handed female?

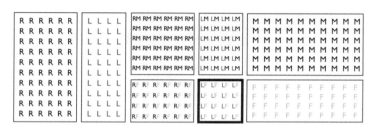

P = 0.4   P = 0.4 x 0.4 = .16   P = 0.4

distributed, what is the probability that one would randomly pick a left-handed person out of the crowd? Again, the probability is 40 percent.

Now, let's consider a *composite probability*. If someone was blindfolded and was to choose just one person at random out of those one hundred, what is the probability one would choose a left-handed female? To figure that out, we take the one distribution of 40 percent left-handed people, and the other distribution, which is 40 percent females, and multiply them together, resulting in a probability of 16 percent. In other words, the way I get the composite estimate of probability is to multiply the probabilities of distribution or occurrence. (There are added factors of advanced statistics that would indicate the probability would be a little rarer, but this simple formula will do for our purposes.)

Let's take this principle of composite probability to our eight prophecies concerning Jesus the Messiah. Since we've used powers of 10, it's easy to multiply our probabilities together. Using this simple formula, and taking all eight prophecies together with the very generous levels of probability we've allowed each one, we arrive at a composite probability for all eight prophecies of 1 in 10^{28}. That's 10 with 28 zeroes following it. Moreover, to be entirely realistic we should divide that by the total population during the past two thousand years, which we will liberally estimate at 100 billion (10^{11}). When we do that, we arrive at a generous composite probability of 1 in 10^{17}.

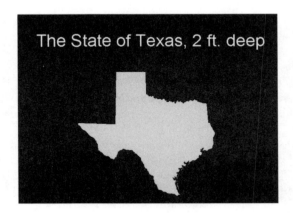

The State of Texas, 2 ft. deep

In a statistics class, the way we try to get a feeling for a particular statistic or probability like "one in one hundred" is to imagine a bucket with one hundred silver dollars in it. We then imagine taking one of those silver dollars, marking it, then putting it back in and mixing it all up. So then the bucket contains ninety-nine unmarked silver dollars, and one marked silver dollar. The chance of reaching in and randomly selecting the one marked silver dollar is one in one hundred. That's an elementary way of visualizing what we mean by one in one hundred.

Well, in regard to these eight messianic prophecies of Jesus, we have a probability of 1 in 10^{17}. So what we need to do is get a bucket and put 10^{17} silver dollars in there. The problem is that it would have to be a pretty big bucket. In fact, what I would need is a bucket the size of the state of Texas, which I can then fill with silver dollars to a depth of two feet. In other words, the chance of one person fulfilling those eight prophecies is equivalent to marking one silver dollar with an X, putting it in a bucket the size of Texas with unmarked silver dollars standing two feet deep, mixing them up in such a way that the marked coin could be anywhere, and then reaching back in at random and drawing out that one marked silver dollar.

That obviously would be pretty unlikely. But we need to bear in mind that we actually have more than three hundred prophecies fulfilled in Jesus to choose from. So far we've used only eight. So let's add another eight; but recognize, too, that because we chose the simplest prophecies for the first eight, the more prophecies we choose, the more technical and specific each selection would become, that is, the more rare they will be in terms of probability.

However, for the purposes of this study, let's assume the next eight are no more rare, or less likely, than the first eight. Assuming there's no decrease in likelihood, we'll multiply 10^{28} by 10^{28}, which is 10^{56}. We then divide by the world population over the past two thousand years (10^{11}), so we now have a composite probability of 10^{45} that we have to deal with. And for a bucket we now need one that can contain 10^{45} silver dollars.

How many silver dollars is that? Well, we would need a ball of silver dollars that has a radius thirty times the distance from the earth to the sun! That would hold about 10^{45} silver dollars. Then, if we took one of those silver dollars, marked it, put it back in, mixed the whole mass uniformly so there's an equal likelihood the marked silver dollar could be anywhere, the chance that I could randomly pick the marked silver dollar would be one in 10^{45}.

For a final example, let's triple our sample: let's take forty-eight prophecies. Remember, we have over three hundred to choose from, so we still haven't scratched the surface. We'll continue in the assumption that even with the more complex prophecies there's no decrease in likelihood, which is actually not the case at all. But even so, we now have 10^{28}, multiplied by itself six times. That turns out to be 10^{168}, but we must divide by the population figure of 10^{11}, so we end up with 10^{157}.

Now we need a model that allows us to imagine this level of probability. Silver dollars will no longer work, because they're too big. In fact, what we need to do now is use the smallest unit we can conceive of, which is an atom. To illustrate this level of probability, we'll make a ball out of every atom in our galaxy (which is about 10^{66} atoms). But that leaves us way short of our target of 10^{157}, so we'll proceed to make one of those balls consisting of every atom in the galaxy *for* every atom of the galaxy. So now I have 10^{66} times 10^{66} atoms, or 10^{132} atoms—but we are still a long way away from having the 10^{157} atoms needed. So what I will do is repeat that mental exercise (make a ball *of* every atom in the universe, *for* every atom in the universe) once every second since the universe began, which is commonly held to be 10^{17} seconds. Believe it or not, that will bring me to only 10^{149} atoms—still short by one hundred million times!

Even so, if we choose to go ahead with that number of atoms, put a mark on one, mix it back into all those atoms we've imagined, and then draw it back out at random—that is a greater probability than the probability of one person in history fulfilling only forty-eight of the more than three hundred prophecies of the Old Testament that Jesus did indeed fulfill.[5] Amazing, and we've only dealt with forty-eight out of three hundred! There are lots of other ways to construct this model, but I'm roughly following the pattern suggested by Peter Stoner in his book, *Science Speaks.*[6]

Going through this list of specific and complex prophecies, we haven't included some of the most unlikely prophecies that Jesus fulfilled, such as the genealogies in Matthew and Luke, or that astonishing prophecy in Daniel—more than four hundred years before Christ—that foretold the exact day when Jesus would ride that donkey into Jerusalem.

The purpose behind our little "thought experiment" is to demonstrate the confidence we can have that Jesus Christ *is* the Messiah who was prophesied in the Old Testament. I cannot conceive of any fact that I can demonstrate with more confidence, more certainty, than the fact that Jesus Christ really was who He said He was. The Designer of the universe actually *did* enter His creation by becoming a man to fulfill a mission on our behalf.

THE SCARLET THREAD

Beginning with Eve and ending with the blood on the Cross, a Scarlet Thread runs all through the Bible. "The seed of the woman" is the first Messianic title introduced in God's Word,[7] the first indication that God would choose to redeem the creation, the heavens and the earth, which had become corrupted by Satan and his mischief.

God does all of this, first of all, through the human race (the "seed of the woman"). He created the human race a little lower than the angels, and He gave them dominion over the earth. They forfeited it, but a Man will regain that dominion. And those who receive Him will rule with Him. We have seen that He is to come from a specific nation, and from a specific tribe within that nation, the tribe of Judah. And finally, He is to come from a specific family, David, whose dynasty will endure, not for one thousand years, but forever.

Satan, of course, watching all this, and recognizing that God has chosen to bypass the angels in His redemption, has tried to thwart the plan of God. That may sound preposterous to us, but this has been his entire career. And he started by trying to destroy the human race by corrupting it with hybrids, by fallen angels, which finally led to the Flood. As God continued to reveal His plan to go through Abraham, Satan focused his attack on Abraham's seed. In Exodus, Satan tried to destroy the male children in Israel . . . but there God raised Moses. After the Ten Plagues, Pharaoh finally released them, but Satan put in his heart to destroy the entire nation. Pharaoh's army drowned instead. When God told Abraham back in Genesis 17 that four hundred years later his descendants would come and occupy the land Canaan, Satan had four hundred years to lay down a minefield. He populated Canaan with the *Nephilim*, tribal groups that were, again, hybrids. The Scripture suggests these hybrids will be part of the end times (Daniel 2:43 suggests they will even be a political constituency on the earth at the time).

As soon as God indicated that the Messiah would come through the family of David, that family was singled out by Satan. Even in the Persian period, in the Book of Esther, Haman, a descendent of king Agag, tried to wipe out all the Jews in the Persian Empire to thwart God's plan of redemption, but he instead met his demise.

In the New Testament, nothing changed. Joseph thought to put away Mary; Herod attempted to murder all the babies in Bethlehem; the villagers in Nazareth tried to throw Jesus off a cliff; the two storms on the sea in Mark 4 and Luke 8 tried to drown Him. And, of course, the ultimate stratagem of Satan was the Cross.

And he's not through; that's the part that mystifies many. Why is Satan still after believing Jews? He's going to actually bring the whole world to war against Jerusalem to get the remnant. But they will have flown to a refuge. And Jesus Christ will come back, personally, and defend them. Why? *Because the prerequisite for Jesus to return is for the believing remnant to petition His return.* Satan believes that if he can wipe them out, he can thwart God's plan.

PROPHETIC SCRIPTURE

Earlier we alluded to J. Barton Payne's estimation that the Bible includes 8,362 predictive verses containing 1,817 predictions on 737 matters. But I think Payne's estimation is, in a sense, incomplete: I believe that every passage—every word, every letter—is there by deliberate design, all part of a comprehensive fabric, and that fabric is largely predictive.

Prophecy is not the study of things to come: prophecy is looking at God's total plan from beginning to end. The apostle Paul was a student of the venerated Gamaliel, who was of the Hillel school of interpretation. They emphasized the *Midrashic* view, which insisted that prophecy is *pattern*, not just prediction. (We'll explore this later in Hour 19.)

Don't apologize for an interest in prophecy. Many groups are uncomfortable studying Bible prophecy, which has suffered at the hands of its enthusiasts as well as from its skeptics. The skeptics have injured the study of prophecy by not approaching it adequately; the enthusiasts have injured it by sensationalism and excessive exuberance in forcing it into some pet theory. Set those extremes aside and realize that Bible prophecy was the first act of ministry that Jesus did after His resurrection. That first Easter afternoon, two of His disciples were walking to Emmaus during

> *If you want to know what time it is on God's clock, look at Israel.*

which Jesus gave them a seven-mile Old Testament prophecy study. Jesus Himself emphasized, "Search the Scriptures, for in them ye think ye have eternal life; they are they which testify of me."[8] And every time they do, it's prophetic.

There are no other religious books on planet earth that have the audacity to hang their track record on their ability to predict the future. Only the Bible is 20/20, on target, and always has been. You *can* prove the Bible is true by what it says and what has happened.

And if the Bible's true, shouldn't that alter our perceptions of what is important? It should alter all of our personal priorities.

TIME IS RUNNING OUT

If you want to know what time it is on God's clock, look at Israel. Understand Israel—it's the only nation that has its origin, history, ups and downs, and destiny all written out in advance for the diligent. Every time you encounter a Jew you are witnessing a miracle. No race on the planet has endured more systematic, heavily resourced attempts to wipe it out than the Jewish race. The fact that there are Jews alive today is a miracle; the fact that their nation has been reestablished in Israel is not only a miracle, it's on schedule! And there's more to come.

How tragic it is when, even in Christian theology, Israel has been substantially dismissed.

Five-sixths of the Bible is about Israel—from Genesis 12 to Revelation 22. And yet how many churches teach that the Church has replaced Israel? Be careful. Do your own homework; check it out.

Other trends to watch for: Russia (Magog) invading the Middle East; the rise of China as a "superstate"; the reemergence of a European "superstate"; the appeal of an ecumenical religion; and global government, the big buzzword. Global government sounds good for many reasons: nuclear proliferation, for one.

Besides political events, there is the rise of the occult. Studying the Bible as a teenager, I could see all these things happening except one thing: I couldn't visualize the idea of a return to witchcraft and sorcery. As a math/science major going toward a Ph.D., I just couldn't see the world taking witchcraft and sorcery seriously until I realized that the word for sorcery is *pharmacia*. The word means "the use and abuse of drugs." But the extent of real occultic practices is also surprising. The whole Nazi regime was occultic, and even some corporate executives, very privately, take these things seriously. How strange it is that we've gone through the age of rationalism and empiricism and emerged with a pronounced preoccupation with metaphysics in all segments of our society.

I challenge you again to research this preposterous statement: You and I are being plunged into a period of time about which the Bible says more than it does about any other period of time in history, including the time that Jesus walked the shores of Galilee and climbed the mountains of Judea.

For every prophecy of Jesus' first coming, there are eight for His Second Coming. And the more we examine the circumstances necessary for that Second Coming, the more we will recognize that they are being nudged into place. It's as if we are backstage watching the future coming together before the curtains are drawn on the final act. And we've read ahead; the climax is in the back of the book; we know how it ends. God wins!

Hour 14

THE NEW TESTAMENT

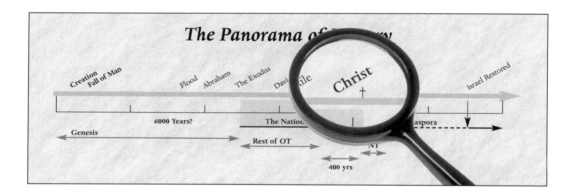

LIKE THE OLD TESTAMENT, the New Testament consists of five historical books: the four Gospels and the Book of Acts. Following that are twenty-one interpretive letters: fourteen epistles written by Paul (although some debate the Book of Hebrews), seven Hebrew Christian epistles, and then the final book, the Book of Revelation. This totals twenty-seven books.

The Old Testament was compiled over several thousand years, but the New Testament was compiled within one lifetime. In fact, Paul's letters, though sent to specific churches, were circulated as a group, often accompanied with the Septuagint version of the Old Testament.

WHEN WAS THE NEW TESTAMENT WRITTEN?

There are events in the New Testament that are conspicuous by their absence. There's no mention of Nero's persecutions which started in about A.D. 64. Also not in the text is the execution of the leader of the Jerusalem church, James, in A.D. 62. There was a Jewish revolt against the Romans in A.D. 66 which is not cited. Nor is the destruction of Jerusalem in A.D. 70 talked about. Why aren't these things mentioned? *Because they hadn't happened yet.* That's a strong authentication of the early dating of these books.

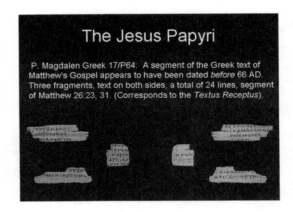

The Jesus Papyri

P. Magdalen Greek 17/P64: A segment of the Greek text of Matthew's Gospel appears to have been dated *before* 66 AD. Three fragments, text on both sides, a total of 24 lines, segment of Matthew 26:23, 31. (Corresponds to the *Textus Receptus*).

And there's something else: the Magdalen papyrus, known as 17P64. It is a segment of Greek text of Matthew's Gospel, Matthew 26:23 and 31, which has been dated before A.D. 66. In 1994, using a scanning laser microscope, Dr. Carsten Thiede compared this fragment with four other manuscripts and concluded that either this is an original of Matthew's Gospel, or an immediate copy written while Matthew and the other disciples and eyewitnesses were still alive! This was a big shock to skeptical scholars who have always maintained that this was written in the second century. Technology has disproved that opinion. Incidentally, the Matthew segment corresponds to *Textus Receptus,* the traditional source documents.

THE DEVELOPMENT OF MODERN TRANSLATIONS

The Jews were distressed that the widely distributed Greek translation, the *Septuagint,* had become the Christian's Bible. So in A.D. 90 they convened a council at Jamnia to pull together a new Hebrew version of the Old Testament. Out of that work came what ultimately was the *Masoretic* text, from which the Old Testament in most of our English Bibles is translated.

In about the fourth century, the *Septuagint,* along with the results of the Jamnia council, came together in what later became known as the *Textus Receptus.* Lucian of Antioch compiled a composite Greek text and it became the primary standard throughout the Byzantine world. From the sixth all the way through the fourteenth centuries, the majority of all the New Testament texts were in Greek. All of the ancient councils were in Greek, not Latin.

In about 1525, Erasmus, using five or six of the Byzantine manuscripts, compiled the first Greek text produced on a printing press. The great innovation that fueled the Reformation was the Gutenberg press and the advent of real printing.

As the Roman Empire began feeling its muscle, Latin began to replace Greek as the official language of the West, and thus Jerome translated the *Vulgate,* drawing on the *Textus Receptus* and *Masoretic* texts. Tyndale, Wycliffe, and others continued the evolution from Hebrew to Greek to Latin to English.

King James VI of Scotland became the King of England and called himself James the First. In 1607, he commissioned fifty scholars to produce a new English translation. They worked in committees, praying at every step; all committees reviewing every word prayerfully. They had 5,556 manuscripts available to them, but they relied primarily on the *Textus Receptus.* The resulting King James Version has been heralded as the noblest monument of English prose.

There are a number of complete New Testament texts that were found that apparently originated in Alexandria in the third and fourth centuries, and, through the agnostic scholarship of Brooke Foss Westcott and Fenton John Anthony Hort, heavily influenced most of the modern translations of the Bible. However, in more recent years, some of the aspects of the Alexandrian codices, and their impact on many of the recent translations, have become suspect and controversial.

KNOWING THE REAL THING

The good news is there is an automatic security monitor watching over every single letter of the text, and it's been running continually for several thousand years. The "fingerprints" of the Author are in the very text we hold in our laps: the designs that the Author has put in the text itself is virtually impossible to compromise. What do I mean by that? Well, let's take a look.

Have you ever noticed the *sevens* in the Bible? They occur in over six hundred passages;

some are very overt, some are simply structural, and some are hidden. The heptadic (the seven-fold) structure seems to act as a signature.

Here's an exercise to demonstrate what I mean. Suppose I ask you to write out a genealogy, a family tree. You can make it up as fiction, but there are some rules I want you to follow:

- The number of words you use must be an exact multiple of seven.
- The number of letters must also be divisible by seven exactly.
- The number of vowels is to be divisible by seven.
- The number of words that begin with a vowel must be divisible by seven.
- The number of words that occur more than once must be divisible by seven.
- The number of words that occur in more than one form must be divisible by seven.
- The number of nouns must be divisible by seven.
- The number of names shall be divisible by seven and only seven other kinds of nouns will be permitted.
- The number of male names shall be divisible by seven.
- The number of generations shall be divisible by seven.

Could you compose a candidate draft that would meet all of these rules? As you've probably guessed, this is the genealogy of Jesus Christ in the opening eleven verses in the Gospel of Matthew, in Greek.

This structure was discovered by Dr. Ivan Panin, born in Russia, December 12, 1855. He was exiled at an early age, caught up in a plot against the Czar. He emigrated to Germany, then the U.S. He graduated from Harvard in 1882 with a Ph.D. in math and then found Jesus Christ. He discovered the heptadic structure of Scripture in about 1890 and committed the next fifty years of his life generating over forty-three thousand pages of research. He went to his Lord on October 30, 1942.

One of the big controversies among some Bible scholars is the last twelve verses of the Gospel of Mark. Your Bible probably has a footnote indicating that the last twelve verses of Mark are disputed or were added by some later scribe. This view comes from an excessive reliance on the Alexandrian manuscripts that were promoted by Westcott and Hort.

But it's simply not true. There are several ways to disprove this claim. First, in A.D. 150

Irenaeus quoted the passage in his commentary, so it must have been around in the second century. Hippolatus, also in the second century, quoted it.

Furthermore, if the last twelve verses of Mark were omitted, the passage would end with the followers of Christ frightened and confused, which is inconsistent with the tenor of the text. There's also another design aspect. First, let's understand the structure of the passage: the first segment (verses 9-11) are an appearance to Mary in the Garden and the disciples' unbelief; the next section (verses 11-18) describes appearances by Jesus Christ; the final verses (19-20) are the conclusion.

> *If the last twelve verses of Mark were omitted, the passage would end with the followers of Christ frightened and confused, which is inconsistent with the tenor of the text.*

In Greek, these last twelve verses contain 175 words (that's 7 times 25). There are 553 letters (7 times 79). The vowels of the letters number 294, and consonants, 259; each exact multiples of seven. The vocabulary used consists of ninety-eight different words (7 times 7 times 2). Eighty-four of those vocabulary words are found earlier in Mark (7 times 12); fourteen are found only here (7 times 2). Forty-two are used in the Lord's address (7 times 6), fifty-six are not (7 times 8). Each one of these conditions is an exact multiple of seven. Rather remarkable "coincidences."

Are these accidental or deliberate? What are the chances of these being the product of random chance? For a single instance, there are six chances of failing, and only one in seven of it coming out correctly. Yet, for two conditions, that's seven times seven, or one chance in forty-nine. For three conditions, that's seven times seven times seven, or one chance in 343. For four conditions, we have one chance in 2,401. The more constraints we put on this, the more rigid the design requirements become. I've given you nine conditions in the description so far. The odds that this was a result of random chance, is one chance in over forty million!

Dr. Panin has identified seventy-five such heptadic constraints! For even just half of those, it would take over one million supercomputers over four million *years* to enumerate the alternatives![1]

Here's another example that blows me away: Matthew uses forty-two words that are not used anywhere else in the New Testament. Those forty-two words (7 times 6) have 126 letters, which is also an exact multiple of seven. Let's assume Matthew set out to do this deliberately, how would he go about it? The only characteristic that these words share was that nobody else used them. How would you determine these words would not be used by anyone else? There are only two ways to do that. Either you would have to get prior agreement with the other authors (assuming you could predict who they would turn out to be), or you would have to write your book after everyone else. You could argue that this proves Matthew's Gospel was *written last*.

Except the same thing is true of the Gospel of Mark! The Gospel of Mark also has a unique vocabulary that is an exact multiple of seven. How did Mark arrange that?

The same thing is true of Luke and John! Someone says, "The Gospel writers must have colluded!" Well, so did James, Peter, Jude, and Paul. Each of them have vocabularies, unique to their writings, that are an exact multiple of seven.

Do we accept our Bible because of Panin's discoveries? No. We accept the Bible, first of all, because the Septuagint authenticates the reality that Jesus Christ was really who He said He was by its precise anticipation of all the details of life of Jesus Christ, centuries in advance. That's the first step. Jesus was authenticated in the Old Testament in the Torah, in Isaiah, in the Psalms; in fact, virtually *every* book of the Old Testament. We accept the Bible because it proves Jesus Christ was who He said He was. And if He was who He said He was, His subsequent authentication of the Old Testament removes all criticism, all questions about who really wrote the Torah, Isaiah, and so forth. We have sixty-six books, penned by over forty authors, over several thousand years, with a design that originated outside the dimension of time itself. Every number, every place name, every detail is there by deliberate design.

And as we apply the insights of cryptography to the text itself, we make new discoveries that are inexhaustible. In addition to the hidden *microcodes*—subtleties of the letters, the numerics, etc.—are the *macrocodes;* these are structural anticipations of what's coming. Abraham offering Isaac on the very spot where another Father would offer His Son for sin (even Abraham knew he was acting out prophecy); the genealogy of Genesis 5, which spells out a summary of God's redemptive plan; and the Book of Ruth, which is the Old Testament Book of the Church. These are only a few examples.

The Old Testament closed with unexplained ceremonies, unachieved purposes, unappeased longings, and unfulfilled prophecies. They are all completed in the New Testament—one book; one integrated whole.

Clearly, the Bible's origin is from outside our physical universe, outside the dimension of time. We serve and worship a transcendent Creator, an awesome Designer who not only created us but chose to enter our creation to undo the damage we've done and to redeem it.

There's another way to know the Bible is true. Jesus gave you a challenge in John 7:17, "If any man will do His will he shall know the doctrine, whether it be of God or whether I speak of myself." That's His challenge. Take Him at His word and see what happens. God will reveal Himself to you as a response to obedience. The revelations of God, throughout the Old Testament, always *follow* obedience; they do not precede it. Take the truth you have, obey it, and God will give you more truth; that's His pattern.

Hour 15

THE GOSPELS

THE DESIGN OF THE GOSPELS

The first thing to notice about the Gospels is they are skillfully designed. Matthew was a Jew, a Levite; he presents Jesus Christ as the Messiah of Israel. Mark (really, Peter's Gospel) presents Him as the suffering servant. Luke, a doctor, presents Him as the Son of Man. And John presents Him as the Son of God. Every detail of each Gospel is tailored to suit its specific perspective.

For example, let's start with the genealogies. Matthew was a Jew so he started his genealogy, as any Jew would, with Abraham. He presented the legal family tree of Jesus. Mark is the only Gospel that doesn't have a genealogy. Why? Because we aren't concerned about the pedigree of a servant. Luke's genealogy started with Adam because, being a physician,

> *In the Old Testament, we see **Christ in prophecy.***
>
> *In the Gospels, we see **Christ in history.***
>
> *In Acts, we see **Christ in the Church.***
>
> *In the Epistles, we see **Christ in our experience.***
>
> *In the Apocalypse, we see **Christ in His coming glory.***

he focused on the fact that Jesus was the Son of Man. In John's Gospel, the first three verses are the genealogy of the preexistent one, the one who had no beginning or end.

A MYSTERY IN THE GENEALOGIES

We know that the Messiah was to come from the royal line of David. But by the time of Jeconiah, God was so fed up with the degeneration of the kings of Judah that He pronounced a blood curse on the line!

> Write ye this man childless, a man that shall not prosper in his days: for no man of his seed shall prosper, sitting upon the throne of David, and ruling any more in Judah. (Jeremiah 22:30)

Again, I suspect that when God declared this blood curse, there must have been a celebration in the councils of Satan. Satan surely must have thought, "Boy, God has shot Himself in the foot on this one because on the one hand He has committed Himself to producing the Messiah from the family of David, yet now there is a curse on the royal family tree of David." But then, I also imagine God turning to the angels saying, "Watch this one!"

From Abraham to David, the two genealogies in Matthew and Luke are identical. But when they get to David, the two genealogies diverge. Matthew went through the first surviving son of Bathsheba, Solomon; through Rehoboam and on to Jehoiachin whose son, Jeconiah, was the subject of this blood curse. It finally ends with Joseph, who is the legal father of Jesus but not the blood father. The curse of Jeconiah was on the bloodline. But Jesus is not of the bloodline of Joseph. He is merely the legal son of Joseph.

The House of David

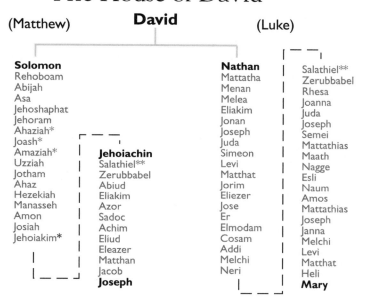

David

(Matthew)   (Luke)

Solomon		**Nathan**	Salathiel**
Rehoboam		Mattatha	Zerubbabel
Abijah		Menan	Rhesa
Asa		Melea	Joanna
Jehoshaphat		Eliakim	Juda
Jehoram		Jonan	Joseph
Ahaziah*		Joseph	Semei
Joash*		Juda	Mattathias
Amaziah*	**Jehoiachin**	Simeon	Maath
Uzziah	Salathiel**	Levi	Nagge
Jotham	Zerubbabel	Matthat	Esli
Ahaz	Abiud	Jorim	Naum
Hezekiah	Eliakim	Eliezer	Amos
Manasseh	Azor	Jose	Mattathias
Amon	Sadoc	Er	Joseph
Josiah	Achim	Elmodam	Janna
Jehoiakim*	Eliud	Cosam	Melchi
	Eleazer	Addi	Levi
	Matthan	Melchi	Matthat
	Jacob	Neri	Heli
	Joseph		**Mary**

When Luke got to David he took a left turn and went through Nathan, the second surviving son of Bathsheba, and on through to Heli, who was the father of Mary and the father-in-law of Joseph.[1] The genealogy of Mary is in Luke.[2] The Virgin Birth, which was hinted in the Garden of Eden[3] and prophesied by Isaiah,[4] was also an "end-run" on the blood curse of Jeconiah.

Every verse, every detail in the Scripture is there by design, and once you make that discovery, it will change your whole approach to understanding the Bible.

CHARACTERISTICS OF THE FOUR GOSPELS

Matthew presents Jesus as the Messiah; Mark presents Jesus as the Servant; Luke presents Jesus as the Son of Man; and John presents Jesus as the Son of God.

Matthew emphasized what Jesus *said*. He recorded the discourses verbatim. (As a customs official, he was a stenographer; his job required that he be able to take shorthand.[5])

Mark's Gospel is actually longer than Matthew's if you dismiss the extensive discourses. He talked about what Jesus *did*. It was like a shooting script, dictated to Mark by Peter, and Peter was a man of action.

Luke, the doctor, emphasized what Jesus *felt*, His humanity. Luke records when Jesus wept, when He trembled with compassion at the gravesite, and so on.

John focused on who Jesus *was*: "These things were written that you might believe that He is the Son of God" (John 20:31).

Matthew wrote to the Jew, Mark to the Roman, Luke to the Greek, and John to the Church. Their relative missions are also supported by the first miracle they record. The first miracle in Matthew was very Jewish: the leper was cleansed and leprosy was, to Jews, a sign of sin. In both Mark and Luke, writing to Gentiles, the first miracles are demons being expelled. John's initial miracle is the mystical event of the water turned to wine. No one knew what happened there except the disciples. What water was used? The water of purification from the Temple. He was showing that Jesus is the Lord of the Torah, undiscerned by anyone but His disciples.

Matthew also ended in a very Jewish way: the Resurrection. Mark ended with the Ascension. Luke, with the promise of the Spirit, setting the stage for "Luke, Vol. 2" (The Book of Acts). What did John finish with? The promise of Christ's return, setting the stage for *his* sequel, the Book of Revelation.

Back in the Book of Numbers, we studied the camp of Israel. Four camps were around the Tabernacle on the east, west, north, and south: the ensign on the east side was that of Judah; on the west side, Ephraim; on the south side, Reuben; and on the north side, Dan. Each one of the tribal standards represented a face: the lion, the ox, the man, and the eagle—the same four faces that appear on the cherubim in the visions of the Throne of God (in Isaiah, Ezekiel, Revelation, etc.).

The Lion of the Tribe of Judah is an emblem of the Messiah, representative of Matthew. The ox was the classic symbol of a servant, as presented in Mark. Luke emphasized the Son of Man; and John, the Eagle. The same four faces that were the ensigns for the camps of Israel and appear on the cherubim seem to also characterize the four Gospels.

BEHIND THE SCENES

The Holy Spirit gave us some anticipatory pre-announcements in the Gospels. In the Upper Room, Jesus promised His followers, "The Comforter, which is the Holy Ghost, whom the Father will send in my name, he shall teach you all things, and bring all things to your remembrance, whatsoever I have said unto you."[6] Later they would remember and understand many things they hadn't understood when they occurred earlier. How? By the Holy Spirit.

Jesus also explained, "Howbeit when he, the Spirit of truth, is come, he will guide you into all truth: for he shall not speak of himself; but whatsoever he shall hear, that shall he speak: and he will shew you things to come.'"[7] Throughout the Old Testament, whenever the Holy Spirit showed up in a type or model, He was always an *unnamed servant*. In Genesis 24, Abraham (the father) sent his *unnamed servant* to get a bride for Isaac (the son). We found out his name in Genesis 15—Eliezer, which means "comforter." But he didn't name himself there; he was true to the model by remaining anonymous. In the Book of Ruth, who introduced Ruth to Boaz? It was an *unnamed servant*.[8]

Jesus is the Second Adam. He's a prophet like Moses; a priest like Melchizedek; a champion like Joshua; an offering in the place of Isaac; a king after the line of David; a wise counselor above Solomon. He was beloved, rejected, and then exalted like Joseph. All these attributes described in the past set the stage for the Coming One.

THE GOSPEL OF MATTHEW

The Lion of the Tribe of Judah is the focus of Matthew. The introduction deals with the genealogy, the baptism, and the temptation. Then Matthew presented the Galilean ministry. Matthew tended to focus on the northern ministry in chapters 5–18 with the tenfold message called the Sermon on the Mount, then ten miracles, and ten rejections. After that, the focus is on the Judean ministry down south, where Jesus presented Himself as a King in chapters 19–25. After that is the Crucifixion itself and the Resurrection. The Gospel of Matthew is very precise, and he emphasized the links to the Old Testament prophecies.

The three major discourses in Matthew are the Sermon on the Mount, the Seven Kingdom Parables, and the Second Coming Discourse in chapters 24 and 25.

Let's review some of the Seven Kingdom Parables because they affect you and me in ways that are not obvious. When you review Matthew 13, you will find seven parables: the Sower and the Four Soils; the Tares and the Wheat; the Mustard Seed; the Woman and the Leaven; Treasure in the Field; the Pearl of Great Price; and the Dragnet.

The Sower and the Four Soils. In the parable of the sower, what's being sowed in each case is the Word of God. The soils are the hearts it falls upon. Some are fruitful and some are not; and Jesus explained why.

The Tares and the Wheat. This parable is similar: the seed is sown, but an enemy came and contaminated what had been sown with false teaching, the tares. Jesus explained these first two to His disciples, but not to the crowd. He didn't explain the others at all.

The Mustard Seed. This parable describes a mustard seed that grew into a tree, where the birds in the air could roost. (Many people preach that it means the Word of God will start small and take over the whole world. Wait a minute! That may be missing the real hidden truth.)

The Kingdom of God is going to be like the tiny mustard seed that grows to a large tree that's so big, even the birds can lodge there. What's Jesus really talking about?

In Israel, the yellow mustard plants are everywhere: they are small plants about two feet tall. And keep in mind that the idioms throughout these parables are consistent. The birds in the third parable are the same emissaries of Satan that appeared in the first parable: the birds are those that come and steal the seed before it can bear fruit.

The Woman and the Leaven. A little parable in one verse:

> Another parable spake he unto them; The kingdom of heaven is like unto leaven, which a woman took, and hid in three measures of meal, till the whole was leavened. (verse 33)

Leaven was a type of sin—always—in the Old Testament as well as in the New Testament. Three measures of meal in Genesis 18 were the three measures of meal Sarah made for the three visitors, the Lord and two angels. From that day on, in the Arab as well as the Jewish cultures, "three measures of meal" was an idiom for the fellowship offering of hospitality. If you're a Jew and you hear a rabbi teach, "The kingdom of heaven is like a woman who hid leaven in three measures of meal," you gasp in horror. That was just not done. The leaven speaks of a growing corruption by puffing up.

The Pearl of Great Price. Pearl is not kosher because oysters are not kosher. A pearl is the only jewel that is a response to an irritation, grows by accretion, and is removed to become an item of adornment. That is a perfect idiom for the Church.

The Dragnet. This signified the Final Judgment. It is possible that the seven letters to the seven churches in Revelation 2 and 3 parallel these seven kingdom parables. It shouldn't surprise us if they do because they were given by the same person. We will explore these in Hour 22.

THE GOSPEL OF MARK

Mark has no nativity narrative or genealogy. He was not interested in Jesus' pedigree since he presented Christ as the suffering servant. Again, if you remove the discourses from

Matthew, Mark is actually longer, but it is more like a shooting script, a graphic perspective of eyewitnesses: names, times, numbers, locations. He was Peter's secretary, and it has been translated from Aramaic. He emphasized the mighty works, the sending of the Twelve, and the Transfiguration in the final week. The finale was the Resurrection and the Ascension.

THE GOSPEL OF LUKE

Luke's Gospel is the most complete narrative. Over twenty miracles are recorded, seven of them unique to Luke, and twenty-three parables are recorded, eighteen of them unique to Luke. The first three chapters present two annunciations, two elect mothers, and two anticipated births: John the Baptist and, of course, Jesus Christ.

John the Baptist's ministry started when he was about nine inches long and weighed a pound and a half: he was Spirit-filled and could jump for joy. That should end the debates about when life begins!

The Galilean ministry occupies the early part of Luke up to chapter 9, including teachings, miracles, and the sending of the Twelve. Chapters 10–19 are a lengthy discussion of the journey toward Jerusalem. In the final chapters Jesus presented Himself as a king riding a donkey, followed by the Passover supper, Gethsemane, and Golgotha.

Luke is the most authenticated historical writer. Sir William Ramsey was a skeptic who set out to debunk Luke, but as a result of his investigation he became a believer, authenticating the precision and the accuracy of Luke's writings.[9]

Luke was a Gentile and a physician, and he wrote more about Jesus' healing ministry than Matthew and Mark put together. He used more medical terms than Hippocrates, "the Father of Medicine," and included the obstetrical details of the nativity. He also probably treated Paul's ophthalmic malady. He may have been a slave—most physicians were in that day. In fact, over half the Roman Empire's population were slaves or employees of a patron.

Luke's Gospel and the Book of Acts were sponsored by a patron named Theophilus. There is some conjecture that these may have been part of the essential documents required for Paul's appeal to Caesar. We know from the Roman law that all the written background had to precede the defendant's arrival. Apparently Luke was dispatched and supported by Theophilus to produce these documents. J. Vernon McGee said this about Luke:

> The religion of Israel could only produce a Pharisee, the power of Rome could only produce a
> Caesar, the philosophy of Greece could only produce an Alexander, who was an infant or child

in art. It was to this Greek mind that Luke wrote. He presents Jesus Christ as the "perfect man," the "universal man" and the very person that the Greeks were looking for.[10]

THE GOSPEL OF JOHN

John opened with a fabulous declaration, using "The Word of God" as a title of Jesus Christ:

> In the beginning was the Word, and the Word was with God, and the Word was God. The same was in the beginning with God. All things were made by him; and without him was not any thing made that was made.
>
> . . . And the Word was made flesh, and dwelt among us, (and we beheld his glory, the glory as of the only begotten of the Father,) full of grace and truth. (John 1:1-3, 14)

Another key verse:

> He came unto his own, and his own received Him not. But as many as received him, to them gave he power to become the sons of God, even to them that believe on his name."
> (John 1:11, 12)

I love the tense confrontation with the rulers in which Jesus declares: "before Abraham was, I am." (8:58). Now any time that you and I might miss the implications of that, the Pharisees come to our rescue. They took up stones to cast at Him. Why were they so upset? Because they recognized what He was saying. Jesus was declaring here that He was the voice of the burning bush!

The Gospel of John is built around seven "I am" statements: I Am the Bread of Life; I am the Light of the World; I am the Door of the Sheep; I am the Good Shepherd; I am the Resurrection and the Life; I am the Way, the Truth, and the Life; and I am the True Vine.

HARMONIZING THE GOSPELS

The best way to learn of the Gospels is to read them. But it may be useful to harmonize them chronologically.

Tiberius was appointed in A.D. 14; Caesar Augustus died on August 19 of that year. Christ's ministry started "in the fifteenth year of Tiberius."[11] "In" (during) the fifteenth year means fourteen years have gone by: thus, Jesus' ministry began in the fall of A.D. 28.

By this reckoning, the fourth Passover, when Jesus was crucified, was April 6, A.D. 32. (which agrees with Sir Robert Anderson's extensive research in dating the Seventy Weeks of Daniel).

(Other chronologies try to support the tradition of a Friday crucifixion. While there are many good scholars who still hold that view, we believe that it was on Wednesday, not Friday. We see three days and three nights between the crucifixion and Sunday morning, as Jesus Himself prophesied.[12] We will explore this further in the next Hour.)

Autumn, A.D. 28. Jesus left Nazareth, where He was raised, and went down to Bethabara for His baptism. Right after the baptism, He went to the Mount of Temptation[13] where He was tempted by Satan. Then He went back to Salem and then Cana, Nathaniel's hometown. The first disciples were from there—John, Andrew, Peter, Philip, and Nathaniel.

Spring, A.D. 29. The first miracle was at the wedding in Cana;[14] Jesus then moved to Capernaum, where he established His base of operations. While Jesus was at the Passover in Jerusalem, Nicodemus, a leader of the Jews, came to Him by night.[15] Jesus explained that he needed to be born again, which gave rise to the most famous verse in the entire Bible,

> For God so loved the world, that he gave his only begotten Son, that whosoever believeth in him should not perish, but have everlasting life. (*John 3:16*)

This was also about the time of John the Baptist's last testimony.

Winter, A.D. 29. Jesus met the woman at the well at Sycar.[16] From there He went back to Cana and healed the son of a royal official. He also healed someone at the Pool of Bethesda.[17]

Spring, A.D. 30. At this time John the Baptist had been imprisoned in Jerusalem. In Galilee, Jesus had begun to broaden His public ministry.[18] At the synagogue in Nazareth He declared His mandate by reading from Isaiah.[19] The townspeople tried to throw Him off a cliff, so He left Nazareth and made His base in Capernaum. There He called four disciples.

Peter and his brother Andrew were fishing partners with James and John. They had fished all night and caught nothing. At midday, Jesus asked Peter to take him a little ways into the Sea of Galilee so He could teach. After He finished, Jesus said, "Let's go out deeper and fish." Peter said, "You're wasting your time. We fished all night and caught nothing."

But they went out anyway and caught so many fish the nets started to break. Then they began to realize they were dealing with more than just a prophet.

During this time Peter's mother-in-law and a leper were healed.

Summer, A.D. 30. In Capernaum, Jesus healed a paralytic. This is about when Matthew was called.[20] Jesus and his disciples picked grain on the Sabbath, and again on the Sabbath, Jesus healed the man with the withered hand.[21] His fame started to spread in the region. The Sermon on the Mount was delivered about this time.[22] Jesus healed a centurion's servant.[23]

Fall, A.D. 30. In Capernaum again, Jesus healed a blind and dumb man, but He was accused of doing this by the powers of Satan. From then on, Jesus spoke publicly only in parables so the truth would be hidden to all but His own.[24] That may shock you, but it was fulfilling a prophesy in Isaiah.[25]

After the seven kingdom parables of Matthew 13, the die was cast; the nation was on its path. They accused the Son of God of being of Satan.

On a ship from Capernaum to Gadara, a very severe storm arose quickly. That is not unusual in that region, but I don't think this was a normal storm because the professional fishermen on board were terrified for their lives. And when Jesus calmed the storm, he "rebuked" the storm. I think Satan was anticipating what was going to happen in Gadara, when Jesus encountered the demoniac who recognized Him as the Son of God and apparently was aware of his destiny!

The demons (two thousand of them) then asked Jesus to be allowed to go into a nearby herd of swine, and Jesus permitted it! Why? To demonstrate to us that demons are real, and not just some idiomatic use of words for some psychiatric disorder. The swine then ran off the cliff and died. Then the disciples went back to Capernaum.

Winter, A.D. 30. Two incidents occurred at the same time: Jairus's daughter was raised and a woman with an issue of blood was healed. Although they appear unrelated, the Holy Spirit seems to link those two events. Jesus was on His way to save a twelve-year-old Jewish girl and on the way a Gentile woman, who had suffered for twelve years, was healed by faith. Was this a model of some broader truth?

Two blind men and a dumb and possessed man were also healed. Jesus arrived in Nazareth; again, people took offense.[26] John the Baptist was beheaded about this time for preaching against the immorality of the administration, and the apostles were sent out in pairs.[27] Jesus then returned to Capernaum.

Spring, A.D. *31.* Back in Capernaum, the Twelve returned. Jesus retired to Bethsaida, which became a major base. During this time He fed the five thousand[28] and returned to Capernaum. And it was on this trip that Jesus walked on the water.[29] His sermon on the Bread of Life occured here. Around this time He was accused of eating with unwashed hands, etc.[30]

In Capernaum, He took a summer cottage up in Tyre.[31] He helped a Canaanite woman and a Gentile and then went to the region of Decapolis.[32] (This is all Gentile country, by the way.)

He healed a deaf and dumb man, fed the four thousand, then went to Magdela where the Pharisees demanded a sign. Then He took a ship to Bethsaida, where He talked about the leaven of the Pharisees.[33]

He then traveled north to Caesarea Philippi. This is where he asked his disciples, "Whom do people say that I am?" (That's the key question in all of our lives: Who do we say Jesus is?) This was Peter's grandest moment: "Thou art the Christ, the Son of the living God." And it was on that foundation that Jesus would build His Church.

Jesus went up to the Mount of Transfiguration[34] (which many scholars believe was Mt. Hermon) where He was transfigured in front of the three "insiders," Peter, James, and John. Peter wanted to make three booths, which is why some people think this was in the fall: it was around the time of the Feast of Tabernacles. (Peter will allude to this heavily in his second letter.) After healing a possessed boy, Jesus went back to Capernaum.

Jesus went down to Jerusalem to celebrate the Feast of Tabernacles where He declared Himself to be the Living Water.[35] He forgave the woman taken in adultery,[36] and returned to Galilee.

Winter, A.D. *31.* During this time the Samaritans rejected Him. He went to Perea, an area east of the Jordan, and, among other things, presented several parables: the Good Samaritan, the Unrighteous Steward, and the Rich Man and Lazarus.[37] This is also when He sent out the seventy.

He traveled to Jerusalem and healed a man born blind. The Good Shepherd discourse occurred there during Hanukkah. (The New Testament authenticates Hanukkah; it's a key to understanding the end times.) And He tarried at Bethabara.

Spring, A.D. *32.* Jesus traveled from Bethabara to Bethany, which was His headquarters when He was in the Jerusalem area because it was within a Sabbath day's journey from the Temple. This is where Lazarus was raised from the dead.[38] Immediately the Jewish leaders plotted to kill both Lazarus and Jesus, so Jesus moved to the village of Ephraim. Traveling again through Perea, He encountered the ten lepers and gave a number of parables.[39] Also at this time was the ambitious request of the mother of James and John, the sons of Zebedee: she wanted her two sons to sit on each side of Him when He entered into His reign.

Jesus traveled back to Jericho where he healed blind Bartimeus.[40] Then Jesus called Zaccheus, the little man in the tree, and presented the Parable of the Ten Talents.[41] Then he went to Bethany for the final week, which we will explore separately in the next Hour.

(The trip from Jericho to Bethany was six days prior to Passover.[42] Jericho was more than a Sabbath day's journey, so as an obedient Jew, Jesus could not have taken this trip on a Saturday. Therefore, Passover could not have been on a Friday that year, another reason why a Friday crucifixion doesn't fit the record.)

Of course, there is no way to adequately summarize the Gospels in just a few pages. But we hope this composite summary will help reconcile the four individual accounts.

And now we are up to that final week—the climax of all human history.

Hour 16

THE PASSION WEEK

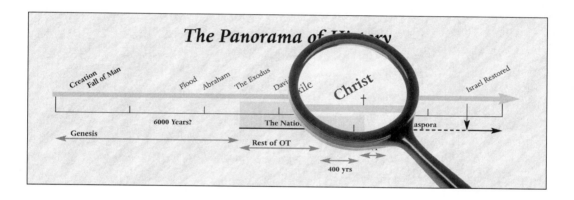

IN THIS CHAPTER we will explore the purpose of all human history, the "passion week," in which we see expressed the agony and love of our Lord and Savior Jesus Christ.

A foundational question to ask about this week is, "When was the Crucifixion?" Many good scholars still defend the traditional Friday view, but many other scholars believe it was on a Wednesday (which is what I believe). Here's why.

As we saw in our review of the previous Hour, the Gospel of John indicates that six days before the Passover, Jesus came to Bethany from Jericho.[1] That's more than a Sabbath day's journey, so six days prior could not have been a Saturday and would eliminate the possibility that Passover that year was on a Friday.

Furthermore, the Greek text of Matthew clearly describes the women coming to the tomb that Sunday morning, "After the Sabbaths were passed," "Sabbaths" being plural.[2]

(There is a mistranslation in English.) Why is that significant? As we reviewed in Hour 5, in addition to the Saturday Sabbaths in the Jewish calendar, there are seven additional high days in their calendar that are "Sabbaths." The first day of the Feast of Unleavened Bread, following Passover, is one of them. The passage indicates that more than one Sabbath had passed in the intervening period between Passover and Sunday, so Passover could not have been a Friday.

A Final Week Chronology

- *Friday was at Bethany.*[4]
- *Saturday was the triumphal entry.*[5]
- *Sunday the fig tree was cursed.*
- *Monday the conspirators counseled.*[6]
- *Tuesday was the Last Supper.*
- *Wednesday was the Crucifixion.*[7]
- *Thursday was the Feast of Unleavened Bread.*
- *Friday the women prepared the spices and so forth.*
- *Saturday they all rested.*[8]

Also, Jesus specifically said He would spend three days and three nights in the heart of the earth.[3] I believe that He says what He means and means what He says. (But in any case there are good scholars who still defend a Friday crucifixion. But we'll assume a Wednesday for our review.)

Sunday morning, "after the Sabbaths," the women came to the tomb.

The Feast of First Fruits is "on the morrow after the Sabbath," after Passover.[9] That morning, at the Temple, as smoke was furling up from the offerings of the Feast of First Fruits, a group of women were discovering an empty tomb.

Sunday He rose, as the "First Fruits" of the "First Resurrection,"[10] as recorded in all four of the Gospels.

THE TRIUMPHAL ENTRY

In both Hours 9 and 13, we noted the prophecy in Zechariah,

Rejoice greatly, O daughter of Zion; shout, O daughter of Jerusalem: behold, thy king cometh unto thee: he is just, and having salvation; lowly, and riding upon an ass, and upon a colt the foal of an ass.[11]

Jesus rode the donkey from Bethany, westward over the Mount of Olives, and into the city. Jerusalem was packed with tourists because the *Torah* required every able-bodied Jew to attend. The Book of Deuteronomy commanded three mandatory feasts: the Feast of Unleavened Bread, Feast of *Shavout* (or Pentecost), and the Feast of Tabernacles. (They commonly call the three feasts in the spring, collectively, "Passover," but that includes Passover, the Feast of Unleavened Bread, and the Feast of First Fruits.[12])

The crowd had heard about Lazarus and they were excited to see Jesus, throwing down their coats and palm branches and singing Psalm 118, "Blessed be the King that cometh in the name of the Lord." This was the only day Jesus allowed Himself to be worshiped as King. The people had tried earlier to make him King, but He slipped away saying, "Mine hour has not yet come" (John 6). But on this day, He not only allowed it; He arranged it and deliberately fulfilled Zechariah 9:9.

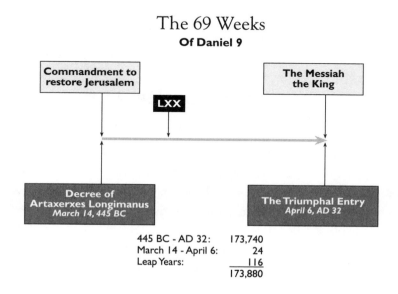

The 69 Weeks
Of Daniel 9

| Commandment to restore Jerusalem | | The Messiah the King |

LXX

| Decree of Artaxerxes Longimanus *March 14, 445 BC* | | The Triumphal Entry *April 6, AD 32* |

445 BC - AD 32:	173,740
March 14 - April 6:	24
Leap Years:	116
	173,880

Any time we risk missing a key point, the Pharisees come to our rescue. The next verse says, "Some of the Pharisees from among the multitude said unto him, Master, rebuke your disciples."[13] They knew that the crowd was proclaiming Jesus as the Messiah, the King. Jesus answered, "I tell you that, if these should hold their peace, the stones would immediately cry out."

Earlier, in Hour 9, we examined Daniel 9 where the angel Gabriel told Daniel that from the commandment to restore and rebuild Jerusalem unto Messiah the King would be 173,880 days, sixty-nine weeks of 360-day years. If you do the arithmetic, you'll discover that the number of days between the Decree of Artaxerxes Longimanus on March 12, 445 B.C., to the triumphal entry which happened on April 6, A.D. 32, is precisely 173,880 days.

As Jesus approached the city He wept over it, saying, "If thou hadst known, even thou, at least in this thy day, the things which belong unto thy peace! but now they are hid from thine eyes" (Luke 19:42). That was a dangerous declaration because now these insights are hidden from Israel as a nation "until the fullness of the Gentiles be come in."[14]

He also announced to them, "The days shall come upon thee, that thine enemies shall cast a trench about thee, and compass thee round, and keep thee in on every side, and shall lay thee even with the ground, and thy children within thee; and they shall not leave in thee one stone upon another" (Luke 19:43, 44).

Thirty-eight years later, the Fifth, Tenth, Twelfth, and Fifteenth Roman Legions laid on a nine-month siege in A.D. 70. One and half million men, women, and children were killed in that battle or died from the famine and disease that followed.

Why was Jerusalem destroyed? While there are many good answers to that, Jesus Himself explained, it was "because thou knewest not the time of thy visitation."[15] Jesus held them accountable to know the last four verses of Daniel 9, and to know that the Messiah had come.

THE LAST SUPPER AND THE GARDEN OF GETHSEMANE

The backdrop to the Last Supper was the plot to kill the Lord. The chief priests, scribes, and elders planned to kill Him, but they were not going to take Him on a feast day.[16] Why? Because they were fearful of the Romans. The Romans almost didn't care what you did as long as you didn't cause an uproar or an insurrection. They were interested in keeping peace in this unruly place called Judea.

It was in the Upper Room, as Jesus and the disciples were celebrating the Passover meal together, that Jesus let the cat out of the bag: "One of you will betray me." One by one, the disciples asked, "Is it I, is it I?" and He announced, "It's the one who dips with me in the sop." He dipped the bread and handed it to Judas.

Who was calling the shots here? *Jesus* was! Judas was now on the spot. He had *not* planned to do it that night. It was a feast day; in fact, it was the highest feast day. But now Judas had a problem. Everybody knew now that a plot was afoot. It was "fish or cut bait," as we often say. Judas had to pull it off that night or it would all be over. As you study this week, you will see that every detail, from the riding of the donkey to the Crucifixion, was precisely timed. And the one orchestrating the entire drama was the Lord Himself.

They sang a hymn and finished three of the traditional four cups. (The fourth cup will be finished in Heaven at the Marriage Supper of the Lamb.) Then they went to Gethsemane for prayer. When the troops arrived, Jesus stepped forward, confronting them. "Whom seek ye?" He asked. They answered, "Jesus of Nazareth." Jesus said, "I am He." Here Jesus used His eternal name, "I Am," and the troops were overwhelmingly stunned. He asked them again, "Whom seek ye?" They answered again, "Jesus of Nazareth." Jesus said, "I told you that I am He. Let these go their way."

Who was giving the orders? Jesus was! The Lord was in charge even of His own arrest and trial. He knew He was fulfilling an eternal destiny.

The crucifixion was not an accident; it was the fulfillment of His mission!

The Trials of Jesus

After Jesus was arrested in the Garden, there were six trials that night. There were three Jewish trials: before Annas, before Caiaphas, before the Sanhedrin. Later, there were three Roman trials; before Pilate, before Herod, and then before Pilate again. I would like to highlight some of the reasons why they were all illegal:

- The binding of a prisoner before he was condemned was against the law.

- Judges participated in the arrest of the accused. That was against the law.

- No legal transactions, including a trial, could be conducted at night. An acquittal could be announced the same day but any other verdict required a majority of two and had to come on a subsequent day.

- No prisoner could be convicted on his own evidence.

- It was the duty of a judge to see that the interest of the accused was fully protected. This was what we would call a "kangaroo court."

- The use of violence during the trial was apparently unopposed by the judges.

- The judges sought false witness against Jesus.

- In a Jewish court, the accused was to be presumed innocent until proven guilty by two or more witnesses.

- No witness was ever called for the defense.

- The court lacked the civil authority to condemn a man to death.

- It was illegal to conduct a session of the court on a Feast day. This was not only a Feast day, but the high Feast day—it was Passover.

- The sentence was finally passed in the palace of the High Priest, but the law demanded that it be pronounced in the Temple in the hall of hewn stone. They broke the law in every detail.

- The High Priest rent his garment. He was never permitted to tear his official robes.[17] And without his priestly robe he couldn't have put Christ under oath, which of course he did.

What is also striking is that Pilate, the personal representative of the ruler of the world, pronounced Christ innocent. The Passover Lamb had to be without blemish.

There was a custom that on some holidays, the Romans would release one prisoner to the crowd. Pilate tried to offer Jesus to the crowd, but his gambit didn't work. Instead, they chose Barabbas, a rebel, murderer, and scoundrel.

We don't know much about Barabbas except the following:

- He stood under the righteous condemnation of the law.

- He knew that the one who was to take his cross and his place was innocent.

- He knew that Jesus Christ was, for him, a true substitute.

- He knew that he had done nothing to merit going free while another took his place.

Think about Barabbas and Jesus. They were changing places. The murderer's bonds, curse, disgrace, and mortal agony were transferred to the righteous Jesus. The liberty, innocence, safety, and the well-being of the Nazarene were transferred to the murderous Barabbas.

Where are you and I? We are in Barabbas's shoes. Everything that is true of Barabbas is true of us. We are in the same position Barabbas was in—all his rights, his immunity, are now ours.

THE CRUCIFIXION

As we saw earlier, death by crucifixion was invented by the Persians about 90 B.C. and then was widely adopted by the Romans. Basically it was death by asphyxiation. A victim had to press down on the spike through his feet to relieve the pressure on his lungs. Although the pain of that was excruciating, it sometimes took as long as nine days to die. Crucifixion was deliberately designed to be agonizing and brutal. It was done publicly as an example to other citizens of the power of Rome.

Where was Jesus crucified? When Abraham offered Isaac, he went to Mount Moriah, which is a ridge system beyond the Temple Mount. The Temple Mount is about 741 meters above sea level, but if you follow this ridge to a peak, at 777 meters above sea level, you come to where Abraham offered Isaac and where Jesus was crucified: a place called Golgotha.

PROPHECIES OF THE FINAL WEEK

We looked at a few Old Testament prophecies quoted in the Gospels, but there are several specifically about the final week, some of which are listed below:

- He would make a triumphal entry in Jerusalem—Zechariah 9:9, Psalm 118.
- He would be smitten like a shepherd—Zechariah 13.
- He would be betrayed for thirty pieces of silver—Zechariah 11:1-13: Psalm 41:9.
- He would be given vinegar and gall—Psalm 69:21.
- They would cast lots for His garments—Psalm 22:18.
- His bones would not be broken—Exodus 12:46; Numbers 9:12; Psalm 34:20.
- His side would be pierced—Zechariah 12:10; Psalm 22:16.
- He would die among malefactors—Isaiah 53:9, 12.
- His dying words were foretold—Psalm 22:1, 31.
- He would be buried by a rich man—Isaiah 53:9.
- He would rise on the third day—Jonah 1:17; Matthew 12:39, 40. Also, Genesis 22:4 with Hebrews 11:19.
- His resurrection would be followed by the destruction of Jerusalem—Daniel 9, 11, 12.

What really held Jesus to that cross? It wasn't the nails!

He was crucified on a cross of wood;
Yet He made the hill on which it stood!

At any time he could have said, "Enough! I'm out of here!" What held him to the cross was His love for us.

It was customary to display the indictment on the cross so that people seeing this grotesque execution would know why the victim was being punished. I am impressed that Pilate was personally on site, personally wrote it, and put it on the cross. He wrote in Hebrew, Greek, and Latin, "Jesus of Nazareth, King of the Jews." [18]

Now again, when we might miss something, the chief priests come to our rescue. The chief priests of the Jews complained, "Write not the King of the Jews, but that He said, 'I Am the King of the Jews.'" They were not happy with the way it was written.

But Pilate said, "What I have written, I have written." The way he wrote it, the first letter of each of the four words in the Hebrew spell out YHWH, the unpronounceable name of God Himself. He apparently did it deliberately to offend the Jewish leadership.

> *At any time He could have said, "Enough! I'm out of here!" What held him to the cross was His love for us.*

SEALING THE TOMB

The religious establishment came to Pilate and said, "Sir, we remember that that deceiver said, while he was yet alive, After three days I will rise again" (Matthew 27:63).

I find this fascinating. His enemies understood that He was going to rise on the third day (even though the disciples apparently didn't!). So they petitioned the procurator, "Command therefore that the sepulchre be made sure until the third day, lest his disciples come by night, and steal him away, and say unto the people, He is risen from the dead: so the last error shall be worse than the first" (27:64).

Were they admitting that the Crucifixion was a mistake? I think so. The day darkened for half a day, there was an earthquake, etc. Since they didn't want to make the second error worse than the first, they wanted a seal on the tomb. Pilate said to them, "You have your watch, go your way, make it as sure as you can."

He gave them permission all right, but do you hear the skepticism in his voice? When the empty tomb was reported, I don't think he was surprised.

THE RESURRECTION

Here is another review from Hour 3 when we examined Genesis 8. When did the Flood end? Remember the Ark came to rest on the seventeenth day of the seventh month (Nisan, on that calendar), on the mountains of Ararat.

Jesus was crucified on the fourteenth of Nisan and He was in the grave three days. So He rose on the seventeenth of Nisan. God's new beginning of the Planet Earth under Noah was on the same date, in advance, as our new beginning in Jesus Christ. I think that's breathtaking! Every detail in God's plan is by design. God, in His predetermined counsel, laid it all out in detail.

After He arose, He appeared to Mary Magdalene that early morning; [19] then the other women; [20] the two on the Emmaus road Sunday afternoon; [21] Peter, some time that day; [22] the Eleven that night without Thomas; and then eight days later with Thomas; [23] then the seven at the seaside breakfast in Galilee; [24] then on the mountain. [25] Over five hundred people saw Him in Galilee, many of whom were present when Paul alluded to this in his letter to the church at Corinth. [26]

(If I said that one November afternoon, President John F. Kennedy was killed in Dallas with a bow and arrow, would you believe me? Of course not! Too many eyewitnesses to the event are still alive and can rebut my false story. Similarly, Paul wrote 1 Corinthians 15 to people who were there. They had seen Him resurrected.)

Then He appeared to James, the Lord's brother, who then became a believer and later became the leader of the church in Jerusalem. Subsequent appearances of Jesus include His ascension[27] and His later confrontation with Paul on the Damascus road. [28]

But I have a problem that I would like to share with you. As I study all this, I notice something very strange: It seems surprisingly consistent that after His resurrection, everyone seemed to have trouble recognizing Him when they saw Him. The first example is Mary in the garden. [29] Mary came there in the morning and peeked into the tomb. He was gone! She turned back to the garden and saw Jesus standing but didn't recognize Him. She thought He was the gardener!

"Woman, why weepest thou?" He asked.

"They have taken away my Lord and I don't know where they have laid Him. Please tell me where they took Him and I'll carry Him away," Mary answered.

He then switched from Greek to Aramaic and said, apparently with emphasis, "Mary!"

She looked at Him and said, "Raboni," which means Master. But it's puzzling. Why didn't she recognize Him at first?

The same thing happened with the two disciples on the road to Emmaus.[30] For seven miles, Jesus spoke with them and taught them from Scripture. But it wasn't until He broke bread at their table that they recognized Him. It seems that the nail prints in His wrists identified Him.[31] But why couldn't they recognize His face right away?

Later that night in the Upper Room the disciples gathered together with the doors locked; they were frightened and confused. As the Emmaus road disciples were describing what they saw, Jesus appeared. They were terrified! Jesus asked them, "Why are you so frightened? I'm not a spirit. Handle me and see. A spirit does not have flesh and bone."

Then Jesus told the disciples to wait for Him in Galilee. While there, the stress, frustration, and confusion of all these events finally got to Peter. "I'm going fishing," he said, and six other disciples joined him. All night long they fished and caught nothing. Just as they were about to give up, in the early morning mist they saw someone standing on the beach.

"Did you catch anything?" he called.

"No."

"Put your net on the other side of the boat." (As if that would make a difference!?)

When they did, the nets were so full of fish that they almost broke. John recognized the similarity to an earlier incident and said, "That's the Lord!" Peter dove right in and swam to shore.

When they got to shore, Jesus had already cooked breakfast—bread and fish were on the fire. "Come and dine," He said.

And then John adds a strange and enigmatic comment:

And none of the disciples durst ask him, Who art thou? knowing that it was the Lord. (John 21:12)

What does that mean? I really wonder.

A CONJECTURE

We have said over and over that the Bible is one book; it has integrity of design. It may surprise you that there are more graphic details of the Crucifixion in the Old Testament than the New.

For instance, Psalm 22 is a description of what it was like to hang on the Cross as if it were dictated by Christ Himself (although it was written by David eight hundred years earlier). Isaiah describes His abusive treatment in detail; in fact, he predicted that He would be beaten so badly He would no longer look human.[32]

But there is another verse most people overlook:

I gave my back to the smiters, and my cheeks to them that plucked off the hair; I hid not my face from shame and spitting. (Isaiah 50:6)

If I understand this verse correctly, and if it was fulfilled on the Cross—and I believe it was—that means *they ripped off his beard!* This is particularly vivid for me because many years ago, I worked for a company that had a large software department and the president of that department happened to have a very full beard. After working with him for over a year, he came to work one day with his beard shaved off. I would not have recognized him but for another employee who happened to call his name.

Maybe that's why Mary in the garden didn't recognize Jesus; she thought He was the gardner! Did He have a disfigured face and scar tissue where His beard had been ripped off?

Maybe that explains why two disciples could walk seven miles with Him and not realize who He was until they saw His nail prints that evening.

Maybe that's another reason some in the Upper Room were terrified as He stood there among them.

That could also be why John, at the seashore in Galilee, said, "We didn't dare ask Him because we knew it was the Lord."

This brings up another question. Does Jesus still bear the marks of His crucifixion? Zechariah predicts,

They shall look on me whom they have pierced. (Zechariah 12:10)

This would seem to indicate that He will indeed bear the scars forever. Some say that the only man-made things in Heaven will be His scars.

In Revelation, John is transported forward in time into Heaven and sees Jesus receiving the Seven-sealed Book:

And I beheld, and, lo, in the midst of the throne and of the four living creatures, and in the midst of the elders, stood the Lamb as it had been slain. (Revelation 5:6)

I think Jesus still bears His marks. They are the marks of His humiliation, but they are also the marks of His glory.

I'm told of a very badly disfigured woman who had a little girl. When the little girl went to school, the kids made fun of her because her mother was so badly disfigured. Often the little girl came home crying because the kids made fun of her. One day when the little girl was old enough, the mother explained what had happened. When the girl was a baby, they were living in an apartment which caught fire. The mother was able to save the little girl, but in doing so the mother was burned and badly disfigured.

From that day on, the little girl was not embarrassed by her mother, because every time she looked, she knew how much she was loved!

We know that the Crucifixion was far more than only a physical event. And I suspect that you and I will spend an eternity discovering what it really cost Him that we might be there with Him and that we might live. It's very possible that when we look into His face, we too will be reminded just how much we are loved . . .

Hour 17

ACTS

SOMETIMES CALLED the Acts of the Apostles, the Book of Acts could be more accurately called the Acts of the Holy Spirit. In the Gospels, Jesus had promised:

> It is expedient for you that I go away, for if I go not away, the comforter will come not to you, but if I depart I will send Him unto you.[1]

Jesus explained His mission:

> The comforter, which is the Holy Ghost, who the Father will send in My name, He shall teach you all things, and bring all things to your remembrance whatsoever I have said unto you.[2]

Jesus also explained His style:

When he, the Spirit of truth, is come, he will guide you into all truth: for he shall not speak of himself; but whatsoever he shall hear, that shall he speak; and He will shew you things to come. [3]

When Jesus became a man, he had locality. But the Holy Spirit indwells every believer.

The Church Receives Its Mission

The Book of Acts covers a little over thirty years of the early church. (Two chapters in Revelation will cover the next several thousand.) In Acts, chapter 1, Jesus told the disciples to await the empowering of the Holy Spirit (which would occur in chapter 2). Then, while the crowd watched, a cloud took Jesus from the Mount of Olives out of their sight, and two angels confirmed that He would return in like manner.

Jesus had given the disciples their marching orders:

But ye shall receive power, after that the Holy Ghost is come upon you: and ye shall be witnesses unto me both in Jerusalem, and in all Judea, and in Samaria, and unto the uttermost part of the earth. [4]

And that is exactly the sequence in which Christianity spread.

The Spirit Given to the Church

On the Feast of Pentecost the Holy Spirit was given to the Church. It was according to the promise and accompanied by the incredible experience of the tongues of fire descending and touching everyone present. Pentecost is one of the feasts the Torah required every able-bodied Jew to attend, so Jerusalem was crowded with Jews from all over the known world. As the disciples were all speaking in unknown tongues, Peter stated, "This is what the prophet Joel talked about." Joel's passage had to do with the end times, so in one sense the end times had already begun since, as he predicted, the outpouring of the Spirit had started and would continue. But it is very provocative that the quote from Joel 2 is really about the very end times, and the events Joel predicted will happen even more specifically with the 144,000 after the Church is raptured. [5]

STEPHEN BEFORE THE SANHEDRIN

Acts, chapter 7, contains one of the most comprehensive commentaries on the Old Testament you can find. Here was young Stephen, called before the Sanhedrin, the most august body of leaders in Judaism. And this young man gave *them* a Bible lesson. I encourage you to notice how Stephen organized his commentary. They didn't allow him to finish, but if you understand how he outlined his speech you can see where he was going. He employed a pattern from the Old Testament. He talked about Joseph in Egypt, about Moses and the Law. He talked about Joshua. *Each of these was rejected the first time and accepted the second time.* He was building up to the fact that Jesus was rejected the first time but will be accepted the second time.

But there are other insights that we gain from Stephen's review. When he spoke of "another Pharaoh," he used the Greek word *heteros*, which means "another of a totally different kind." This was an allusion to Isaiah where we discover the Pharaoh of the Exodus was not Egyptian but an Assyrian.[6]

Stephen also revealed Abraham's delay in obeying God's call.[7] Contrary to God's instructions, Abraham didn't really leave his country or family; he simply moved "up river" a little way until his father died; then he moved on. This sin of Abraham is hidden in Genesis, and yet Stephen gave us a clue as to what was really going on.

Stephen was then stoned to death. A man standing by, holding their coats was a character named Saul. We'll hear much more about him shortly.

PHILIP AND HIS INFLUENCE

After the stoning of Stephen, the believers in Jerusalem were scattered. Philip's story is just one example of how they took the Good News with them as they went.

Philip was one of the seven leaders of the Jerusalem church. He went to the capital of Samaria and preached Christ. So many people were saved and healed that Peter and John went to Samaria to investigate, and the Samaritan believers received the Holy Spirit.

Then God sent Philip to the Jerusalem-Gaza road to intercept the treasurer of Ethiopia who was reading the scroll of Isaiah but couldn't understand it. Philip joined his chariot, interpreted the passage for him, and led him to Christ. Returning to Ethiopia this senior official planted a church which became very influential.[8]

Philip then traveled north to Caesarea, preaching in every town on the way. He finally settled in Caesarea with his wife and daughters.

THE CONVERSION OF PAUL

A zealous Pharisee named Saul, although he was a Jew, was born a Roman citizen and raised in Tarsus, an important Roman city. Tarsus was the seat of a very famous university, one with a better reputation than even those in Athens and Alexandria, the only others that then existed. Saul's education in Greek was outstanding. At Mars Hill, he quoted classic Greek poets and could speak to that community very eloquently. But as a boy he was educated by the well-known Jewish teacher Gamaliel. When Stephen was stoned, Saul was there giving his approval, and he became a violent persecutor of this radical sect later called Christians. He was given the authority to imprison Christians and even traveled to foreign cities to rout them out. During the time span covered by the book of Acts most of the persecution that the church experienced was at the hands of the Jewish leadership.

One day, on the way to Damascus, Saul was confronted by Jesus Christ: "Saul, Saul, why persecutest thou? Jesus told him to go to Damascus and find a believer there named Ananias. At the same time, Ananias had a vision that told him to receive this Saul. He was shaken because he knew Saul to be a killer of Christians.

Saul was blinded by this vision of Christ, and he remained blind until he met Ananias and was baptized. But we know from the Galatian letter that Paul continued to have eye problems. He mentioned that the Galatians loved him so much they would have plucked out their eyes and given them to him.[10] Apparently his eyes were weak and very unsightly. That may be why Luke became his physician, to help treat his eyes, and the thorn in the flesh he spoke of may have been his eye problem.

Saul stayed in Damascus for three years, then spent three years in the desert in Arabia. We know very little about this crucial period.

Three years after his conversion as he began his ministry, Saul got in trouble everywhere he went. He had to sneak out of Damascus in a basket lowered from a window at night. Barnabas then took him to meet Peter in Jerusalem. The church in Jerusalem had their doubts about Saul's conversion but after he talked with Peter and James, he was accepted. After two weeks, he was smuggled out of Jerusalem and taken to Caesarea and then to Tarsus where he spent ten years. During this time he visited Cilicia and Syria. He was still largely unknown to believers in Judea, but he was maturing, teaching, and doing the Lord's will.

Barnabas ultimately brought Saul to Antioch where they taught together for a year. Saul, Barnabas and Titus brought famine relief money for Judea and met privately with the church leaders who acknowledged that Saul's ministry was to the Gentiles.

Peter and Paul are both contrasting and parallel figures in Acts.	Here are some similar highlights from Paul's ministry:
1. Peter preached his first sermon in Acts chapter 2.	1. Paul preached his first sermon in chapter 13.
2. A lame man was healed in chapter 3.	2. Elymas the sorcerer was rebuked in chapter 13.
3. Even his shadow had influence in chapter 5.	3. A lame man was healed in chapter 14.
4. Peter and John laid on hands in chapter 8.	4. People tried to worship Paul in chapter 14.
5. Simon the Sorcerer was rebuked in chapter 8.	5. Even his handkerchief had influence in chapter 19.
6. People tried to worship Peter in chapter 10.	6. Paul laid on hands in chapter 19.
7. Tabitha was raised from the dead in chapter 9.	7. Eutychus was raised in chapter 20.
8. Peter was imprisoned in chapter 12.	8. Paul was imprisoned in chapter 28.

THE RISE OF ANTIOCH

Antioch in Syria became a strategic center of the church. Antioch was the third largest city in the Roman Empire. It was mostly non-Jewish, made up of many different races, but soon became the center of Gentile Christianity and the base from which a great missionary outreach took place. Initially, believers who traveled from Jerusalem to Antioch preached only to the Jews there. Some believers from Cyprus and from North Africa came and preached to the Gentiles. To investigate the situation, the Jerusalem church sent Barnabas, a trusted leader. He took his friend Saul, now calling himself Paul, and they stayed to preach. Finally a strong Antioch church sent relief money to Jerusalem. All through the epistles Paul collected relief money for the poor church in Jerusalem. It was about this time the word *Christian* was coined.

PETER AND PAUL IN ACTS

The Book of Acts can be divided into two major sections. In the first twelve chapters, Jerusalem was the center of the action and Peter was the chief figure. The Gospel was taken as far as Samaria. The Jews of the homeland generally rejected the Messiah and Peter was imprisoned for his teachings.

In chapters 13-28, Antioch, in the northern part of Syria, became the center of the Gentile church, and Paul became the chief figure. The Gospel reached as far as Rome itself. The Word was rejected by the Jews of the dispersion, and Paul was imprisoned more than once.

PETER

At Pentecost in Acts 2, Peter preached and many became believers. He healed a lame man and was arrested with John and warned not to preach (a warning they did not heed). Peter and John followed Philip to Samaria and many believed there. Peter went to Lydda and then on to Joppa where he raised Dorcus from death.

In Acts, chapter 10, a pivotal event took place: the door was opened to the Gentiles. Cornelius was a centurion in Caesarea, which was the main headquarters for the Romans in Judea. He was a Gentile, but a man of faith. God gave him a vision and told him to send for Peter. Meanwhile, Peter, who was down in Joppa, had a vision of a sheet coming down filled with both clean and unclean animals. Three times Peter was told to eat this non-kosher food. The essence of the vision was that the door was being opened to the Gentiles by faith. As he was puzzling over this vision, those sent from Cornelius arrived and summoned him. He went to Caesarea, and many became believers there.

All of this was quite shocking to the Jewish believers, but the Jerusalem church, at a special council (see below) in Acts 15, accepted the testimony that the Gospel was now open to the Gentiles, too. And although God used Peter to open the door to the Gentiles, Paul was to be the missionary to the Gentiles; Peter would continue to be the apostle to the Jews.

After Peter was arrested and miraculously set free in a very dramatic episode, we don't know a lot about the rest of his ministry. We do know that he met Paul in Antioch;[11] that he was in Corinth;[12] and that he visited the churches in north Asia Minor.[13]

He wrote his first epistle from Babylon, and he was ultimately executed in Rome as the Lord had predicted. There is strong evidence that Mark was Peter's scribe and composed his Gospel in Rome.

THE FIRST MISSIONARY JOURNEY

Saul and Barnabas were sent out by the Antioch church with John Mark.[14] When they arrived at the Island of Cyprus, they encountered Bar-Jesus, a false prophet and friend of the governor. Bar-Jesus was struck blind, and the governor believed.[15] At Paphos, Saul became Paul.

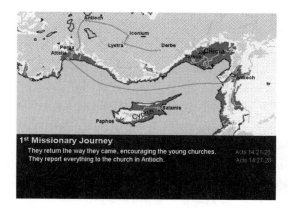

1st Missionary Journey
They return the way they came, encouraging the young churches.   Acts 14:21-26
They report everything to the church in Antioch.   Acts 14:27-28

For some reason, John Mark decided to return to Jerusalem.[16] There are hints that he may have been from a very wealthy background. They were heading into Galatia, which is rough country, and some scholars suspect that he just didn't want to go. Whatever it was, Paul wrote Mark off.

Barnabas, Mark's uncle, defended him, but to no avail. (This dispute between Barnabas and Paul was so severe that they would later split up: Barnabas would take Mark with him, and Paul would take Silas. Mark later would regain Paul's respect.)

When they arrived in Antioch (of Pisidia, not the Syrian Antioch), Paul preached to Jews and Gentiles. They stayed a long time, and many Jews and Gentiles became believers. The non-believing Jews became jealous and stirred up opposition in the form of a Gentile plot on their lives which forced them on.[17]

In Lystra, Paul healed a cripple, and he and Barnabas were hailed as gods. They were almost killed by enemies who arrived from Antioch and Iconium.[18] Each place they went, they won people and planted churches but always under the threat of violence and death.

They returned back the way they had come, encouraging the young churches they had planted, and reported everything back to their base in Antioch and Syria.

THE COUNCIL OF JERUSALEM

After a couple of decades, a huge argument started within the church over the obligations of Gentile believers. In the Jewish world, if a Gentile wanted to come to faith, he was circumcised and then adopted into Judaism. The Jewish believers took for granted that the pattern would remain the same: If you wanted to become a Christian you first needed to become a Jew. This also implied that these Gentile believers would have to keep the Mosaic laws. Paul and Peter disagreed. So Paul, Barnabas, Titus, and others went to Jerusalem for a showdown at the Council of Jerusalem. James, the brother of Jesus, was the leader in Jerusalem. Peter was there, too.

The council began, and after much disputing, Peter stood and said, "Now therefore why tempt ye God, to put a yoke upon the neck of the disciples, which neither our fathers nor we were able to bear?"[19] This was a rather candid assessment by a Jew. "But we believe that through the grace of the Lord Jesus Christ we shall be saved, even as they." (Notice his provocative reversal: he didn't say, ". . . *they* shall be saved even as *we*.") They were finally convinced the Holy Spirit was really reaching out to the Gentiles.

There were really two issues here. The obvious issue was, what must a Gentile do to be saved? James dealt with that. But there is also an implicit question: If this is true, what was to become of Israel? Were the centuries of the Law and the Prophets all for nothing? If Gentiles can be saved just by faith without the Law, does that mean it's all over?

James answered in a very interesting way:

Men and brethren, hearken unto me: Simeon hath declared how God at the first did visit the Gentiles, to take out of them a people for His name. And to this agree the words of the prophets; as it is written, After this I will return, and will build again the tabernacle of David, which is fallen down; and I will build again the ruins thereof, and I will set it up.[20]

James responded to both questions. He formally announced that the Gentiles didn't have to be circumcised and become Jews to be saved. That was very controversial news. But he also confirmed a future for Israel. He answered the implied question. After the Gentile believers are taken out for a people for His name, God says, "I will return and build again the Tabernacle of David." God is not finished with Israel.[21] Their destiny will yet be reestablished.

The resolutions that James announced at the council, which were written in letters of authority and distributed to the churches, were that Gentiles should abstain from idols, from fornication, from things strangled and from blood. But there was no commitment to the ceremonial laws, circumcision, or any Mosaic practices. These were not required of a Gentile.

PAUL'S SECOND MISSIONARY JOURNEY

Paul's second missionary journey covered Philippi, Thessalonica, Berea, Athens, Corinth, and Ephesus. On the way to Galatia, Paul and Barnabas had argued over Mark because Mark had decided to go home, so Paul would not let Mark go on this trip. Paul and Barnabas split over the issue. Barnabas took Mark with him to Cyprus and Paul took Silas, one of his secretaries, to Galatia.

At Lystra, Paul met Timothy. It's not clear that Paul converted Timothy, but he did adopt him as his son in a sense, and asked Timothy to join them.

Paul tried to go north to Bithynia but was blocked by the Holy Spirit. Then one night Paul had a vision: In it a Macedonian urged him to come to Macedonia. He then met Luke, whom some scholars suspect may have been the character in the dream. Luke joined them, and they sailed to Philippi.

In Philippi, Paul cast an evil spirit from a girl medium. The girl could prophesy through the power of a demonic spirit and made a lot of money for her owners. After she was saved, she lost the gift. This meant her owners lost their income, so they incited a mob to attack Paul and Silas, who were flogged and imprisoned. At midnight, while they were praising God, an earthquake destroyed the jail and freed them. Through this incident, the jailer and his family were converted.

From there they traveled to Thessalonica where they spent only a few weeks planting a church. They later had questions for Paul, which he responded to in letters which become major cornerstone documents in the New Testament. What's startling is that the questions they asked were about the Rapture of the Church, the Second Coming of Christ, and the Great Tribulation. Paul, in his letters, reminded them that he had taught about these very things in those first few weeks when they planted the church. The Thessalonian letters are among the earliest by Paul and the most foundational regarding eschatology, the study of the "last things" or "end times." (We will summarize these in Hour 21.)

Paul and Silas had to leave Thessalonica because some Jews stirred up a riot. They went to nearby Berea, where they were well-received, and many Greeks and Jews were converted.

But when Jews from Thessalonica heard Paul was in Berea, they came and stirred up another mob. Paul immediately left for Athens while Silas and Timothy stayed behind.

THE MARS HILL DISCOURSE

In Athens, Paul spoke at the Areopagus (Mars Hill). Areopagus was the court of the judges and also constituted an informal debate forum. Paul preached to the Athenians very differently from the Jews in the synagogues. His whole approach, the outline of his message, and his whole style changed because he was dealing with a different audience.

(We need to learn that. We too often talk in irreverent "Christianese" and "Bible-babble." People don't know what we are talking about because they don't know our vocabulary or have any Biblical background.)

Paul began where the people were. Where were they? They were in idolatry. They had thirty thousand gods and idols of all kinds. Paul found their idol "to the unknown god" and used that as his hook. He was going to tell them more about this *unknown* god. But he started out by complimenting them for being devout and god-fearing. He was not being snide or sarcastic; he was trying to win the people, not the argument. And then he quoted, not Scripture, but the poems of classic Greek authors. Six hundred years earlier, Epimenides had said, "For in him we live, and move, and have our being." "For we are also his offspring" is from a poem by Aratus, a Cilician who lived three centuries earlier.[22] He also quoted from a religious hymn of Cleanthes, a contemporary of Aratus. This was the literature in which the Athenians would have been educated and from which Paul learned his education in Tarsus.

Paul and his companions finally departed for Corinth. They spent about two years there and then sailed to Ephesus. From there, they finally sailed back to Antioch.

PAUL'S THIRD MISSIONARY JOURNEY

After spending some time in Antioch, Paul revisited the churches in Galatia, then went on to Ephesus where he spent the next three years. Paul planned to go to Macedonia and sent Timothy and Erastus ahead.

Paul was worried about the church in Corinth. Corinth was the Las Vegas, or Bourbon Street, of the old world, a center of debauchery and sexual excess. He had also been visited by three members of the church from the household of Chloe who brought him news of cliques and dissensions. Although there may have been an earlier letter, the letter we know

> *Corinth was the Las Vegas, or Bourbon Street, of the old world, a center of debauchery and sexual excess.*

as 1 Corinthians was written at this time in response to those problems.

He was to return through Macedonia to Troas. Paul arranged to meet with Titus to get news of the Corinthian situation. While in Ephesus, he was at the center of a riot organized by the silversmiths because his message threatened the sale of silver statues of Diana. After this, he traveled to Troas to meet Titus, but Titus wasn't there as arranged, so Paul went to Macedonia to search for him. Along the way he encouraged the churches and collected some money for the church in Jerusalem. Finally, Paul and Titus met and Paul was pleased to hear that the severe letter had been taken as intended. In response, Paul wrote what we call 2 Corinthians, recounting his former visit and expressing his joy over their reforms. Titus took the letter to Corinth to prepare the church for Paul's third visit.

Paul stayed in the Achaia region for about three months, probably in Corinth. From here he wrote the letter to the Romans. He had planned to travel to Jerusalem by sea via Syria, but a plot by his enemies forced him to return through Macedonia.

Arriving in Troas from Philippi he preached one night until midnight, about six hours. A young man named Eutychus fell asleep and tumbled out of a three-story window and died, but Paul raised him from the dead.

Just across the peninsula from Ephesus, at Miletus, Paul summoned the Ephesian elders for a farewell meeting. (He wanted to avoid the crowd in Ephesus.) He was going back to Jerusalem and knew he would never see these people again. It's a very touching address.[23]

He then went to Patara, changed ships and sailed for Tyre. After landing at Tyre, Paul spent a day at Ptolemais, and then stayed at Philip's house in Caesarea. Here Agabus the prophet took Paul's belt, tied it around his own hands and feet and said, "This is what they are going to do to you when you get to Jerusalem." He was saying that Paul would be bound by Jews and handed over to the Gentiles. But Paul was determined to go despite all this well-intentioned advice.

At Jerusalem, Paul was welcomed by the church but recognized by some Jews from Asia. A mob tried to kill him, and he actually had to be rescued by Roman troops. They arrested and bound him, but Paul surprised them by announcing he was a Roman citizen. He insisted upon a defense before the Jewish council but that turned out to be too violent. He was sent under armed guard to Governor Felix at Caesarea, the main capital of the Romans in the region. Why? Because about forty men had sworn a blood oath that they would kill Paul, but he found out about the plot and tipped off the leadership.

He was in prison in Caesarea for several years. While before the Sanhedrin, the arguments again turned violent.[24]

Paul appeared before Governor Felix, but Felix deferred judgment. After two years, Festus replaced Felix, and Paul finally appeared before Governor Festus. He realized he would not have any success, so he invoked his right as a Roman citizen to appeal to Caesar. He was sent back to King Agrippa while waiting for his appeal, but even King Agrippa couldn't release him because he had appealed to Caesar. (An appeal to Caesar required the one appealing to supply all the supporting documentation for his case. Many people believe Luke wrote his Gospel and the book of Acts to fulfill this requirement.)

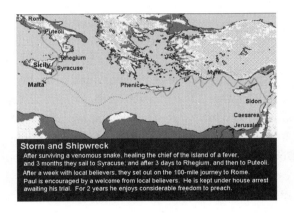

Storm and Shipwreck
After surviving a venomous snake, healing the chief of the island of a fever, and 3 months they sail to Syracuse; and after 3 days to Rhegium, and then to Puteoli. After a week with local believers, they set out on the 100-mile journey to Rome. Paul is encouraged by a welcome from local believers. He is kept under house arrest awaiting his trial. For 2 years he enjoys considerable freedom to preach.

Paul, a prisoner now, was taken from Jerusalem to Caesarea then to Sidon to pick up a ship. It was getting to be autumn, very late in the season to sail, yet they went to Myra and found an Alexandrian granary ship headed for Rome. They managed to find a harbor from bad weather at a place called Fairhaven. Their desire was to get around the coast to winter in Phenice. A big discussion ensued: Should they stay put or risk getting into better harbor? Paul advised them not to go, but they didn't listen. They decided to try for Phenice, but a fierce storm blew them out to sea and put them in desperate straits. Paul prophesied that they would lose all the cargo but no one would die. Finally, after jettisoning their gear and their cargo, and staving off a mutiny after fourteen nights of this storm, the ship broke up on a sand bar off Malta. No lives were lost.

Three months after surviving a venomous snake and healing the chief of the island of a fever, they sailed to Syracuse, and after three days to Rhegium, and then to Putoeli. Paul was under house arrest awaiting his trial, but the centurion had become very comfortable with Paul from his experience with him aboard ship, so for two years he enjoyed considerable freedom to preach.

PAUL IN ROME

The book of Acts closes with Paul in Rome. By the time he wrote a letter to his protégé, Timothy, he was released from house arrest in Rome and headed to Macedonia. He left Timothy in Ephesus to continue the work there, and he left Titus in Crete.

His last letter, again from prison in Rome, was his second letter to Timothy. He had been rearrested by this time and was awaiting his execution.

In conclusion, the book of Acts describes the birth of the Church (as quite distinct from Israel, although there is much confusion on this point) and is the gateway to the incredible epistles. In our next Hour, we will focus on the cornerstone of Christian theology—Paul's letter to the Romans.

Hour 18

THE EPISTLE TO THE ROMANS

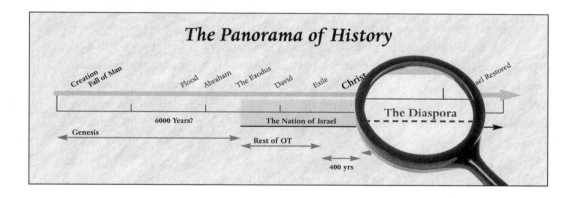

THE EPISTLE TO THE ROMANS is a cornerstone in the Scriptures. Sometimes called the Gospel according to Paul, it is the most comprehensive book in the New Testament. If you are going to study the New Testament, you must diligently address this book.

Romans was written at the close of Paul's third missionary journey during the three months he was in Greece in either the late winter or the early spring of A.D. 57 or 58[1] This was just before he returned to Jerusalem with the offering from the Macedonian churches.

The historical impact of Romans is probably unequaled by any other book. The Church thrived on the great truths of God's grace until grace began to erode into forms of legalism, plunging the world into the Dark Ages from the sixth to the sixteenth centuries.

The Great Reformation brought grace back into the picture. "By grace are we saved through faith." The Epistle to the Romans really altered the whole course of the world.

209

The book of Romans has a very international outlook. Paul was a Roman citizen. Since he was educated in Tarsus, he had a Greek cultural background and was well versed in the Greek philosophers. He was also a "Hebrew of the Hebrews," taught by Gamaliel himself, who was among the most venerated of the rabbis. Paul was bright, learned, and intellectual, yet he was also very sensitive. He knew how to reach people; he tailored his message to his audience.

This book will delight the greatest logician; it will hold the attention of the wisest of men; yet it will bring the humblest soul gently to the feet of the Savior. Romans emphasizes that a God small enough for our mind is not large enough for our need.

The name *Paul* means "the least; the little one." He, of all writers, really understood the grace of God. He acknowledged that he himself was the chief of sinners, and yet he was the most devoutly religious man who ever lived. But if he was the most religious man who ever lived, and yet could also call himself the chief of sinners, that's really good news for you and me. God has already saved one far worse than us, by Paul's own testimony in the Scriptures.

Romans wasn't written to the world, but to believers. It wasn't written to the church at Rome, but rather to the individuals, to the believers, who were in Rome. This letter does not preach to the unsaved; the unsaved are never called "God's beloved," a term reserved for God's own children. Romans is intended to teach the saints. What are saints? I prefer Donald Grey Barnhouse's definition:

> Saints are a group of displaced persons, uprooted from their natural home, and on their way to an extraterrestrial destination, not of this planet, neither in its roots or in its ideals.[2]

That describes us. If you feel a little estranged sometimes, rejoice in that. When you pick up the newspaper and see all of the nonsense and evil in the world, you can take comfort that we are just passing through.

THE OUTLINE OF THE BOOK

The first section, chapters 1–8, is doctrinal, a masterpiece on the doctrine of faith. The first three chapters are the most complete diagnosis of sin in the Bible. They speak of three basic types of people: the Pagan Man, who has never heard the Gospel;[3] the Moral Man, who strives to live a good life;[4] and the Religious Man, who keeps all the rules and regulations.[5] All three stand condemned because their righteousness is not adequate to avoid offending a perfect and holy God.

The second section, chapters 9–11, deals with God's greatest predicament: How can God love us and save us without violating His own nature? Without violating His justice? Without impugning His own holiness?

God has a problem but He found a way to solve it by giving us the greatest gift conceivable—His Son. These chapters can also be called *dispensational* because they focus on Israel's past, present and future. We are interested in Israel, not because we are Jewish, but because even as Gentiles we are heirs through them.

The third and last section, chapters 12–16, explains sanctification, the peace of God. We are not only delivered from the penalty of sin in the past tense, we can be delivered from sin in the present sense.

The three sections can be summarized as "Faith, Hope, and Love," or Doctrinal, Dispensational, and Practical.

The Gospel of Paul

The word "Gospel" is not a code of ethics or morals. It's not a creed to be accepted. It's not a system of religion to be adhered to. It's not good advice to follow. So what is the Gospel? It is a message concerning a Divine Person. My friend Lou Phelps suggested to me the word *GRACE* could be an acronym to summarize Romans: "God's Righteousness At Christ's Expense."

God's grace is what Romans is really all about, and, specifically, God's predicament. Romans presents the most complete and penetrating statement of God's divine plan for redemption. Christ did not come to make bad men good, but to give dead men life! An illustration of that is the case of the Prodigal Son.[6] When the son came home, his father did not say, "My son has become good." Rather, he said, "My son was dead and is alive again! He was lost and now is found!" The point of the Prodigal Son is that, despite his misdeed, he *never lost his sonship.*

Paul's entire commitment can be summarized,

> For I am not ashamed of the gospel of Christ: for it is the power of God unto salvation to every one that believeth; to the Jew first, and also to the Greek.[7]

The power of God unto what? Unto salvation—*not* unto reformation, education, progress, development, nor for the "fanning of some innate flame."

A TRILOGY AROUND A KEY VERSE

As we have reviewed in Hour 12, the Epistle to the Romans is part of a trilogy on a key verse from the prophet Habakkuk, "The just shall live by faith."[8]

- Who are *the just*? The answer to that question is the very focus of the Epistle to the Romans.[9]

- How shall they *live*? The Epistle to the Galatians is the definitive guide.[10]

- The just shall live by what? By *faith*. The Epistle to the Hebrews focuses on faith in unparalleled terms.[11]

These three epistles, Romans, Galatians, and Hebrews, are a trilogy on Habakkuk's declaration: *The just shall live by faith.*

New Testament

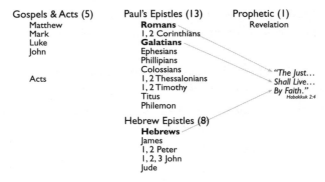

Gospels & Acts (5)	Paul's Epistles (13)	Prophetic (1)
Matthew	**Romans**	Revelation
Mark	1, 2 Corinthians	
Luke	**Galatians**	
John	Ephesians	
	Phillipians	
	Colossians	"The Just…
Acts	1, 2 Thessalonians	Shall Live…
	1, 2 Timothy	By Faith."
	Titus	*Habakkuk 2:4*
	Philemon	

Hebrew Epistles (8)
Hebrews
James
1, 2 Peter
1, 2, 3 John
Jude

SECTION ONE: DOCTRINE, CHAPTERS 1 - 8

What is the greatest possible thought? Daniel Webster's provocative declaration: "Our responsibility to our Maker." To meet this ultimate challenge of life, we have to know something about God. What is He like? What is His personality? What does He require?

Doctrine, the telling forth of Truth, helps us know what God is like. The first eight chapters of Romans emphasize doctrine.

The first part of this section deals with the judgment of pagan humanity. They are judged for suppressing God's truth, for ignoring God's revelation, and for perverting God's glory. What about those primitive savages who have never heard the Gospel? Romans, chapter 1, nails it directly:

> For the invisible things of him from the creation of the world are clearly seen, being understood by the things that are made, even his eternal power and Godhead; so that they are without excuse:
>
> Because that, when they knew God, they glorified him not as God, neither were thankful; but became vain in their imaginations, and their foolish heart was darkened.
>
> Professing themselves to be wise, they became fools. [12]

You can't deny God; just look at the night sky. Examine the DNA. No one has an excuse to deny God exists. It takes willful ignorance to deny the Creator.

And what was the result of their denying their Creator? Abandonment to a depraved lifestyle:

> For this cause God gave them up unto vile affections: for even their women did change the natural use into that which is against nature: and likewise also the men, leaving the natural use of the women, burned in their lust one toward another; men with men working that which is unseemly, and receiving in themselves that recompence of their error which was meet. [13]

As a matter of history, all the great cultures for the last six thousand years can be measured in their decay by the rise in homosexuality and all of the depravity that accompanies it.

> And even as they did not like to retain God in their knowledge, God gave them over to a reprobate mind, to do those things which are not convenient. [14]

Paul then takes up the Moral Man, and the Religious Man. All fall short of the requirements of a perfect and holy God. These passages are the great leveler: All men are equally accountable and all fall short of God's requirement.

This leads to God's greatest problem: How does He justify unrighteous man without violating His nature, His holiness, and His justice? [15] Even Socrates could not imagine a way God could forgive and not compromise His own nature:

213

It may be that the deity can forgive sins,
but I do not see how.
—Socrates, writing to Plato in 500 B.C.

But the dilemma was solved by God giving His greatest gift, Jesus Christ, the Son of the living God.[16]

THE PATH TO MATURITY

Chapter 5 starts with the path to maturity, and the first step is through tribulation. Troubles are God's way of helping us grow, because from tribulation comes perseverance, and through perseverance, we get experience. And you know what the climax of all of this is? *Hope!* The depth of our hope is the measure of our spiritual maturity.

THE THREE TENSES OF SALVATION

There are three tenses of being saved:

Past tense. You *have been saved* from the penalty of sin. Positionally you are saved from sin.[17] That is technically called justification: You've been saved in the sense that the penalty of your past sins has been removed.

Present tense. You are also *being saved* from the power of sin. That is present tense and continuing. That is sometimes called *sanctification*.

Future tense. You also *shall be saved* from the presence of sin. That's called the redemption of our bodies.

Paul contrasts the two Adams.[18] Here are some characteristics of the first Adam, the one that we all know from Genesis.

- By one man's offense many died.
- By one (Adam), judgment and condemnation.
- By one man's offense, death reigned.
- By one man's offense, condemnation came to all men.

- By the disobedience of one, many were made sinners.
- Sin reigned in death.

The last Adam (Jesus Christ) has other characteristics.

- By one Man's free gift, righteousness came to many.
- Through one Man, believers reign in life.
- The righteousness of One brings justification to all.
- The obedience of One causes many to be declared righteous.
- Grace reigns—eternal life.

Why did God introduce the Law? The answer may surprise you!

Moreover the law entered that the offence might abound. But where sin abounded grace did much more abound.[19]

The Law was given that sin might abound? Realize what the Scripture is telling us. There is a perversion in us that the Law highlights. The Law was given so that the offense might abound, but where sin abounded grace did much more abound. That is good news because the Law eliminates any way for man to rationalize away his sin nature.

Not only did grace abound to forgive us from the penalty of sin; sin no longer has dominion over us.

Let not sin therefore reign in your mortal body, that ye should obey it in the lusts thereof[20]

That imperative is a present imperfect: In other words, "Do not let sin continue to reign in your life." Will you stumble from time to time? Certainly. But you have the power of the Holy Spirit residing in you, and sin does not have to continue to reign in your life. How do you do that? By your insisting that what God says is true. It's a matter of faith and applying it. Now, the dominion of sin is your choice. You never had a choice before; you were a slave to sin. But if you have accepted Jesus Christ—if you are a believe—then the Holy Spirit reigns in you, or *can* reign in you if you give Him a chance. It's now your choice.

And committing your life to Christ is just step one. It is a beginning, much like launching a ship; you are on a whole new adventure. How do you keep sin from ruining your life? By choosing moment-by-moment to follow, not your feelings or impulses, but the Spirit's leading. They are faith choices. God will subsequently align your feelings to your choices.

From the Book of Genesis on, revelation always follows obedience. God gives you some truth and sees what you can do with it. If you act on it, He'll give you some more. That's the pattern. We may say, "Seeing is believing." But the opposite is the actual truth: "Believing is seeing."

Paul then explains more about why the Law was given. The Law was given to expose our sin nature;[21] to incite the sin nature to sin more;[22] to drive us to despair of self-effort.[23] You don't have a chance if you think you can clean yourself up before you come to the Lord. You come to the Lord first, *then* He will clean up your life. A fisherman cleans the fish *after* the fish are caught.

- The Law was given to drive us to dependence upon the Holy Spirit alone. The Law can't save; it just reveals our need to be saved. The only way you can be saved is through the Spirit of God.
- The Law depends upon the flesh; the Spirit depends on God's power.
- The Law produces rebellion; the Spirit produces God's desires and places those desires in our hearts.
- The Law results in more sin; the Spirit produces righteousness.
- The Law brings wrath; the Spirit brings joy, and peace.
- The Law is not of faith; the Spirit is by faith.
- The Law kills, but the Spirit gives life.

ROMANS 8: VICTORY!

The first eleven verses of Romans 8 are about being delivered from the flesh by the power of the Holy Spirit. The next few verses are about the realization of our sonship. Remember that the term "sons of God" refers to a direct creation of God. That's why it is used of angels. Adam was a direct creation of God; he was a son of God. Cain and Abel were not; they were sons of Adam. You and I are not, by nature, sons of God; we are sons of Adam.

He came unto His own but His own received Him not, but to as many as received Him, to them gave He the power to become the sons of God.[24]

Paul continued to explain the concept of adoption, where someone achieved legal status as a son.

Finally there is a climactic hymn of praise for victory, which is one of the most exhilarating passages in the Bible.

Romans 8 opens with no possibility of condemnation; it closes with no possibility of separation! Chapter 8 is quite a contrast from chapter 5.

5: A summation of the saving work of Jesus Christ;

8: A summation of what Christ did to provide victory.

5: Justification (declared righteous) by faith is forever;

8: Godly life is insured through the power of the Holy Spirit.

5: Our performance is based on understanding of God's love;

8: Our performance is based on the power of the Holy Spirit.

5: Our relationship to God;

8: Our relationship to the world, conflict, the flesh.

5: The Holy Spirit is mentioned only once (v.5);

8: The Holy Spirit is available to us to give us assured victory.

5: The capstone on our salvation in Christ;

8: The capstone on our victory in Christ!

THE PURPOSE OF TRIALS

Why do Christians have trials? We have trials for at least ten reasons:

- To glorify God (Daniel 3).
- Discipline for known sin (Hebrews 12:5-11; James 4:17, Romans 14:23; 1 John 1:9).
- To prevent us from falling into sin (1 Peter 4:1-2).
- To keep us from pride (Daniel 4).
- To build faith (1 Peter 1:6-7).
- To cause growth (Romans 5:3-5).
- To teach obedience and discipline (Acts 9:15-16; Philippians 4:11-13).

- To equip us to comfort others with those same kinds of trials (2 Corinthians 1:3-4).
- To prove the reality of Christ in us (2 Corinthians 4:7-11).
- For testimony to the angels (Job 1, Ephesians 3, 1 Peter 1).

Someone has said, "If you squeeze a lemon, you should get lemon juice. If you squeeze an orange, you should get orange juice. If you squeeze a Christian, you should get Christ."

THE CERTAINTY OF SANCTIFICATION

One of the most comforting assurances is this:

And we know that all things work together for good to them that love God, to them who are the called according to his purpose. (Romans 8:28)

What are its three most important words? "And we know . . . "! We don't *hope* this is true. We don't *suspect* this might be true. We *know* all things work together for good. But then Paul goes on:

For whom he did foreknow, he also did predestinate to be conformed to the image of his Son, that he might be the firstborn among many brethren. Moreover whom he did predestinate, them he also called: and whom he called, them he also justified: and whom he justified, them he also glorified. (verse 29)

We have a sequence here. I suspect Paul may have had Genesis in mind as he was writing this: Abraham was predestined. Through Isaac the seed was called. Jacob, He justified. And through Joseph, He was glorified.

PREDESTINED, CALLED, JUSTIFIED, GLORIFIED

This leads to the classical paradox—fate, or predestination versus free will—which has puzzled philosophers for thousands of years. Do we have free will, or are we predestined? Did Judas really have the choice of betraying Christ? It was predicted in Psalm 41:9, and it was fulfilled in Judas. Did Judas really have a choice?

When God prophesies a future event, does that mean it's inevitable? Of course it does, because He sees the end from the beginning. Do people have any choice? *Yes, they do.*

This whole paradox should go away if we realize something that was not known before the twentieth century: Time is a *physical* property. Living in time, we view events as a sequence. Behind us is the past; ahead is the future. (The time dimension is strange since you can only go in one direction; you can move forward and look back. You can't move back or look forward.)

But God is outside time, so He can see what we are going to do. That doesn't mean He relieves us of the choice; it just means that He, in his infinite knowledge, knows the choice we are going to make. The climax of all this is found in verses 31–34:

> What shall we then say to these things? If God be for us, who can be against us? He that spared not his own Son, but delivered him up for us all, how shall he not with him also freely give us all things? Who shall lay anything to the charge of God's elect? It is God that justifieth. Who is he that condemneth? It is Christ that died, yea rather, that is risen again, who is even at the right hand of God, who also maketh intercession for us.

What is Paul saying? That the prosecutor is our defense council. He has our case wired: His Father is the judge. Paul continues in verses 35–39:

> Who shall separate us from the love of Christ shall tribulation, or distress, or persecution, or famine, or nakedness, or peril, or sword? As it is written, For thy sake we are killed all the day long; we are accounted as sheep for the slaughter. Nay, in all these things we are more than conquerors through him that loved us. For I am persuaded that neither death, nor life, nor angels, nor principalities, nor powers, nor things present, nor things to come, nor height, nor depth, nor any other creature, shall be able to separate us from the love of God, which is in Christ Jesus our Lord.

It doesn't get any better than that.

SECTION TWO: AN ISRAEL TRILOGY, CHAPTERS 9–11

The next three chapters are a change of focus. They follow very logically from the foregoing, but they center on Israel. Romans 9 focuses on Israel's past; Romans 10, on Israel's present; and Romans 11, on Israel's future.

The reason Paul raises the issue of Israel is to answer the logical question that comes out of the first eight chapters: If God has said that none can be condemned whom He has justified, and that none in Him can be separated, then why have the Israelites, who were sovereignly chosen and given unconditional promises, completely failed and been rejected?

There is also the problem of how the Gentiles are to relate to the Jews. If circumcision is of no value without faith, then what advantage has the Jew? What is the benefit of circumcision (which symbolizes the whole Law)?

From Genesis 12 to Acts 2, the Bible is all about Israel. The emphasis is that God keeps His promises. What about the promises to Israel? Doctrinally, we need to understand that all of our benefits as Gentiles derive from God's unconditional promises to Abraham:

> I will make of thee a great nation.
> I will bless thee. I will make thy name great, and thou shalt be a blessing.
> I shall bless them that bless thee and curse him that curseth thee.
> And in thee shall all families of the earth be blessed.[25]

These promises didn't just apply to Israel. Every benefit we have as believers derives from this unconditional covenant. When God confirmed the covenant, He followed a divinely ordered ritual. It was customary when undertaking a solemn covenant, that the two participants would divide a sacrifice into two parts, and then, together, walk between them, in a figure eight pattern, reciting the terms of the agreement. But before this one began, God put Abraham in a deep sleep and performed the covenant ritual alone. It was unilateral, and was declared to be eternal and unconditional. God reaffirmed the covenant to Abraham's descendants, even when they had been unfaithful.[26] The New Testament also declares it to be immutable and unchangeable.[27] So how do we benefit from it? We rely entirely on our derivative benefit from the Root of David, the Lion of the Tribe of Judah, the Lamb who takes the Seven-sealed Book in Revelation.

Romans, chapter 9, also enumerates ten blessings of the Jew for his own sake:

- Received the Words of God

- Called "the Princes of God"

- Adopted

- The Glory

- The Covenants

- The Law

- The Temple services (they have all benefits)
- Special promises (earthly promises)
- Fathers of the Faith: Abraham, Isaac and Jacob
- The Messiah would come from them.

Yet they were blinded. They rejected Jesus, and He said these things were now hidden from their sight.[28] For how long? Paul will tell us in chapter 11:

> For I would not, brethren, that ye should be ignorant of this mystery, lest ye should be wise in your own conceits; that blindness in part is happened to Israel, until the fullness of the Gentiles be come in.[29]

(The "fullness of the Gentiles" is not the same as the "times of the Gentiles." The fullness of the Gentiles refers to the Church. The Church will be complete when it reaches a divinely appointed number. The "fullness" implies there is a limit: God is looking for a specific number. When the "fullness of the Gentiles be come in," the Father will say to the Son, "Go get 'em.")

There are three prerequisite conditions for the restoration of Israel:

The first "until": "until the fullness of the Gentiles be brought in" (above).

The second "until": "until the times of the Gentiles are fulfilled."[30] The "times of the Gentiles" began with Nebuchadnezzar and will end with the Antichrist.

The third "until": "until they recognize their offense."[31] As we reviewed in Hour 12, Israel has to acknowledge that Jesus is the Messiah, formally and officially. The remnant will do that when they are in refuge in Edom at the climax of Armageddon.[32]

SECTION THREE:
PRACTICAL LIVING, CHAPTERS 12-16

In chapter 12, our responsibilities as a result of the gifts that God has given us are delineated. Even our practical considerations will be profoundly impacted by our world view, and there are only two:

We are an accident of random chance with no destiny.

We are the product of deliberate and purposeful creation.

What are the key questions of life? They would include: Who am I? Where did I come from? Where am I going? To whom am I accountable? If I come from a Creator, I am His product. I am accountable to Him.

Chapter 13 rehearses our civil responsibilities to government. In the first eleven verses of Genesis, God created four major institutions: personal volition; marriage; the family; human government. Satan is attacking each one of these today.

Christian maturity is the subject of chapter 14. Paul inverted our unguided presuppositions about spiritual maturity:

> Him that is weak in the faith receive ye, but not to doubtful disputations. For one believeth that he may eat all things; another, who is weak, eateth herbs.[33]

The point here is that when one is weak in the faith, he puts certain restrictions on himself. There are many reasons for being a vegetarian. But the one who does it for religious reasons is weaker in the faith than the one who has the strength and liberty in Christ.

> Let not him that eateth despise him that eateth not; and let not him which eateth not judge him that eateth: for God hath received him.[34]

The one who is weak is orientated to legalistic externals. But Christ has removed us from the ceremonial law. The one who is strong enjoys his full liberty in Christ. And that's not measured by what we give up, nor is it a license to sin.

> One man esteemeth one day above another; another esteemeth every day alike. Let every man be fully persuaded in his own mind. He that regardeth the day, regardeth it unto the Lord; and he that regardeth not the day, to the Lord he doth not regard it. He that eateth, eateth to the Lord, for he giveth God thanks; and he that eateth not, to the Lord he eateth not, and giveth God thanks.[35]

In his epistle to the Colossians, Paul dealt with the same issues:

Let no man therefore judge you in meat, or in drink, or in respect of an holyday, or of the new moon, or of the Sabbath days; which are a shadow of things to come; but the body is of Christ.[36]

All these old rules in the Old Testament were anticipatory. They are there by design and that design will always relate, in some way, to Jesus Christ. Paul confirmed this to us in Romans 15:

For whatsoever things were written aforetime were written for our learning, that we through patience [perseverance] and comfort [encouragement] of the scriptures might have hope."[37]

THE SCRIPTURE CONSTANTLY DISPLAYS AN INTEGRATED DESIGN

Chapter 16 contains more personal greetings than in any other epistle. There are thirty-three people by name, and on the list are some slaves and some royalty.

Paul's Epistle to the Romans is the definitive statement of Christian doctrine and can command a lifetime of study in itself. It will challenge the greatest minds and philosophers, and yet any of us can understand it and embrace its precepts.

In our next Hour we will summarize the remainder of Paul's epistles.

Hour 19

THE PAULINE EPISTLES

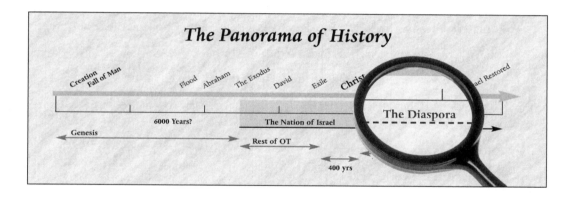

IN THIS CHAPTER we will explore the remaining Pauline, or Church Epistles. Paul wrote nine epistles to seven different churches: Corinth (two), Ephesus, Philippi, Colossae, and Thessalonika (two). (There may be a mystical parallel between these seven and the seven churches Jesus wrote to in Revelation; we'll explore that in Hour 22). Three of the epistles, Ephesians, Philippians, and Colossians, are called the "prison epistles" as they were written by Paul while he was imprisoned in Rome.

Paul also wrote four personal letters to three different pastors: Timothy (two), Titus, and Philemon. These letters were also intended for circulation in the churches, but they were specifically to encourage, instruct, and warn pastors faced with the burden of ministering.

(I also attribute the unsigned Epistle to the Hebrews to Paul, but we'll explore that in the next Hour.)

The early church was composed of real people just like you and me. They had real problems, just as we have now. They had different styles and different personalities, but they were just regular people, struggling against the powers of darkness, armed with the Word of God and the Holy Spirit.

Paul wrote, in his second letter to his protégé, Timothy:

All scripture is given by inspiration of God and is profitable for doctrine, for reproof, for correction, for instruction in righteousness.[1]

"Doctrine" is, of course, fundamental teaching. "Reproof" means rebuke for wrong conduct. "Correction" means rectifying wrong doctrine.

The arrangement of Paul's epistles in the New Testament reflects the order of 2 Timothy 3:16.

- Romans comes first, which is the definitive statement of Christian doctrine.

- 1 and 2 Corinthians are reproof, correction of conduct.

- Galatians is for correction of doctrine: "The just shall live by faith."

- The Book of Ephesians also stresses doctrine, in this case *ecclesiology*, the study of the church.

- Philippians deals with reproof again.

- Colossians is the correction of doctrine.

- 1 and 2 Thessalonians focus on doctrine having to do with *eschatology*, the study of "last things" or the "end times."

THE CORINTHIAN EPISTLES

As we learned in Hour 17, Corinth was the Las Vegas, or Bourbon Street, of the old world, a center of debauchery and sexual excess. Very early in the life of the church some members from the household of Chloe brought Paul news of cliques in the congregation. The situation was serious enough that Paul wrote "First Corinthians" tackling the problems. There are allusions to an earlier letter, so 1 Corinthians could well be the second letter Paul wrote to them. Then Paul made a very painful visit to the church and likely wrote another letter, this one very severe, which has been lost. To find out the response to this "severe" letter, Paul arranged to meet Titus in Troas. The good news from Titus was that the church received the letter as Paul had intended. So then Paul wrote "Second Corinthians," which is full of joy.

If you track this carefully, you will see that there seem to actually have been four letters and three different visits.

THE FIRST EPISTLE TO THE CORINTHIANS

Paul divided everyone into two camps: those who perish and those who are saved.

> For the preaching of the cross is to them that perish foolishness; but unto us which are saved it is the power of God.[2]

Everyone is in one of these categories: "them that perish" or "those who are saved." (Which are *you*?)

> For ye see your calling, brethren, how that not many wise men after the flesh, not many mighty, not many noble, are called: but God hath chosen the foolish things of the world to confound the wise; and God hath chosen the weak things of the world to confound the things which are mighty; and base things of the world, and things which are despised, hath God chosen, yea, and things which are not, to bring to nought things that are: that no flesh should glory in his presence.[3]

The "foolishness of God" sounds like an oxymoron. But you may have noticed that God seems to go out of His way to do things unconventionally. He saved only eight people out of the old world with an Ark. He saved the people in Egypt by having them splatter blood on the doorposts. He ordered the Israelites to conquer Jericho by blowing trumpets and marching around the city. The Creator of the universe made His entrance into Jerusalem riding a donkey. A group of unlettered fishermen affected the entire Roman world. And of course the ultimate ostensible "foolishness" was the Cross.

Stewardship and rewards are a key part of 1 Corinthians. We talk a lot about salvation; salvation gives you admission to heaven, but that's all. Rewards are about what you are going to do when you get there.

Concerning rewards, there are only two different foundations to build on: gold, silver, and precious stones; or wood, hay, and stubble. And they are going to be tried by fire. When they are tried, your works, your fruits, your labors will either be destroyed or purified by the fire. But even if your works are consumed in the fire, you yourself will still be saved.[4]

Chapters 12–14 are about spiritual gifts. Chapter 12 teaches that the Holy Spirit gives gifts—to each of us, spiritual gifts, supernatural gifts—but not everybody gets the same gifts. That's very important. If we have a spiritual gift and do not exercise it, we defraud the body, for the gift was not given for us but for the body of Christ. One of the greatest adventures is for each of us to discover his or her spiritual gift because that's a clue to what his or her ministry will be. Diversity of service but one Church; diversity of gifts, but one Spirit; diversity of members, but one body—this is the essential message of chapter 12.

Chapter 14 deals with the abuse of gifts. The greatest of the gifts is prophecy. It most edifies the church, it most convinces outsiders, but its use should be orderly. The discussion of prophecy is a counterbalance to an overemphasis on tongues. Is the gift of tongues for today? Yes, but there is a lot of nonsense going around. The real answer to questions about spiritual gifts is inserted right between chapters 12 and 14: that most famous chapter in Corinthians, Chapter 13. All these gifts, whatever they are, are valueless without love.

Chapter 13 is about the utter necessity of love, the moral excellency of love, and the abiding supremacy of love. The Holy Spirit is looking for fruit—we should be inspecting fruit, not gifts.

> Though I speak with the tongues of men and of angels, and have not charity [love], I am become as sounding brass, or a tinkling cymbal. And though I have the gift of prophecy, and understand all mysteries, and all knowledge; and though I have all faith, so that I could remove mountains, and have not charity, I am nothing. And though I bestow all my goods to feed the poor, and though I give my body to be burned, and have not charity, it profiteth me nothing.[5]

What counts is what is done in response to the Spirit. The next four verses give us the characteristics of love:

- Love suffereth long, and is kind;
- Love envieth not;
- Love vaunteth not itself, is not puffed up,
- Doth not behave itself unseemly,

- Seeketh not her own,

- Is not easily provoked, thinketh no evil;

- Rejoiceth not in iniquity, but rejoiceth in the truth;

- Beareth all things, believeth all things,

- Hopeth all things, endureth all things.[6]

We can learn the character of Christ by substituting His name for "love" in this passage—Christ suffers long and is kind, Christ envies not, and so on.

But what happens when we put *our name* in place of "love"? The disparity is embarrassing, but as we grow in grace and the knowledge of our Lord and Savior Jesus Christ, that disparity narrows, because His goal is for us to fit that description. We grow by walking moment-by-moment with the Holy Spirit.

We hear the term "Gospel" a lot. What is the Gospel? The word means more than simply "good news." Paul defines the Gospel in the first few verses of 1 Corinthians 15:

Moreover, brethren, I declare unto you the gospel which I preached unto you, which also ye have received, and wherein ye stand; by which also ye are saved, if ye keep in memory what I preached unto you, unless ye have believed in vain. For I delivered unto you first of all that which I also received, how that Christ died for our sins according to the scriptures; and that he was buried, and that he rose again the third day according to the scriptures.[7]

That is the Gospel. What is shocking is what Paul did *not* mention. He did not mention Christ's teachings, His moral example, or His miracles. What are the critical issues here? Three specific things:

1. Christ died for our sins according to the Scriptures.

2. He was buried. Paul emphasizes this because baptism is a model of us being buried with Him.

3. He rose again the third day according to Scriptures.

That's the essential truth for you to grasp, embrace, and hang on to. Our eternal destiny hangs on the truth of this Gospel. The crucifixion was not a tragedy: it was the fulfillment of a mission.

Because of what comes next, 1 Corinthians 15 is known as the Resurrection Chapter. Paul would probably argue that it's the most important chapter in the Bible because if Jesus did not rise from the dead, then you and I have no hope. His resurrection authenticates and validates what He did for us.

The Resurrection body of Jesus is a model for us. First of all, He was tangible. He challenged the apostles to handle Him to see that He was flesh and bone. There is a very important physics lesson included in the Scriptures:

> It doth not yet appear what we shall be: but we know that, when he shall appear we shall be like him; for we shall see him as he is.[8]

That means whatever dimensionality He has, we'll also enjoy. Now Jesus was obviously not limited to four dimensions. That is why Jesus could enter and leave a room by passing through the floors, the ceiling, or the walls. Clearly, whatever the Resurrection involves, we are going to enjoy it. The Greek word that refers to the resurrection body is *oiketerion*. It's a term used only twice in the New Testament: it's the body that believers aspire to, and it's the body the angels disrobed from in order to participate in the mischief they did in Genesis 6.[9]

Our resurrection body will encompass seven transitions:

- Corruption to Incorruptible
- Dishonor to Glory
- Weakness to Power
- Physical to Spiritual
- Earthly to Heavenly
- Flesh and Blood to Transcendent
- Mortal to Immortal

People think that Physical to Spiritual is the same as Tangible to Intangible, but it's actually the other way around. What we experience in this physical dimension is actually a digital simulation. At the resurrection, we will go into the real reality.

Paul also talks about the translated generation. There will be a generation that does not see death:

Behold, I shew you a mystery [a secret that I am revealing to you]; We shall not all sleep, but we shall all be changed, in a moment, in the twinkling of an eye, at the last trump: for the trumpet shall sound, and the dead shall be raised incorruptible, and we shall be changed. For this corruptible must put on incorruption, and this mortal must put on immortality.[10]

What is the "twinkling of an eye"? (It's not a blink.) It's related to the time it takes for light to travel the thickness of your eye. I suspect that it's about 10^{-43} seconds, which is the smallest quantum of time possible. In that instant we are going to be transformed. We shall be incorruptible.

THE EPISTLE TO THE GALATIANS

Titus delivered a disturbing report that detractors were attacking Paul's character. They insinuated that he was a coward and they sowed doubts about his credentials. So Paul was forced to respond for the health of the Gospel there and throughout that region. Some call this an impassioned self-defense of a wounded spirit. Some say it was written with a quill dipped in tears from the apostle's anguish of heart. It contains far more pathos than any of his other letters.

Galatians is a polemic against the perversion of the Gospel. Romans instructed us to be grounded in doctrine; Corinthians, to be guided in our practice; Galatians, to be guarded against error. Galatians became the battle cry of the Reformation because it teaches liberation through the Gospel. In this letter Paul said that anyone who preaches any other gospel, or any other Jesus, is damned. Paul had visited Galatia twice, and his second visit was far less reassuring. He had to admonish them against errors of all kinds.

The first couple of chapters show the authenticity of the Gospel, its origin and nature; the superiority of the Gospel, the new relation it effects, and the privileges it releases; and the true liberty we have in Christ. Love and Service replace Law and Bondage. The Spirit ends the bondage of the flesh. Galatians reveals a series of contrasts and surprises.

- *Faith vs. Works.* You don't earn your salvation. It's a gift of God. If you have saving faith, it will be demonstrated through works.
- *Grace vs. Law.* Grace has a tendency to become leavened with legalism.

- *Spirit vs. Flesh.* Do you walk by your own choices and emotions, or do you walk by faith and the Spirit of God? It's a moment-by-moment daily challenge.

- *Truth vs. Error.* Do we really guard our doctrine from error?

- *Church vs. State.* We are watching that unravel in our own culture.

- *Christianity vs. Paganism.* Our government schools are forcing paganism on our kids. Biblical Christianity is becoming increasingly "politically incorrect."

- *Christ vs. Pseudo-christ.* We will see this in the future.

In Galatians it is pointed out that Abraham was saved 430 years before the Law. Paul argued that the promises of God preceded the Law and cannot be annulled. Ishmael and Isaac in the Old Testament were modeled here as different sons with different principles: the flesh and the spirit. Ishmael was born in unbelief. The son of the bondwoman would not be heir, Paul declared. Isaac was a promise in response to faith. The ultimate triumph in God was the offering of Isaac, just as our final challenge of faith is our response to the offering of Jesus Christ on the Cross.

The fruits of the Spirit are listed: Love, Joy, Peace, Longsuffering, Gentleness, Goodness, Faith, Meekness, Self-control. The first three are of the heart; the next three relate to your neighbor; the last three relate to God. So how is your love life? The secret of your love life should be the utter monopoly of your heart by the Holy Spirit.

Four "bearings" are in Galatians:

- *Fruit-bearing*, nine fruits of the Spirit
- *Burden-bearing*, bearing one another's burdens
- *Seed-bearing*, whatsoever a man sows, that shall he reap.
- *Brand-bearing*, I bear the marks of the Lord Jesus.

The slaves had a brand that was a mark of ownership. Soldiers had a brand that was a mark of allegiance to the leader. Criminals had a brand, one of indictment. Those that were abhorred (the lepers) had a mark of reproach. Devotees had marks of consecration. *Paul's body had all five.*

The Epistle to the Galatians can be summarized by this admonition: Are ye so foolish? Having begun in the Spirit are ye now made perfect by the flesh?[11]

Galatians is a call out of religious externalism.

The Epistle to the Ephesians

The Book of Ephesians is the first of the prison epistles and is considered by many scholars to be the most majestic of all the epistles. Ephesians is fundamental to the doctrine of ecclesiology. Chapter one opens with,

> According as he hath chosen us in him before the foundation of the world, that we should be holy and without blame before him in love.[12]

"Chosen in Him"—the Greek verb for *chosen* means once and for all. English has an active voice and a passive voice, but Greek also has a middle voice which includes a sense of choosing. We are chosen out of the world once and for all for God's peculiar treasure.

> Having predestinated us unto the adoption of children by Jesus Christ to himself, according to the good pleasure of his will.[13]

Adoption was a different concept in the Greek culture than today. Then, when a son became of age, he was formally adopted and thus gained legal standing in the family. The adoption was a public attestation of adult sonship and confirming of his privileges.

> *The Epistle to the Galatians can be summarized by this admonition: Are ye so foolish?*

In whom we have redemption through his blood, the forgiveness of sins, according to the riches of his grace.[14]

What do we mean by redemption? Redemption is a release by ransom. The ransom was paid on the Cross in respect to eternal principles of righteousness which govern the universe—the holy law of God—which the human predicament has outraged. Our sins are evil because of the magnitude of holiness of the one we are sinning against.

The concept of our being *sealed* is also in Ephesians:

> In whom ye also trusted, after that ye heard the word of truth, the gospel of your salvation: in whom also after that ye believed, ye were sealed with that holy Spirit of promise, which is the earnest of our inheritance until the redemption of the purchased possession, unto the praise of his glory.[15]

Sealing is a term signifying ownership and security. We are His. We are not our own. And we are safe in Him. This sealing is the earnest, or guarantee, of our inheritance.

We should all memorize this fundamental passage:

> For by grace are ye saved through faith; and that not of yourselves: it is the gift of God: not of works, lest any man should boast. For we are his workmanship, created in Christ Jesus unto good works, which God hath before ordained that we should walk in them.[16]

We are His workmanship (*poema*, in the Greek).

Many people ask, "Didn't God know Adam was going to sin?" Yes, He did. He created Adam with a free will, knowing he would rebel. Why did He bother? The answer is in the preceding verse to that above:

> That in the ages to come he might shew the exceeding riches of his grace in his kindness towards us through Christ Jesus.[17]

It has all been a demonstration for ages yet to come. How does the God of the universe demonstrate infinite love? By allowing man to get in a predicament that only God's death could solve. No greater love hath any man than he that lays down his life for his friends. And nothing less than the death of God Himself availed to satisfy His holiness and justice.

THE GREAT MYSTERY

Paul went on to reveal a mystery that was hidden before time began. Jesus said,

> Verily I say unto you, Among them that are born of women there hath not risen a greater than John the Baptist; notwithstanding he that is least in the kingdom of heaven is greater than he.[18]

No man was greater than John the Baptist (which is quite a statement!). But at the end of that very sentence, Jesus was talking about something John was *not* part of. Jesus explained,

> For all the prophets and the law prophesied until John.[19]

John the Baptist was the last of the Old Testament. Most of us take for granted that all believers are in the same category, but there are a couple: Old Testament believers, and, now,

The Armor of God

Another key topic Paul wrote to the Ephesians about was the cosmic warfare we are all engaged in.

> For we wrestle not against flesh and blood, but against principalities, against powers, against the rulers of the darkness of this world, against spiritual wickedness in high places.[21]

Those last phrases in Greek mean ranks of angels. Paul didn't have in view a battle with leaders of an administration we might disagree with, or the promoters of paganism in our culture, etc. Our real warfare is not with flesh and blood, but with ranks of angels, powerful beings who serve the power of darkness.

Paul gave us our imperative (this is not optional):

> Put on the whole armour of God, that ye may be able to stand against the wiles of the devil.[22]

Paul then detailed seven key elements of our spiritual armor. And when should we put on the armor? Before the battle begins; yet the battle has already started and we are already on enemy turf. It's time we put on our armor. We should be girded with truth. We must have the breastplate of righteousness. Our feet must be shod with the preparation of the gospel of peace. Our shield of faith must be intact. We must have our helmet of salvation. We have the sword of the Spirit. And the heavy artillery—prayer!

Each of these elements deserve careful study and preparation.

something entirely new: the Church. You and I are part of something which was not revealed in the Old Testament. This entirely new thing was revealed to Paul and he announces it in this letter:

> How that by revelation he made known unto me the mystery . . . Which in other ages was not made known unto the sons of men, as it is now revealed unto his holy apostles and prophets by the Spirit; That the Gentiles should be fellowheirs, and of the same body, and partakers of his promise in Christ by the gospel.[20]

The mystery Paul was given to reveal is not the Gospel, or that Gentiles would be saved. Those issues are manifest throughout the Old Testament. Paul is declaring something not revealed in the Old Testament.

What was not revealed? An entirely new thing: to make of both the Jew and Gentile a new body of *fellow heirs*—the Church, the Body of Christ. Many Christians fail to appreciate the uniqueness of the Church, and its distinctiveness over other categories of believers. The benefits you and I enjoy were mind-blowing to Paul's Pharisaical mind.

THE EPISTLE TO THE PHILIPPIANS

Philippians can be called Resources through Suffering. The book is about Christ in our life, Christ in our mind, Christ as our goal, Christ as our strength, and joy through suffering. It was written during Paul's imprisonment in Rome, about thirty years after the Ascension and about ten years after he first preached at Philippi.

Here are some of the memorable passages:

- For me to live is Christ, and to die is gain.[23]
- What things were gain to me, those I counted loss for Christ.[24]
- I can do all things through Christ which strengthens me.[25]
- Rejoice in the Lord always. Again, I say rejoice.[26]

Also in Philippians we have a declaration known as the *Kenosis*:

> Let this mind be in you, which was also in Christ Jesus: who, being in the form of God, thought

it not robbery to be equal with God: but made himself of no reputation, and took upon him the form of a servant, and was made in the likeness of men: and being found in fashion as a man, he humbled himself, and became obedient unto death, even the death of the cross.[27]

That's the ultimate humility. The God of the universe did all that on our behalf.

THE EPISTLE TO THE COLOSSIANS

In Colossians, Christ Preeminent is the main theme. At this time, a group of heretics (later known as the Gnostics) were active and mixing angel worship and Jewish mysticism with asceticism and Greek mythology. Alexandria was their main headquarters. (The word *gnostic* comes from *gnosis,* which means knowledge.) The book of Colossians is a response to gnosticism. Christ is preeminent in all things. Paul talks about the fullness of Christ and the sufficiency of Christ. Seventy-eight of the ninety-five verses resemble Ephesians.

One of the themes in Colossians is "the fullness of Christ in creation, redemption, and the Church."

Christology, the study of Christ Himself, is a major theme. Christ is the visible form of the invisible God, the prior head of all creation. In Him the universe was created. He is before the universe; in Him the universe coheres. He is the head of the body, the church, and the firstborn from among the dead. He's above all of the angels, including Satan. His preeminence is clearly declared:

For by him were all things created, that are in heaven, and that are in earth, visible and invisible, whether they be thrones, or dominions, or principalities, or powers: all things were created by him, and for him: and he is before all things, and by him all things consist. And He is the head of the body, the church: who is the beginning, the firstborn from the dead; that in all things he might have the preeminence. For it pleased the Father that in him should all fullness dwell. [28]

Colossians also speaks of Christ as the Redeemer:

And, having made peace through the blood of his cross, by him to reconcile all things unto himself; by him, I say, whether they be things in earth, or things in heaven.[29]

THE EPISTLES TO THE THESSALONIANS

There are two letters to the Thessalonians, both of which are among the most important eschatological passages in the New Testament. (*Eschatology* is the study of the last things, or the end times.) We will include a review of these two critical letters in Hour 21 when we will specifically review this fascinating and controversial area.

THE PASTORAL EPISTLES

If you are saved, you are in the full-time ministry whether you realize it or not. All of the letters to pastors are for you and me also, not just pastors. Paul's four pastoral letters anticipate the very challenges we face today.

THE EPISTLES TO TIMOTHY

Paul wrote two letters to his young protégé, Timothy. In his first letter, Paul exhorted Timothy to guard the wonderful beginning God had given him. He advised him on the conduct of the assembly, how to have order in the church, and listed the qualifications for elders and deacons.

Second Timothy addresses challenges to faithfulness, and warns of dangers. Some have turned aside. Some have made a shipwreck of their faith. Some shall fall away. Some have turned after Satan. Some have been led astray. Some have missed the mark. All these were real issues then and they are real issues today.

What's our challenge? *To finish well!* We celebrate when someone receives Jesus Christ. But salvation is really a beginning, not a climax. You say you are saved; Praise God! What have you *done about it*? Our challenge is to finish well.

> I have fought a good fight, I have finished my course, I have kept the faith: henceforth there is laid up for me a crown of righteousness, which the Lord, the righteous judge, shall give me at that day: and not to me only, but unto all them also that love his appearing.[30]

TITUS

Titus was Paul's troubleshooter. One of Paul's most trusted workers, he accompanied Paul and Barnabas on the difficult visit to the Jerusalem council. (He was probably the only

Gentile there.) He was sent on a diplomatic mission to Corinth with a severely worded letter that he was charged to deliver and enforce. Paul and Titus traveled to Crete, where Paul left him. Paul later wrote a letter to Titus which shows Titus again in charge of another difficult situation. Paul ordered him to combat the quarreling and slander by rebuking the hearers and using his full authority to bring order.

PHILEMON

The finest art galleries usually reserve a space for choice miniatures. This private, personal note from Paul is a masterpiece of courtesy, tact, and even playful wit. It also serves as an example of intercession.

Paul lived in Colossi, and Onesimus was a slave owned by Philemon. Onesimus had run away, met Paul, and had been converted. Paul encouraged him to turn himself in to Philemon who had also been converted by Paul. Onesimus delivered the epistle to the Colossians and took this private note to Philemon. Philemon had every legal right to kill Onesimus as a runaway slave, but Paul knew Onesimus was a changed person; he just had to convince Philemon. Paul praised Philemon and offered, "Whatever he owes you, charge it to me." But then he pointed out, "By the way Philemon, you owe me your life—keep that in the balance." There was some playfulness there, but Paul gave his pledge of assurance and benediction. It is a charming little letter, but it is also a model of intercession and sponsorship.

In our next Hour we will explore a group of letters written to Hebrew Christians.

Hour 20

THE HEBREW CHRISTIAN EPISTLES

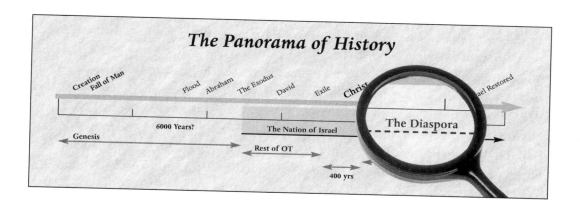

HEBREWS, JAMES, 1 and 2 Peter, 1, 2, and 3 John, and Jude are known as the Hebrew Epistles because they were, in large measure, written to the Jews, and yet they have important lessons for all of us.

THE EPISTLE TO THE HEBREWS

The epistle to the Hebrews is one of the two greatest theological treatises in the New Testament, the other being Romans. One main theme is the priesthood of Christ versus the priesthood of the covenant with Israel. The Lord's priesthood began after He offered himself on the Cross. In Leviticus, the priest could only offer what had already been sacrificed. Aaron did not wear his high priestly garments until after the already-slain burnt offering was on the altar. The Passover lamb was instituted before Aaron was appointed and offered by the head of the household. All these subtleties are very important. It is a very rabbinical book.

Hebrews was written to Jewish Christians, not unbelievers. The epistle functions almost like a Leviticus of the New Testament, but it focuses on how Christ supercedes and fulfills the Aaronic priesthood.

The Temple was still standing at this time, and that was a real dilemma for the Jewish Christian. Try to imagine yourself as a Jew embracing a Messiah, which your leadership has rejected. The Temple is still operating. The traditional culture is still going through all of its routines. Yet you are at variance with all that and are trying to find your way. How do you deal with this? Divinely appointed priests are officiating in the divinely appointed Temple accomplishing a divinely ordered service that has been ennobled through the centuries. You face the reality that it was a Jewish religious world that crucified Jesus. You have some very deep emotional troubles.

To complicate this, you are facing persecution, especially in Jerusalem. Stephen was martyred in Acts 7. James the apostle was executed in Acts 12, about A.D. 62. Others were killed in Acts 8 and 26. In Galatia, many Jewish believers were tempted to resort temporarily to apostasy to avoid persecution. The persecution in those days did not come from Rome; it was from the Jewish leadership. If you were a Jew trying to maintain a position within that culture, and yet you were a Christian, you were an outcast, part of a weird sect. And you were being persecuted.

The author's objectives in writing to these believers were to combat possible apostasy, encourage them to press on to spiritual maturity, and comfort those who were enduring persecutions. To do this, he demonstrated the superiority of the Messiah over Judaism by focusing on His superiority over the three pillars of Judaism: the role of angels, the role of Moses, and the Levitical priesthood under Aaron. He deviated from his logical arguments five times to put in special warnings.

Jesus is the new and better deliverer in the first seven chapters. The God-man is better than the angels in the first two chapters. He is an apostle better than Moses in the third chapter. He is a leader better than Joshua in the fourth chapter. And he is a priest better than Aaron in the last part of chapter four. The writer then built on this foundation.

He wrote about Calvary and a new and better covenant which offered better promises, better sanctuary, was sealed by a better sacrifice, and achieved better results. These were very Jewish arguments to an audience with a good grasp of the Old Testament. The author then focused on faith, which is the true and better response.

Some other themes in Hebrews include the Son of God as the Final Revealer. He's the heir of all things. Through the Son, the ages were made. He is the brightness of God's glory. He is the image of the Father. He upholds all things by His power. He made purification of sin. And he sat down in Majesty on high. These things are obvious to us having read the epistles, yet the author must hammer this through to the Jewish mind to really establish his foundation.

In the first two chapters, the Son is shown to be superior to the angels by virtue of His deity, His humanity, and the salvation He provided. Why His deity? The Old Testament reveals the answers.

- The Son's position is unique—Psalm 2:7.

- The Son is head of the Davidic Covenant—2 Samuel 7:14.

- Angels worship the Son—Psalm 97:7.

- Angels serve the Son—Psalm 104:4.

- The Son is to rule the Kingdom—Psalm 45:7-8.

- The Son is the Creator—Psalm 102:25-27.

- The Son is enthroned at the right hand of God—Psalm 110:1.

The writer was establishing these points from the recognized authority, the *Tenach*—the Jewish Old Testament. I believe the writer was Paul, but he did not sign it, since that would be arguing from his own authority. He wanted the arguments to stand on their own rabbinical logic.

The Son's superiority because of His humanity was the second line of argument in this book. Why his humanity? Because sovereignty over the earth was promised to man, not angels (Genesis 1). Through sin, man lost this sovereignty to Satan and his angels. But the Messiah has regained dominion for man. Man will be associated with Him in rule. The Messiah became a man to reclaim dominion of the earth, which was originally committed to man. That was the end run on Satan's presumed victory in Eden.

The Son is also superior in the salvation He offers. Why His salvation? Because He manifested divine grace. Here the writer cites Psalm 22 and Isaiah 8. The Son was to overcome the Prince of Death to free the believer from the fear of death and to help man. All these reasons are why He is superior to the angels.

Jesus is also superior to Moses in His person, His work, and His position. Here the writer inserts one of the warnings: the warning against disobedience. He reminds them that the Israelites failed to enter into Kadesh Barnea because of unbelief. The very people God rescued from Egypt failed to enter into God's promised rest. So he is saying, "Don't make the same mistake your fathers did. They failed by lack of faith to enter into God's rest. Don't do the same thing. Enter into the present rest—your spiritual maturity." He's drawing an analogy.

Jesus is greater than the Aaronic priesthood. Why? Because he's in a better position; He's heavenly rather than earthly. He is a better priest because He, too, is divinely appointed. The writer cites Psalm 2:7 and 110:4. And then there is another warning; a warning to progress to maturity. He urges them to progress from the *milk* of the word to the *meat* of the word. They are no longer babes. It's time to grow. And then he makes a very key point: a return to Judaism is not an option available to them, even to avoid the persecution.

> *Jesus is also superior to Moses in His person, His work, and His position.*

Hebrews 6:4-6 describes another option that they cannot take. This passage causes a lot of confusion. These were saved believers. They were once enlightened; they tasted the heavenly gift; they were partakers of the Holy Spirit; they tasted the good Word of God and the powers of the age to come. Some commentators try to argue that they were not really saved, they were just exposed. No! That's simply twisting the text. They clearly were believers. But the option they do not have is to temporarily give up their salvation, go back to Judaism until the persecution subsides, and then hope to be saved later.

Only two options were available to them: 1) Go back to Judaism (confirming their immaturity) and be subject to the judgment of A.D., 70 physical death now and loss of rewards later; or 2) Make a clean break from Judaism once and for all and press on to maturity. The author advocated the latter.

In chapter seven, the writer discusses the priesthood of Melchizedek. Melchizedek is mentioned briefly in Genesis 14 and once again in Psalm 110, but the writer of Hebrews puts a big emphasis on this peculiar character. Melchizedek was a priest-king (Genesis 14). He was a priest of the Most High God and the king of Salem. He was not Jewish. In fact, we don't know a lot about him. Vitally important to the writer, though, is that Melchizedek received tithes from Abraham. This was significant for a rabbi because Levi hadn't been born yet; in concept, he is "in the loins of Abraham." So if Abraham, the father of the Jews, was offering tithes to Melchizedek, Melchizedek was a priest of a higher level than Levi or Aaron or Moses. His role was apparently independent of his genealogy, which was not recorded and was irrelevant. His birth and death are not recorded, so he was viewed as timeless. Thus Melchizedek is presented as a type or a model foreshadowing the Messiah. The Melchizedek priesthood preceded, and then replaced, the Aaronic priesthood.

The Levitical priesthood could never achieve perfection. Psalm 114 implies there will be another (non-Levitical) order through David. The priesthood was of the line of Aaron. David was of the line of Judah. Under this system, the kings and the priests never mixed. But there is a priesthood that will combine kings and priests. Melchizedek was the example given here. The Messiah will be a king and a priest. And the body of Christ—believers—will be kings and priests. The writer argued that the Levitical priesthood was temporary, and it was weak because, although it doled out penalties for disobedience, it did not impart the strength to keep its commands. It did not bring perfection or completeness. It was weak as the Law was weak.

We, however, are the beneficiaries of a better covenant. According to Jeremiah 31, the Mosaic covenant was destined to be replaced by a superior one, and that's where the New Testament (or New Covenant) got its name. The New Covenant has better promises, a better priesthood, a better sacrifice, and a better sanctuary.

The limitation of the old sanctuary was that it was temporary and restrictive. Only one man, out of one tribe, out of one nation, could enter the sanctuary, and he could only do that on one day of the year and never without blood.

We have a better sacrifice. The Mosaic sacrifices were inadequate; they had to be repeated. Since they used animal blood, sins were covered but not removed. In Psalm 40, we read that only obedience can bring perfection. But the Messiah can impart perfection. The Mosaic sacrifices were never intended to be permanent. They were foreshadowing; they were prophetically anticipating the sacrifice that would occur on that cross in Judea some two thousand years ago. The writer of Hebrews emphasizes these contrasts:

- Levitical priests/Messiah
- Many priests/One
- Standing/Sitting (finished)
- Daily/One specific day
- Repeated/Once and for all
- Many sacrifices/Only one
- Covered sins/Took sins away

There is an interesting chapter on the dangers of willful sin. If these Jewish believers now apostatize from the faith and once and for all return to Judaism, there remains no more sacrifice for their sin. If they choose to apostatize, there is no more return. Why? Because it's a rejection of the work of the Trinity, which includes the unpardonable sin. And God will judge His people (Deuteronomy 32). "It is a fearful thing to fall into the hands of the living God."

Chapter 11 is sometimes called "the Hall of Faith." It is a "Who's Who" of Old Testament heroes who demonstrated faith.

- **Abel** demonstrated his faith because his offering indicated that blood was the only way.
- **Enoch** demonstrated his faith through fellowship; he didn't die.
- **Noah** was obedient and saved his family.
- **Abraham** departed from the land, being a foreigner in a strange land; was willing to sacrifice his miracle son, Isaac, believing that he would be resurrected.
- **Moses** was hid against the law of Pharaoh, refused to be called the son of Pharaoh, and kept the first Passover.
- **Rahab** saved the spies.

Also Sarah, Isaac, Jacob, Joseph, Joshua, Gideon, Barak, Samson, Jephthah, David, Samuel, and the prophets, each in their own way, demonstrated faith.

After cataloguing the heroes of faith, the writer offers an exhortation to endurance:

Wherefore seeing we also are compassed about with so great a cloud of witnesses, let us lay aside every weight, and the sin which doth so easily beset us, and let us run with patience the race that is set before us, looking unto Jesus the author and finisher of our faith; who for the joy that was set before him endured the cross, despising the shame, and is set down at the right hand of the throne of God. (Hebrews 12:1)

Here is a summary of the five warnings:

- The danger of drifting.
- The danger of disobedience.
- Progress toward maturity—interim apostasy not an option.

- The danger of willful sin.

- Warning against indifference.

Again, the Book of Hebrews details that *"the just shall live by faith,"* completing the trilogy on Habakkuk 2:4 with Romans and Galatians.

JAMES

Next is the Book of James. From Matthew 13, Mark 6, and Galatians 1, we know James was a half brother of Jesus. He was an unbeliever until after the resurrection when Christ appeared to him. He was married, and was the leader of the church in Jerusalem, which, incidentally, has been confirmed by some recent excavations.

When Peter was released from prison (Acts 12), he instructed the disciples to go tell James. James issued the verdict of the Jerusalem Council and confirmed the Proclamation of Gentile Christianity (both in Acts 15). When Paul arrived in Jerusalem, he reported to James in Acts 21. In Galatians 2 we find that his name was being used without permission by the Judaizers. (James was executed in A.D. 62, which confirms the early dating of the New Testament as there is no mention of his death.)

The Epistle of James to the Twelve Tribes is a little different from the letters by Paul. He dealt with conduct, not creed; behavior, not belief; deed, not doctrine. He spoke of endurance, faith, outward trials, and inward temptations in the first chapter. And he gave ways to test the genuineness of faith—our response to the Word of God. These include our response to social situations, the production of good works, the exercise of self-control, our reaction to worldliness, and our resort to prayer in all circumstances. These are not ways to get saved; they are demonstrations of faith that show we are.

Faith without works is a major theme in James.

Yea, a man may say, Thou hast faith, and I have works: show me thy faith without thy works, and I will shew thee my faith by my works. (James 2:18)

He was not writing about being justified before *God* by your works, but being justified before *men.* If you say you have faith and don't have a changed life, there is still something lacking. He was not in conflict with Paul, he was just tackling a different issue. Paul wrote about justification before the throne of God; James dealt with justification in society.

Fifty-four imperative verbs are in the 108 verses of this epistle: It was a call to action all the way through. James closed with an appeal to restore those who may have failed any of these tests.

THE EPISTLES OF PETER

The first epistle of Peter was written to the Jews of the dispersion. In it, Peter presented the status of the believer, and then discussed the practical aspects of our pilgrim life. He offered many instructions about our citizenship, marriage, and how we should treat our servants or employees. Then he warns of the fiery trial to come. He encourages us to rejoice, commit and be vigilant.

First Peter was actually penned and carried by Silas, a professional secretary. The Greek in this letter is much more polished than Peter's second epistle, which he apparently penned himself.

By the time he wrote the second epistle, Peter was old. In John 21, Jesus had signified that Peter would die a martyr's death, so Peter wrote this letter trying to encourage his Jewish friends.

Second Peter speaks of the need to grow in virtue and knowledge, self-control, patience, godliness, kindness and love. He emphasized his personal witness to the Transfiguration. But then he makes a strange remark. He said,

"We have also a more sure word of prophecy." (2 Peter 1:19)

The messianic prophecies are there for all to see. (We reviewed some of them in Hour 13,)

He then warned that false teachers would infect the church with slander and immorality. He did that by highlighting how God delivered to and from judgment. The first example was how God confined the fallen angels of Genesis 6 to judgment, and God delivered Noah and his family. (This is an important confirmation of our understanding of the strange events of Genesis 6. Second Peter 2 is one of the key places that corroborate our view which is no different from the traditional Jewish teachings and the view of the early church. Fallen angels engaged in some very bizarre mischief. Second Peter confirms this as Jude will too.)

The second example was from Genesis 19: God judged Sodom and Gomorrah on the one hand, yet delivered Lot and his family. An important point was that Sodom and Gomorrah would not be destroyed *until* Lot was delivered. In the same way, I don't believe the wrath of God can be poured out on the earth until the Body of Christ is removed.

The last chapter characterized the end times. Peter pointed out:

Knowing this first, that there shall come in the last days scoffers, walking after their own lusts, and saying, Where is the promise of his coming? for since the fathers fell asleep, all things continue as they were from the beginning of the creation. (2 Peter 3:3,4)

Here Peter contrasted the concept of the Second Coming with *uniformitarianism*—that all things continue the same without interruption. The premise that God created the universe also implies that He is willing and able to intervene. Uniformitarianism, of which the theory of biogenesis ("evolution") is an example, attacks the idea that God intervenes in the history of the earth.

THE EPISTLES OF JOHN

John wrote five books in the New Testament: the Gospel, these three letters, and the book of Revelation. These three little letters are gems. First John is the longest and deals with "truth versus error" by highlighting seven contrasts:

- Light vs. Darkness—1:5–2:11.
- The Father vs. the World—2:12–2:17.
- Christ vs. the Antichrist—2:18–2:28.
- Good Works vs. Evil Works—2:29–3:24.
- Holy Spirit vs. Error—4:1–4:6.
- Love vs. Pious Pretense—4:7–4:21.
- The God-Born vs. Others—5:1–5:21.

He also poses seven tests:

- Profession—1:5–2:11.
- Desire—2:12–2:17.
- Doctrine—2:18–2:28.
- Conduct—2:29–3:24.

- Discernment—4:1–4:6.

- Motive—4:7–4:21.

- New Birth—5:1-5:21.

As in other places in Scripture, 1 John has a heptadic structure:

- The seven traits of being born again.

- The seven reasons why this epistle is written.

- The seven tests of Christian genuineness .

- The seven tests of honesty and reality.

John described the spiritual fundamentals as all-inclusive commandments in 3:23: that we believe on Jesus Christ and that we love one another. Verses 17-18 are a profession of love for others.

The second epistle of John is a personal one to the "elect lady." I'm fascinated that no one speculates about who this lady is, but I think it's obvious—it must be Mary. At the Cross, Jesus consigned his mother to the apostle John. (He didn't consign her care to his half brothers Jude, James, or the others. And that was appropriate because she obviously was a believer and they were not at the time.)

So when John wrote a letter late in his life, to the "elect lady," I suspect that, unless there is any evidence to the contrary, it was to Mary.[1]

John here concentrated on the practical walk in love, the divine insistence on love, and the human expression of love.

The doctrinal elements are warnings against error, false teachers, and false charity. (He instructs her to not extend the slightest hospitality to false teachers because it could be construed as an endorsement of their teachings, etc.[2] This is in contrast to the admonitions to the rest of us.)

In some respects, 2 John is a rebuttal to the Gnostics who denied that Jesus came in the flesh, but that subject is not the main focus. John covered that in his first letter, which was really a sermon.

The third epistle is a very short report card to Gaius, who had done well, and to two others: Diotrophes who was said to have been evil by way of his pride and strife; and Demetrius who was commended.

JUDE

The epistle of Jude is just one chapter, but is full of surprises!

Jude was the half brother of Jesus.[3] He also was an unbeliever while Christ was alive, but became a believer after the resurrection.[4]

In this letter, Jude attacked apostasy and argued for his readers to contend for the faith because some people would fall away. He argued against subtle perversions which included at least two basic denials: denying grace by turning it to lasciviousness (just because we have liberty in Christ does not give us a right to sin); and denying our Lord and Master Jesus Christ.

Apostasy will lead to certain doom, and he used three examples: Egypt, the angels in Genesis 6, and Sodom. He also pointed to three apostates by using the examples of Cain, Balaam, and Korah; and then emphasized the utter falsity of these teachers by using six awful metaphors.

An analysis of 2 Peter deals with many of these same things, but in Peter they are future tense; in Jude, they are past tense. Apparently the prophecies in 2 Peter were fulfilled by the time Jude wrote his letter.

In light of the fact that apostasy has been foretold, Jude told his readers how to contend: they should build, pray, keep, and look. And they should support those who contend.

Jude focused on the certainty of judgment, and he used an extremely provocative example.

> *Jude was the half brother of Jesus.[3] He also was an unbeliever while Christ was alive, but became a believer after the resurrection.[4]*

And the angels which kept not their first estate, but left their own habitation, he hath reserved in everlasting chains under darkness unto the judgment of the great day. Even as Sodom and Gomorrah, and the cities about them in like manner, giving themselves over to fornication, and going after strange flesh, are set forth for an example, suffering the vengeance of eternal fire. (Jude 1:6,7)

Jude argued that these false teachers were going to be judged. Then he linked the errors of Sodom and Gomorrah in "going after strange flesh" with the angels in Genesis 6. (The

Scripture always confirms the truth by two or three witnesses, and 2 Peter 2:4 and Jude 1:6,7 refer to the angels in Genesis 6.)

Here is something extremely provocative—Jude quotes a prophecy given by Enoch.

> And Enoch also, the seventh from Adam, prophesied of these, saying, Behold, the Lord cometh with ten thousands of his saints, to execute judgment upon all, and to convince all that are ungodly among them of all their ungodly deeds which they have ungodly committed, and of all their hard speeches which ungodly sinners have spoken against him. (Jude 1:14,15)

Jude was quoting this prophecy of Enoch, as it was presumably familiar to his readers; but let's stop and realize what was going on. The oldest prophecy uttered by a prophet, *uttered before the Flood of Noah*, is a prophecy of the Second Coming of Christ.

But Jude did something else that should disturb us. He made the case that we should not speak evil of dignities, even if they are against us. He chose a bizarre example to make his case.

> Likewise also these filthy dreamers defile the flesh, despise dominion, and speak evil of dignities. Yet Michael the archangel, when contending with the devil he disputed about the body of Moses, durst not bring against him a railing accusation, but said, The Lord rebuke thee. (Jude 1:8, 9)

Here again, Jude alluded to some background familiar to his readers, but which has been lost to us. First of all, the fact that there was a dispute between Michael and the devil regarding the body of Moses is a surprise. Where did that happen? And why would Satan want the body of Moses?

In any case, the point is that even when Michael was contending with Satan, he didn't speak evil of Satan. He said, "The Lord rebuke you." Jude would tell us to not speak evil of dignities, and he chose Satan himself to make the point. Don't speak evil of him; don't rail directly against him. Let the Lord deal with him. If you are ever confronted with a demon, rely on the authority of Jesus Christ. Don't try to confront a demon on your own.

In this chapter we have taken a very superficial look at these Hebrew Christian epistles:

- Hebrews—the New Covenant

- James—Faith Demonstrated

- 1 Peter—Persecuted Church
- 2 Peter—Coming Apostasy
- 1 John—Love
- 2 John—False Teachers
- 3 John—Preparation of Helpers
- Jude—Apostasy

We have looked at the Hebrew Epistles and those of Paul, but we have yet to deal with the seven most important letters often overlooked on the list of epistles. They are the seven letters by Jesus Christ himself: to Ephesus, Smyrna, Pergamos, Thyatira, Sardis, Thessalonica, and Laodicea. We will review these in Hour 22.

But first, it will be useful to review, in summary, the topic of eschatology, the study of last things, or end times. We cannot see the world from God's perspective without understanding His coming climax, and also understanding where we are today.

Fasten your seat belts!

Hour 21

ESCHATOLOGY

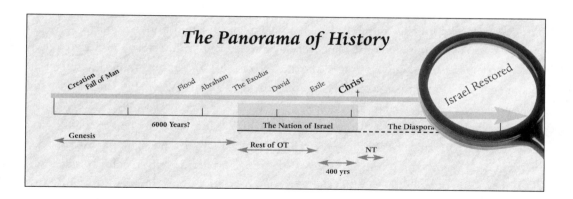

IN THIS HOUR we are going to depart from our usual pattern and attempt to put in broad perspective the subject of *eschatology*, the study of the "last things" and the end times. No other aspect of Biblical study has suffered more from its enthusiasts as well as from its critics. Zealous enthusiasts have promoted unfounded conjectures and speculations while critics have failed to recognize the scope, depth, and precision of God's Word. No other area of study will more challenge the validity of your approach to interpretation and your grasp of "the whole counsel of God."[1]

One of the key issues that confronts the church and creates a great deal of division is the literal return of Christ to rule on the earth. Over 1,845 verses refer to Christ's rule in the Old Testament alone; seventeen books give prominence to the event. In the New Testament, there are at least 318 references to the return of Jesus Christ. Twenty-three out of the twenty-seven books give prominence to the event. For every prophecy of Christ's first coming, there are at least eight of His Second Coming.

There are two basic views in eschatology regarding the promises of the return of the Messiah of Israel to rule the earth, and, in particular, in a thousand-year period known as the millennium:[2] *amillennialism*, which views these allusions as merely symbolic, and *premillennialism*, which regards them as literal. These two viewpoints derive from the *hermeneutics* (the theories of Biblical interpretation). Those who take the promises in the Bible literally will tend toward *premillennialism*: they look for a literal return of Christ to rule on the earth for a thousand years. Those who view major portions of Scripture as merely symbolic or allegorical do not anticipate a literal return of the Messiah to rule politically on the earth, and are designated as *amillennial* ("no millennium").

THE TRAGEDY OF AMILLENNIALISM

The great tragedy for the church has been amillennialism, an attempt to explain away the idea that Jesus will literally come back to rule. This started with Origen, an early churchman whose hermeneutics encouraged the allegorization of Scripture. Augustine relied on this allegorical method to formulate an amillennial eschatology, which claimed that the thousand-year rule revealed in the book of Revelation was merely figurative. Subsequently this view was adopted by the Roman Catholic Church and remains their eschatological view to this day. Tragically, although the reformers did a diligent job shedding the shackles of tradition by returning to the authority of the Bible, especially with regards to salvation, they didn't adequately reexamine the eschatological doctrines of the Church. Most Protestant denominations today, therefore, remain amillennial in their interpretation of end-time prophecy.

Several tragic ideas or logical assumptions are derived from amillennialism. First, all of the Messianic promises throughout the Old Testament are at risk, promises that point to the dynasty of David ruling the earth through Jesus Christ, the Messiah.

Second, amillenialism allowed the early church to become extremely anti-Semitic. Jews have suffered through nineteen hundred years of persecution, much under the banner of Christ, because of these views.

Third, it caused the Church to lose its moorings, its roots. We serve a Jewish King. We serve a church founded by Jewish leaders. And we venerate a Jewish Scripture. God is not through with Israel, yet the destiny of Israel is denigrated by amillennialism.

Fourth, the promise given to Mary by the angel Gabriel is rendered indeterminate. She was specifically told that her child would rule on the throne of David. The throne of David did not exist during those days. It has yet to be reestablished.

The fundamental issue is really hermeneutics. How do you go about interpreting the scriptural text? To the extent that you take it literally, you will be driven to a premillennial point of view. To the extent you are willing to treat the text symbolically or allegorically, you will drift toward the amillennial perspective, rationalizing these promises in figurative terms.

It is the discovery that God says what He means, and means what He says, that raises the fog of diffidence and energizes the most exciting adventure of anyone's lifetime!

Two other viewpoints we will mention briefly are *preterism* and *reconstructionism*. Preterists say that everything in Revelation has already taken place and is all past history. Reconstructionists claim the Church has replaced Israel and has inherited the promises that were given to her. *Neither of these are Scriptural doctrines.*

THE PROBLEM: A MISSING THEOLOGICAL DIVISION

Missing from most lists of formal theological categories of study is a subject that occupies five-sixths of the Bible: *Israelology: the study of Israel as an element of God's plan.* When you put this issue into its proper Biblical perspective, then all of the other areas of study take on an entirely different significance.

We must be very careful to discern the distinction between Israel and the Church. They have different origins and different destinies. The prevalent "replacement theology" views the church as replacing Israel in regards to the promises of the Old Testament. This view denies Israel its place in God's program, arguing that because Israel rejected her Messiah, she forfeited the promises of the Old Testament, and those promises have now devolved upon the Church. But some of the most critical promises to Israel were *unconditional*: She couldn't forfeit them if she tried. The Mosaic Promises had some conditions attached, but the Abrahamic Covenant was unconditional. This is not just a matter of having a different point of view. If you accept the idea that Israel is not going to receive those promises, commitments which reconfirmed repeatedly under oath, then you make God a liar and impugn His character!

The Seventy Weeks prophecy (the pivotal prophecy in Daniel 9) dealt specifically with Israel, *not* the Church.[3] Paul taught that during the dispensation of the Church the distinction between Jew and Gentile was set aside;[4] but in Revelation 4 onward, those distinctions reappear;[5] the Jewishness of Revelation—particularly chapters four through nineteen—is key to understanding this section of Scripture. (We will address this over the next two Hours.)

Many who are confused about some of the issues in eschatology also haven't done their homework in *ecclesiology* (the study of the Church). It is important to understand the distinctiveness of the *mystical* body of Christ, in contrast to other categories of the faithful.[6]

THE RAPTURE

Another subject which causes divisions and controversy is the "rapture" (Greek, *harpazo*; the Latin Vulgate equivalent is *"rapiemur,"* from which is derived "the rapture" as an English equivalent). The word means "to be forcibly snatched up," "to be taken away." This view, I have to confess, is probably the most preposterous Biblical view in Christianity. It reminds me of what a Nobel Prize winning physicist said about quantum physics:

> I think it is safe to say that no one understands quantum mechanics . . . In fact, it is often stated that of all the theories proposed in this century, the silliest is quantum theory. Some say that the only thing that quantum theory has going for it, in fact, is that it is unquestionably correct.
>
> *Richard Feynman, California Institute of Technology.*

That's a good description of this strange doctrine of the "rapture"!

Among the most significant doctrinal epistles dealing these issues in the New Testament are 1 and 2 Thessalonians. They were actually the first of Paul's epistles and yet we have left them for last because they are so relevant to this particular topic.

OUR BLESSED HOPE

Part 1

The first three chapters of 1 Thessalonians review things Paul had already taught them—their conversion, evangelism, and after-care. Then he looked ahead—the comfort of our calling and the challenge of our calling.

Paul had originally landed in Thessalonica, and while he was there for two to three weeks, he planted a church and taught them the basics. Later, while in Corinth, he learned they had become concerned over the death of some of their members. They were worried that those who had died would not see the return of Christ. So Paul wrote this very key passage, reminding them about the *harpazo*:

> But I would not have you to be ignorant, brethren, concerning them which are asleep, that ye sorrow not, even as others which have no hope. For if we believe that Jesus died and rose again, even so them also which sleep in Jesus will God bring with him. For this we say unto you by the word of the Lord, that we which are alive and remain unto the coming of the Lord shall not prevent them which are asleep. (1 Thessalonians 4:13-15)

Then he explained how this is going to happen:

> For the Lord himself shall descend from heaven with a shout, with the voice of the archangel, and with the trump of God: and the dead in Christ shall rise first: then we which are alive and remain shall be caught up together with them in the clouds, to meet the Lord in the air: and so shall we ever be with the Lord. (1 Thessalonians 4:16, 17)

This idea didn't begin in 1 Thessalonians. Remember what Jesus announced to the disciples in the Upper Room that last night before Gethsemane:

> Let not your heart be troubled: ye believe in God, believe also in me. In my Father's house are many mansions: if it were not so, I would have told you. I go to prepare a place for you. And if I go and prepare a place for you, I will come again, and receive you unto myself; that where I am, there ye may be also. (John 14:1-3)

In 1 Thessalonians 5 there is another very key passage.

> But of the times and the seasons, brethren, ye have no need that I write unto you. For yourselves know perfectly that the day of the Lord so cometh as a thief in the night [to children of darkness]. For when they shall say, Peace and safety; then sudden destruction cometh upon them But ye, brethren, are not in darkness, that that day should overtake you as a thief. Ye are all the children of light, and the children of the day: we are not of the night, nor of darkness. . . . For God hath not appointed us to wrath, but to obtain salvation by our Lord Jesus Christ. (1 Thessalonians 5:1-9)

He is talking about the children of darkness: Jesus will come as a thief in the night to *the children of the night*. The children of the day will know the season; they won't be caught by surprise!

But the key passage is verse 9: *"We are not appointed unto wrath."* There is a time of God's wrath coming, which the Lord Jesus Christ Himself labels as the Great Tribulation, which the Church will *not* be subject to.

Part 2

The first letter to the Thessalonians alleviated their concerns for awhile. But then another letter was being circulated in Thessalonica, a forgery claiming to be from Paul. Paul wrote 2 Thessalonians in response to that upsetting letter.

The second chapter of 2 Thessalonians is one of the most important prophetic chapters in the New Testament. We will look at it carefully because it deals with the order of events around which there is much confusion.

The Thessalonian church was starting to come under intense persecution, so they assumed they had entered into the Great Tribulation. They were very upset because that implied either they had missed the Rapture or Paul had taught them incorrectly. (Otherwise, if you assume Paul had taught them that Rapture would *follow* the Tribulation, why would they be upset? They would be rejoicing at the prospect that their redemption was drawing near!)

In the letter we know as "2 Thessalonians," Paul dealt with their misapprehensions caused by the false letter being circulated "as if from us:"

> Now we beseech you, brethren, by the coming of our Lord Jesus Christ, and by our gathering together unto him, that ye be not soon shaken in mind, or be troubled, neither by spirit, nor by word, nor by letter as from us, as that the day of Christ is at hand. (2 Thessalonians 2:1,2)

If they had been taught a post-tribulational view, they would have rejoiced at the tribulation because that would mean the Second Coming was that much closer. But they are troubled because they had been taught they would be raptured *before* the Tribulation. Because they thought the Tribulation had started, they figured one of two things: either Paul had not taught them correctly or they had somehow missed the Rapture.

In the second chapter Paul talks about events that had to *precede* the Tribulation:

> Let no man deceive you by any means: for that day shall not come, except there come a falling away first, and that man of sin be revealed, the son of perdition; who opposeth and exalteth

himself above all that is called God, or that is worshipped; so that he as God sitteth in the temple of God, shewing himself that he is God. Remember ye not, that, when I was yet with you, I told you these things? (2 Thessalonians 2:3-5)

It is interesting to realize that these topics were issues that Paul had already taught them in those few brief weeks when he first founded the church! Paul is actually reminding them of issues that he had taught them from Daniel 9, et al. Let's analyze this critical passage carefully:

Let no man deceive you by any means, for that day shall not come except first there come a falling away . . .

The easiest assumption is that this is referring to a general apostasy in the church. (Some exegetical experts suggest that this, too, may be alluding to the rapture. But this is not on what our view rests.)

. . . and that man of sin be revealed, the son of perdition . . .

This person will oppose *"and exalt himself above all that is called God,"* including *Allah* and any other name.

. . . so that he as God sitteth in the temple of God, shewing himself that he is God . . .

This is how we know the Temple is going to be rebuilt. Jesus, Paul, and John all make reference to it.[7] The Temple had been similarly desecrated previously, over two centuries before this. But it will happen again during the seven-year period known as the "Seventieth Week" of Daniel. This world leader, "The Man of Sin," the "Son of Perdition," commonly called the "Antichrist," is going to be an ecumenical world leader. He will be accepted by the Jews as their Messiah; he'll be accepted as the Twelfth Imam by the Muslims; he'll be the Leader of the World for a time. He will be incredibly attractive in every respect, and the whole world will worship him. But something else has to happen *first*.

And now ye know what [restraineth] that he might be revealed in his time. For the mystery of iniquity doth already work: only he who now [restraineth] will [restrain], until He be taken out of the way. And then shall that Wicked be revealed, whom the Lord shall consume with the spirit of his mouth, and shall destroy with the brightness of his coming. (2 Thessalonians 2:6-8)

Who is the Restrainer? The Greek structure points to a *person* as the Restrainer—the Holy Spirit as He embodies the Church. (Other conjectures have been suggested, but they do not fit the relevant texts.)

Let's get each of these events clearly laid out. When that Restrainer is removed (at the Rapture), *then* shall that Wicked One be revealed. The revealing of this Man of Sin is a prerequisite condition to the Day of the Lord; the removal of the Restrainer is a prerequisite to the revealing of the Man of Sin. The Apostasy is also a prerequisite to the Restraint being removed. First apostasy, then the Rapture, then the Man of Sin will be revealed, and only then does the "Day of the Lord" occur.

But Paul goes on about this Man of Sin:

Even him, whose coming is after the working of Satan with all power and signs and lying wonders, and with all deceivableness of unrighteousness in them that perish; because they received not the love of the truth, that they might be saved. And for this cause God shall send them strong delusion, that they should believe [the] lie. (2 Thessalonians 2:9-11)

This passage seems to indicate that those who *reject* the message of the Gospel before the Rapture will be especially susceptible to the Great Lie that will assure their destruction. So it is dangerous to say, "Well, I'll just wait and take my chances during the Tribulation." No, the time for salvation is now.

THE SECOND COMING CONTRASTED WITH THE RAPTURE

The list of all the primary passages having to do with the Second Coming is quite extensive.[8] These are passages that speak of the Second Coming in the sense of Jesus coming in power to take over the earth. There is another list of passages which appear to allude to a distinctively different event: the Rapture.[9] Rather than go through each of these individually, let's summarize them in contrast to one another:

Obviously, many good scholars hold different views. I feel that the Scripture clearly indicates that we're dealing with *two* distinct events. You need to study diligently and come to your own conclusions; but be sure to reconcile *all* the relevant Scriptures as you do so.

Rapture	*Second Coming*
Translation of believers	No translation involved
Translated saints go to heaven	Translated saints return to the earth with Him
Earth is not judged	Earth is judged
Imminent, could happen at any moment	Occurs after a period of seven years after many detailed events
Not in the Old Testament	Predicted in the Old Testament
Involves believers only	Involves all men and women on earth
Occurs before the day of wrath	Concludes the day of wrath
No reference to Satan	Satan is bound for 1,000 years
He comes *for* His own	He comes *with* His own
He comes in the air	He comes to the earth
He claims his Bride	He comes with his Bride
Only His own see Him	Every eye shall see Him
Great Tribulation begins	Millennium begins
Church age believers only	Old Testament saints raised after the millennium

THE GREAT TRIBULATION

There has been, of course, tribulation and oppression of believers throughout time. However, there will be a specific period of time called "the Great Tribulation" that is pivotal in understanding the final climactic conclusion of the era in which we live. It is defined by Jesus Himself:[10]

> For then shall be great tribulation, such as was not since the beginning of the world to this time, no, nor ever shall be. And except those days should be shortened, there should no flesh be saved: but for the elect's sake those days shall be shortened. (Matthew 24:21-22)

"The elect?" There are at least three different categories of believers: The Old Testament group closed with John the Baptist ("the Law and the Prophets were until John");[11] The

Church period is what we are in now. Then there will be those who will be saved after the Rapture; they are known among scholars as the Tribulation saints.

But there is something else rather provocative about Jesus's statement above. If you had read the above passage one hundred years ago, you would have been puzzled: How could man completely wipe himself out with bayonets and muskets?

But today, the cloud of self-destruction hangs over every geopolitical decision on the Planet Earth. Twenty-seven countries are presently building ICBMs (intercontinental ballistic missiles), and over a dozen have nuclear weapons. Technology is now available to wipe out all of mankind. Think of it—the Holocaust in Europe killed one Jew in three; the prophetic Scriptures indicate that the Tribulation will wipe out two out of three.[12] That is why Jeremiah calls it "the time of Jacob's trouble."[13] It will be worldwide, but focused on Israel.

> And at that time shall Michael stand up, the great prince which standeth for the children of thy people: and there shall be a time of trouble, such as never was since there was a nation even to that same time: and at that time thy people shall be delivered, every one that shall be found written in the book (Daniel 12:1).

God will bring them to desperation in this unprecedented time of oppression, and they will then petition Jesus for His return.[14]

Let's review the critical passage from Daniel 9 that we covered in Hour 9. Remember, verse 25 contained that astonishing prediction of the very day in which the Messiah presented Himself as the *Meshiach Nagid,* the Messiah the King.

Verse 26 described an interval between the sixty-ninth and the seventieth weeks which included the Crucifixion and the destruction of the city and sanctuary. We know that this interval included thirty-eight years; we have now experienced it as having lasted about two thousand years.

Verse 27, the final week, the so-called "Seventieth Week of Daniel," is that final week (of years) defined by the enforcement of a covenant for seven years by a coming world leader. However, in the middle of that seven-year period, he will become so powerful that he will set himself up to be worshiped with an event that has a specific title: the Abomination of Desolation. From the middle of that week to the end is definitively the Tribulation. Jesus labeled it that way. (So technically, the tribulation isn't seven years; it will be three and a half years.)

The Tribulation will climax with the Battle of Armageddon, which will be interrupted by the Second Coming of Jesus Christ and the establishment of His kingdom on the Planet

The Second Coming (a)

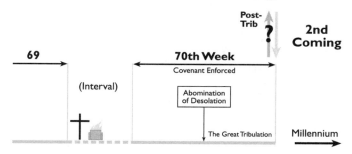

Earth and specific rule for one thousand years, as detailed in Revelation 20, Isaiah 65, and elsewhere.

THREE VIEWS

Obviously I am presenting the premillennial view, and within that are three variations of viewpoint: (a) those who believe the Rapture will occur before the Tribulation—these are called "pretribulationists"; (b) those who see it as occurring in the middle of the Tribulation—called "mid-tribulationists"; and (c) those who believe it will occur at the end or after the Tribulation—called "post-tribulationists."

Post-tribulationists

Post-tribulationists believe that the rapture occurs virtually coincident with the Second Coming. While it requires relegating numerous passages as simply symbols or allegories, this is the view of many denominations within the Church. This view results in many difficulties if one takes the Biblical text literally. Among the most serious is the issue of imminency. We are clearly taught to expect the return of the Lord at any moment. This view requires seven years of specifically detailed events to precede the Lord's return for the believers.

Another difficulty emerging from post-tribulationism is presence of the Church on the earth during the seventieth week. In several places the Church has been promised that it would not experience God's wrath,[15] which is an explicit aspect of the Tribulation.

There are other difficulties. How can the Bride come *with* Him? Who is going to populate the millennium if the saved are immortal and the unsaved are dealt with? How can the virgins of Matthew 25 buy oil without the Mark of the Beast?

The Second Coming (a)

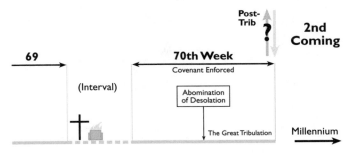

Mid-tribulationists

The mid-tribulationists, on the other hand, are technically correct on one point: they recognize that the Rapture occurs prior to the Tribulation but the Tribulation really starts in the middle of the week, which leads to the belief that the Rapture could occur in the middle of the week. But this view still puts the Church on the earth during the seventieth week of Daniel, which ignores the apparent mutual exclusiveness between the Church and Israel.

Pretribulationalists

The view which we have presented is that the Rapture occurs prior to, not just the Tribulation, but the entire seventieth week of Daniel.

(Incidentally, you may see many pre-tribulation charts that assume the Tribulation starts

The Second Coming (b)

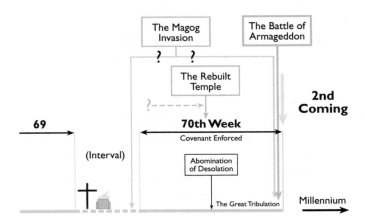

at the beginning of the seventieth week, but this is technically incorrect. The Tribulation is the last half—the last three and a half years—of the "week." What defines the seventieth week is the Antichrist enforcing a covenant. In order for him to do that, he has to be in power. In order to be in power, he has to be revealed. He can't be revealed until the Church has been removed.[16] So there is an interval between the Rapture and the beginning of the seventieth week, until he is strong enough to enforce the covenant. It could be one day, it could be thirty years. We don't know. Yet, the more we know about some of the prophecies, and the more we see what is going on in the world, the closer the Rapture seems to be.)

Let's summarize the above with an end-time order of events surrounding the Day of the Lord. First, the Church will become apostate. There will be a one-world ecumenical church, but it will be Satanic. The restrainer (the Holy Spirit) will be removed with his containers (the Church). And then the wicked one (the man of sin) will be revealed. He will enforce a covenant for seven years; but after three and a half years, he will establish himself as the center of worship with a specific event that will trigger what the Bible calls "the Great Tribulation." Believing Jews in Jerusalem will flee to the mountains of Edom. This ultimately climaxes with the Battle of Armageddon which will be interrupted by the Second Coming of our Lord Jesus Christ to establish His reign on the earth.

Those of us who hold a pre-tribulational and premillennial point of view believe that Jesus will come back twice: once for his Church; once for Israel.

PRETRIBULATIONALISM IN HISTORY

Some people believe the pretribulational view is of recent origin, but that is not true. You'll find this viewpoint in the history of the early church.[17]

ENOCH AND THE RAPTURE

The Hebrew *Midrash* emphasizes that "prophecy is pattern not just prediction." So let's examine the judgments of God in the Scripture. There were three groups of people who faced the judgment God at the Flood of Noah:

1. Those who perished in the Flood;
2. Those who were preserved through the Flood in the Ark;
3. Those who were removed prior to the Flood.

The one removed was Enoch. You say, "Well, that's just one person." Yes, but the Body of Christ in the Scripture is also treated as one. There are many members but one body. Paul says it that way. And that will come up when we study the Book of the Revelation.

(It is interesting that there is a Hebrew tradition that Enoch was born on the day they presently celebrate as the Feast of Pentecost; furthermore, they also believe he was "translated" ("raptured") on his birthday. Is it possible that the church will also be raptured on its birthday?)

This brings us to the problem of date setting. Throughout history various people have been convinced that Jesus was coming back at a certain date. These have included: Joachim of Flores, 1260; Militz of Kromeriz, 1365; Joseph Mede, 1660; John Napier (the famous mathematician), 1688; Pierre Jurieu of France, 1689; William Whitson, 1715 (then 1734; then 1866); J. A. Bengal, 1836; Joseph Worlf, 1847; William Miller, 1843 (then Oct. 22, 1844); C. T. Russell, 1874; E. C. Whisenant's "88 reasons for 1988"; Harold Camping, September 1994; and they continue.

The Lord said,

But of that day and hour knoweth no man, no, not the angels of heaven, not the Son, but my Father only" (Mark 13:32).

"Watch therefore: for ye know not what hour your Lord doth come" (Matthew 24:42).

"Therefore be ye also ready: for in such an hour as ye think not the Son of man cometh" (Matthew 24:44).

"Watch therefore, for ye know neither the day nor the hour wherein the Son of man cometh" (Matthew 25:13).

"Be ye therefore ready also: for the Son of man cometh at an hour when ye think not" (Luke 12:40).

And he said unto them, 'It is not for you to know the times or the seasons, which the Father hath put in his own power.' (Acts 1:7).

How many times does He need to say this?

Signs of the Times

There is an old seaman's proverb:

> Red sky at night, sailor's delight;
> Red sky in the morning, sailor take warning.

This was a well-known proverb even in Jesus' day. He quoted it to the Pharisees and Sadducees, and then chided them that they could discern the face of the sky, but could not discern the signs of the times!

If that was true then, how much more, for us, today!

I believe that you and I are being plunged into a period of time about which the Bible says more than it does about any other period of time in human history—including the time that Jesus walked the shores of Galilee and climbed the mountains of Judea!

That is, intentionally, a rather preposterous statement. It is my earnest desire for you to *challenge* it! To do that, you need to do two things:

1. Find out what the Bible says about the end times;

2. Find out what is really going on.

The first challenge is direct, and you have already begun by this review. The second is bit more difficult; you won't find out on the ten o'clock news! But with the alternative media, talk radio, and, above all, the Internet, you can easily find out what is really happening anywhere and everywhere. Here are some things to watch for:

- *The Magog Invasion:* The Russian invasion of the Middle East.[18]

- *The Rebuilding of the Temple.* Seven different groups are pushing for the rebuilding of the Temple. We know that it is going to be rebuilt because Jesus, Paul, and John all make reference to it.[19]

- *The Rebuilding of Babylon.* Saddam Hussein has made a modest start. Isaiah and Jeremiah each refer to a real Babylon being destroyed, like Sodom and Gomorrah, which has yet to happen.[20]

- *The Rise of a European Superstate.*[21]

- ***The Battle of Armageddon.*** The battle of Armageddon is at the climax of the seven-year period and is interrupted by the Second Coming. The four major world powers will participate.[22]

- ***The Refuge in Edom.*** The believing remnant in Israel will flee to Edom (modern Jordan), the one place that escapes the rule of the Antichrist.[23]

CONCLUSION

Our challenge to you is to be like the Bereans:

> These were more noble than those in Thessalonica, in that they received the word with all readiness of mind, but searched the scriptures daily, to prove whether those things were so. (Acts 17:11)

This is where Luke tells you not to believe anything that Chuck Missler tells you; but rather, with an open mind, search the Scriptures daily, to prove whether those things be so! Then find out what is going on in China, Europe, the Middle East, and around the world, and form your own conclusions.

Hour 22

REVELATION 1-3
LETTERS TO SEVEN CHURCHES

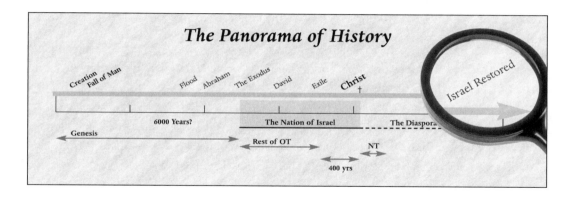

IN THIS HOUR, we will explore the Church in prophecy by examining the first three chapters of one of the most awesome books in the entire Bible. (The Book of Acts covers the first thirty years; these three chapters in the Book of Revelation cover the next two thousand.) Many places in the Bible admonish you, in general, to read the Word of God. But only this book has the audacity to say, "Read me, I'm special." We are going to claim that special promise as a student of this unique book.

In the Old Testament we have Christ in Prophecy. In the Gospels, Christ in History. In Acts, Christ in the Church. In the epistles, Christ in Our Experience. In the apocalypse we have Christ in His Coming Glory.

The Old Testament says, "Behold He comes." The New Testament Gospels say, "Behold He died." Acts says, "Behold He lives." The epistles say, "Behold He saves." But the Book of Revelation says, "Behold He reigns."

The word "Revelation" is the *Apocalypsis,* which means "the unveiling." The word is singular: It is *the* revelation. It is *the* unveiling. It is the unveiling of Jesus Christ; and it will come as a surprise to many to discover who He really is!

The book's 404 verses contain over eight hundred allusions from the Old Testament. If it seems strange to us, it is simply because we haven't done enough homework in the Old Testament. It presents the climax of God's plan for mankind. And it is the consummation of all things. Everything that was begun in Genesis finds its consummation in Revelation.

So let's take a look at the first verse:

"The Revelation of Jesus Christ, which God gave unto him ..."

This was a presentation *to* Jesus Christ. Because He did not know some things during His ministry (such as the time of the Second Coming),[1] some scholars suspect that He came into His full knowledge at this time.

> . . . to show unto his servants things which must shortly come to pass; and he sent and signified it by his angel unto his servant John: who bare record of the word of God, and of the testimony of Jesus Christ, and of all things that he saw. (Revelation. 1:1-2)

We will see, in his text, the things John saw, but which he rendered them into signs, or codes (*sememes*), each of which is explained somewhere in the Scriptures. It is, thus, one of the most illuminating illustrations of the integrity of the entire Bible. And it is the most exciting treasure hunt imaginable to search each of these out. One of the most exciting projects you can undertake is a study of the Book of Revelation. With a good concordance you can track down every allusion, every phrase that sounds strange, and find out where in the Scripture it is explained. Nothing will give you a greater appreciation, a more complete grasp of the integrity of the sixty-six books of the Bible, than doing a diligent study of this book.

> Blessed is he that readeth, and they that hear the words of this prophecy, and keep those things which are written therein: for the time is at hand. (Revelation 1:3)

No other book of the Bible has this kind of promise. Then it continues:

John to the seven churches which are in Asia:

> Grace be unto you, and peace, from him which is, and which was, and which is to come [three tenses—past, present and future]; and from the seven Spirits which are before his throne; and from Jesus Christ, who is the faithful witness, and the first begotten of the dead, and the prince of the kings of the earth. Unto him that loved us, and washed us from our sins in his own blood, and hath made us kings and priests unto God and his Father; to him be glory and dominion forever and ever. Amen. (Revelation 1:4-5)

The Trinity is mentioned here: "From him which was, and is, and is to come" is obviously God the Father. And we have Jesus Christ, "the faithful witness." But there is also this strange phrase in the middle—"the seven spirits which are before his throne"—which is an Old Testament idiom for the seven-fold Holy Spirit as referenced in Isaiah 11:2:

1. And the Spirit of the YHWH shall rest upon him,

2. the Spirit of Wisdom,

3. and Spirit of Understanding,

4. the Spirit of Counsel,

5. the Spirit of Might,

6. the Spirit of Knowledge,

7. and the Spirit of the Fear of the LORD.

Also notice verse 5: "Unto him that loved us, and washed us from our sins in his own blood, and hath made us kings and priests unto God and his Father; to him be glory and dominion forever and ever. Amen." Angels are not kings and priests; only the redeemed are kings and priests. This will prove important later.

Chapter one is a vision of the risen Christ, with numerous descriptive allusions drawn from the Old Testament: The description of His hair is from Daniel 7:9; His eyes as a flame of fire from Hebrews 1 and 4; His feet are brass, speaking of judgment and referencing the brazen serpent in Numbers 21; His voice is like many waters, from Ezekiel 1 and 43, and Daniel 10. These are all familiar labels from the Old Testament.

In His right hand are seven stars, and He is also seen in the midst of the seven lampstands. Both the seven stars and the seven lampstands are idioms for the Church.[2] Out of his mouth comes a two-edged sword which is an idiom for the Word of God.[3] These poetic and majestic idioms are all drawn from elsewhere in the Scripture, and for the rest of the book these descriptors will be used as identifiers of Jesus Christ.

The Book of Revelation also includes a divinely given outline of itself to the reader. Jesus says to John,

> Write the things which thou hast seen, the things which are, and the things which shall be hereafter. (Revelation 1:19)

These are the three major divisions of the Book. "The things which thou has seen" is the vision just seen in earlier in Chapter 1.

"The things which are" are the letters by Jesus Christ to the seven churches in Chapters two and three. These epistles are often overlooked, yet are among the most important letters in the entire Bible. The Lord Himself dictated them to the seven churches.

Chapter four begins "the things which shall be hereafter;" in other words, those things which will follow *after* the church. (Chapter 4:1 starts with the phrase *meta tauta,* "after these things," which signals this major division.)

In all of Revelation, the two chapters most important for us today are the ones most often overlooked—chapters two and three. At the end of chapter one, Jesus himself says,

> The mystery of the seven stars which thou sawest in my right hand, and the seven golden lampstands. The seven stars are the angels of the seven churches: and the seven lampstands which thou sawest are the seven churches.
>
> *Revelation 1:20*

These idioms speak of a church, as a lampstand, bearing light. In chapter four these lamps will be in Heaven.[4]

THE SEVEN CHURCHES

Why did Jesus pick *these* seven churches to write letters to? The seven churches are Ephesus, Smyrna, Pergamus, Thyatira, Sardis, Philadelphia, and Laodicea. There are several dozen others he might have picked. Where's the church in Jerusalem? The church at Rome? The church in Antioch? Why these seven? For one thing, in the Bible, seven implies completeness. These seven, somehow, are completely representative of the Church in total. The degree to which they are *anticipatory* is astonishing!

There are at least four levels of understanding within these seven letters. The first is local: These were actual churches. Sir William Ramsey researched each of these and discovered these letters were related to real problems in those churches at that time. There was a local, immediate application.

> *Sir William Ramsey researched each of these and discovered these letters were related to real problems in those churches at that time.*

Second, the letters are also admonitions for all churches in general. In each letter, the Holy Sprit concludes with a repeated catchphrase,

He that hath an ear let him hear what the spirit says to the church(es).

Note the plural: In other words, each church should pay attention to what was said to each of the other churches. Each letter applies to every church to some extent.

Third, there is a homiletic (personal) application of each letter to each of us. "He that hath an ear, let him hear . . ." means everyone who has an ear: That's each of us!

And fourth, most astonishingly, these letters lay out, in advance, the history of the Church. The book of Acts covers about thirty years. The book of Revelation extends the book of Acts for the next two thousand years. If these letters were in *any other order* than the one presented, they would not fit the historical model. (In this particular order, they fill that gap, that interval in Daniel 9:26, between the sixty-ninth and seventieth weeks.)

Within each of the seven letters are seven design elements:

The name of the church: Each church name proves to be significant to its particular unique message.

The title of Christ chosen: Jesus will select a title, from those listed in chapter one, to represent Himself to each church, a title characteristic for the unique letter.

*A **commendation***: Some good news;

*His **concerns***: the bad news;

*An **exhortation***: what to correct;

*A **promise to the overcomer***. (this will proved to be an interesting structural element.)

The close (a structural closing phrase): "He that hath an ear, let him hear what the Spirit says to the seven churches."

Every detail will prove important; even the placement of the closing phrase will prove illuminating.

The Church at Ephesus

The word Ephesus means "my darling," or "the desired one."

> Unto the angel of the church of Ephesus write;
> These things saith he that holdeth the seven stars in his right hand, who walketh in the midst of the seven golden lamp stands;
> I know thy works, and thy labor, and thy patience, and how thou canst not bear them which are evil: and thou hast tried them which say they are apostles, and are not, and hast found them liars: And hast borne, and hast patience, and for my name's sake hast labored, and hast not fainted. (Revelation 2:1-3)

In Acts 20, when Paul was on his way back to Jerusalem, he didn't go through Ephesus itself because the crowd would be too big. He went to Miletus on the other side of the peninsula and let the elders come to meet him. There he gave them his farewell address. But he warned them to be on the alert for false doctrine and false teaching. Apparently they heeded that admonition because Jesus here compliments them on their diligence; they did well in that regard. But then there is this horrible word, *nevertheless.*

Nevertheless, I have somewhat against thee, because thou hast left thy first love. (Revelation 2:4)

They got so busy doing the work of the Kingdom that they didn't have time for the King! The weak link here was their devotional life. (Is that also true of *us*?) So Jesus gives them an exhortation.

Remember therefore from whence thou art fallen, and repent, and do the first works; or else I will come unto thee quickly, and will remove thy lamp stand out of his place, except thou repent.

But this thou hast, that thou hatest the deeds of the Nicolaitans, which I also hate. (Revelation 2:5-6)

Who were the Nicolaitanes? It's an untranslated word: but *nicao* means "to rule over," and *laitans* are the laity, the common people. It means "ruling over the common people." The idea of the clergy over the laity was introduced in the organizational church. However, Jesus taught us about His organizational concepts when He washed the disciples' feet. "He who will be the greatest ought to be the servant."[5] Then we encounter this little closing code phrase:

He that hath an ear, let him hear what the Spirit saith unto the churches.

And then we come to the promise to the overcomer:

To him that overcometh will I give to eat of the tree of life, which is in the midst of the paradise of God. (Revelation 2:7)

In this letter, the promise to the overcomer is a postscript, a tag after the closing phrase that closes the letter proper. This is true of the first three letters, but we will notice that there is a strange design change in the last four letters; in fact, several aspects of the last four letters are distinctively different from the first three.

The Church at Smyrna

The word *Smyrna* means "myrrh," an aromatic embalming ointment; the name *myrrh* thus suggests death. When the Magi gave the three different gifts to the baby Jesus in accordance with the secret prophecy that Daniel had conveyed some five centuries earlier, they gave gold as an emblem for His deity, frankincense for His priesthood, and myrrh for His death.

The very name Smyrna, myrrh, tells us, up front, this will be to the persecuted church.

And unto the angel of the church in Smyrna write; These things saith the first and the last, which was dead, and is alive; I know thy works, and tribulation, and poverty, (but thou art rich) and I know the blasphemy of them which say they are Jews, and are not, but are the synagogue of Satan. (Revelation 2:8, 9)

This letter is to a suffering church. That's why Jesus chose an identity of Himself that would be precious to them: "These things saith the first and the last, which was dead and is alive." That's an encouragement to those facing death. "I know thy works of tribulation and poverty." Yes, they are going through all kinds of tribulation and persecution.

"I know the blasphemy of them that say that they are Jews but they are not." Some people say the promises which God made to Israel were forfeited because Israel rejected her Messiah, and that the church has now replaced Israel. However, the promises in question were unconditional! Israel couldn't forfeit them if she tried. So, beware of the blasphemy of those non-Jews who would deny God's expressed commitments to His chosen people. The idea that the Church has replaced Israel would make God a liar! (This is a widespread controversy; study it diligently for yourself, discerning the distinctiveness of both Israel and the Church in God's program.)

His exhortation:

Fear none of those things which thou shalt suffer:
Behold, the devil shall cast some of you into prison, that ye may be tried; and ye shall have tribulation ten days: be thou faithful unto death, and I will give thee a crown of life. He that hath an ear, let him hear what the Spirit saith unto the churches; He that overcometh shall not be hurt of the second death. (Revelation 2:10, 11)

Death and life is all through this letter. Again, the promise to the overcomer is an add-on, after the catchphrase, "He that hath an ear . . ." He that overcometh shall not be hurt of the second death." Jesus is encouraging them in their trials. (He that is born once, dies twice; he that is born twice, dies once.)

The Church at Pergamos

The first clue to the significance of this letter is the name Pergamos; it means "mixed marriage." Pergamos was a perverted marriage.

278

The "Ten Days"?

It has been suggested that the persecution of the early church happened in ten distinct periods:

1. *Nero* A.D. *54-68; beheaded Paul, crucified Peter upside down.*

2. *Domitian* A.D. *95-96; who exiled John to Patmos, where he wrote this letter.*

3. *Trajan* A.D. *104-117; Ignacious was burned at the stake.*

4. *Marcus Aurelius* A.D. *161-180; Polycarp was martyred on the Sabbath and burned at the stake.*

5. *Septimus Severus,* A.D. *200-211.*

6. *Maximus,* A.D. *235-237.*

7. *Decius,* A.D. *249-251.*

8. *Velarian,* A.D. *257-260.*

9. *Aurelian,* A.D. *270-275.*

10. *Diocletian* A.D. *303-313; the worst of the bunch.*

And to the angel of the church in Pergamos write; These things saith he which hath the sharp sword with two edges; I know thy works, and where thou dwellest, even where Satan's seat is: and thou holdest fast my name, and hast not denied my faith, even in those days wherein Antipas was my faithful martyr, who was slain among you, where Satan dwelleth. But I have a few things against thee, because thou hast there them that hold the doctrine of Balaam, who taught Balac to cast a stumblingblock before the children of Israel, to eat things sacrificed unto idols, and to commit fornication. So hast thou also them that hold the doctrine of the Nicolaitans, which thing I hate. Repent; or else I will come unto thee quickly, and will fight against them with the sword of my mouth. (Revelation 2:12-16)

Jesus is alluding to the Old Testament story of Balaam, a prophet for hire. Balac, the enemy king, was trying to figure out a way to conquer Israel, so he hired Balaam to advise him. Balaam told him that God would support Israel so long as they were faithful; so to conquer them, he had to lead them to unfaithfulness and God would then turn His hand against them. In other words, he advised Balac to cast a stumbling block before the children of Israel.

Balaam's strategy in the Old Testament was characteristic of what was going on in Pergamos: the church was beginning to marry the world.

Also, the "deeds" of the Nicolaitans had become "doctrine." The remedy for all these concerns was to return to the Word of God.

> He that hath an ear, let him hear what the Spirit saith unto the churches; To him that overcometh will I give to eat of the hidden manna, and will give him a white stone, and in the stone a new name written, which no man knoweth saving he that receiveth it. (Revelation 2:17)

Again, the promise to the overcomer, glorious though it is, is an appendage *after* the closing catchphrase.

The Church at Thyatira

At one time this town was named Semiramis, who was the consort of Nimrod, the first world dictator.

> And unto the angel of the church in Thyatira write; These things saith the Son of God, who hath his eyes like unto a flame of fire, and his feet are like fine brass; I know thy works, and charity, and service, and faith, and thy patience, and thy works; and the last to be more than the first. (Revelation 2:18, 19)

They have done some good things, but they also have some problems:

> Notwithstanding I have a few things against thee, because thou sufferest that woman Jezebel, which calleth herself a prophetess, to teach and to seduce my servants to commit fornication, and to eat things sacrificed unto idols. (Revelation 2:20)

Again, an idiom from the Old Testament: Queen Jezebel was bad news. She introduced idol worship into Israel. (False worship is always termed a form of spiritual fornication.) After the great standoff between Elijah and the priests of Jezebel on Mt. Carmel, when the Lord demonstrated who was really God, Elijah slaughtered the priests of Jezebel.

> And I gave her space to repent of her fornication; and she repented not.
>
> Behold, I will cast her into a bed, and them that commit adultery with her into great tribulation, except they repent of their deeds. And I will kill her children with death; and all the churches shall know that I am he which searcheth the reins and hearts: and I will give unto every one of you according to your works. (Revelation 2:21-23)

In 1 Kings 21, King Ahab wanted a vineyard that belonged to a Naboth, but Naboth didn't want to sell. Ahab was upset, so Queen Jezebel arranged an inquisition and bribed everyone to lie so that Naboth was condemned and executed. Then she took the property for the king. Does that procedure sound familiar? Like the practices the Medieval Church indulged in during the Inquisition?

> But unto you I say, and unto the rest in Thyatira, as many as have not this doctrine, and which have not known the depths of Satan, as they speak; I will put upon you none other burden.
>
> But that which ye have already hold fast till I come.
>
> And he that overcometh, and keepeth my works unto the end, to him will I give power over the nations: and he shall rule them with a rod of iron; as the vessels of a potter shall they be broken to shivers: even as I received of my Father. And I will give him the morning star. (Revelation 2:24-28)

One of this representative church's problems was a desire for temporal power. Does that summarize the history of the medieval church in European history?

> He that hath an ear, let him hear what the Spirit saith unto the churches. (Revelation 2:29)

Two things distinguish this letter (in fact, the last four letters) from the previous three. First, it has an explicit reference to His Second Coming: "till I come." But also, the promise to the overcomer is brought into the body of the letter.

Bear in mind, we believe there is no detail, no number, no place name, no subtlety, in the original text, that isn't there by the deliberate design of the Holy Spirit.

The Church at Sardis

The name *Sardis* means "remnant."

And unto the angel of the church in Sardis write; These things saith he that hath the seven Spirits of God, and the seven stars;

I know thy works, that thou hast a name that thou livest, and art dead. (Revelation 3:1)

The word *name* will appear all through this letter. This church seems to be the denominational church.

> *If you are caught by surprise, you are not doing the will of God. He desires for you to expect Him at any moment.*

Be watchful, and strengthen the things which remain, that are ready to die: for I have not found thy works perfect before God.

Remember therefore how thou hast received and heard, and hold fast, and repent. If therefore thou shalt not watch, I will come on thee as a thief, and thou shalt not know what hour I will come upon thee. (Revelation 3:2-3)

Apparently, if they repent, they *won't* be caught by surprise. They still won't know the day or the hour, but they won't be surprised. If you are caught by surprise, you are not doing the will of God. He desires for you to expect Him at any moment.

Thou hast a few names even in Sardis which have not defiled their garments; and they shall walk with me in white: for they are worthy.

He that overcometh, the same shall be clothed in white raiment; and I will not blot out his name out of the book of life, but I will confess his name before my Father, and before his angels.

He that hath an ear, let him hear what the Spirit saith unto the churches. (Revelation 3:4-6)

Again, the promise to the overcomers is in the body of the letter, included *before* the closing phrase.

The Church at Philadelphia

Every church believes they are the Philadelphians. The word means "brotherly love."

And to the angel of the church in Philadelphia write; These things saith he that is holy, he that is true, he that hath the key of David, he that openeth, and no man shutteth; and shutteth, and no man openeth;

I know thy works: behold, I have set before thee an open door, and no man can shut it: for thou hast a little strength, and hast kept my word, and hast not denied my name.

Behold, I will make them of the synagogue of Satan, which say they are Jews, and are not, but do lie; behold, I will make them to come and worship before thy feet, and to know that I have loved thee.

Because thou hast kept the word of my patience, I also will keep thee from the hour of trial, which shall come upon all the world, to try them that dwell upon the earth. (Revelation 3:7-10)

Verse 10 is a key verse for all of us. There are two groups of people in the Book of Revelation: Those who get caught up to heaven, and those who are "earth dwellers." The earth dwellers do not just live on the earth; their focus and orientation is earthly. These are the lost. There will come an hour of trial upon all the world to try them that dwell upon the earth. This is the Great Tribulation, the last half of the Seventieth Week of Daniel. The promise to this particular church is that they will be kept, not from tribulation, but the *hour* of tribulation. In other words, they aren't protected *through* the trials; they won't even be around.

"Behold, I come quickly: hold that fast which thou hast, that no man take thy crown" (3:11). You can't lose your salvation,[6] but you can lose your rewards. Be diligent.

Him that overcometh will I make a pillar in the temple of my God, and he shall go no more out: and I will write upon him the name of my God, and the name of the city of my God, which is new Jerusalem, which cometh down out of heaven from my God: and I will write upon him my new name.

He that hath an ear, let him hear what the Spirit saith unto the churches. (Revelation 3:12-13)

Here again, "promise to the overcomer" is within the body of the letter.

The Church at Laodicea

Laodicea means "the rule of the people." That's an interesting phrase. Many churches across the country are doing market research, trying to make their pulpits "user-friendly." and the message of the Church more palpable to the easily offended. But we are called to preach the Gospel. What is the Gospel? How Christ died for our sins according to Scripture, that He was buried, that He rose again, according to the Scriptures.[7]

Jesus Christ is to rule the Church; here we have the people running things instead of God.

And unto the angel of the church of the Laodiceans write; These things saith the Amen, the faithful and true witness, the beginning of the creation of God; I know thy works, that thou art neither cold nor hot: I would thou wert cold or hot. So then because thou art lukewarm, and neither cold nor hot, I will spew thee out of my mouth.

Because thou sayest, I am rich, and increased with goods, and have need of nothing; and knowest not that thou art wretched, and miserable, and poor, and blind, and naked:

I counsel thee to buy of me gold tried in the fire, that thou mayest be rich; and white raiment, that thou mayest be clothed, and that the shame of thy nakedness do not appear; and anoint thine eyes with eyesalve, that thou mayest see.

As many as I love, I rebuke and chasten: be zealous therefore, and repent. (Revelation 3:14-19)

Even though they have fancy cathedrals and much worldly goods, they are actually poor, blind and naked.

The next verse is one of the most quoted verses, but we have all heard it out of context.

Behold, I stand at the door, and knock: if any man hear my voice, and open the door, I will come in to him, and will sup with him, and he with me. (Revelation 3:20)

That's a wonderful verse, but read it in its *context* and it's a disturbing indictment: Where is Jesus with respect to this church? "Behold I stand at the door." He's out there. He is outside, trying to get in. And the promise isn't to the church; it's to the individual inside this church. "If any of you hear my voice, and open the door, I will come into him and sup with him and he with Me (individually)."

To him that overcometh will I grant to sit with me in my throne, even as I also overcame, and am set down with my Father in his throne.

He that hath an ear, let him hear what the Spirit saith unto the churches. (Revelation 3:21-22)

CHARACTERISTICS OF THE CHURCH LETTERS

Although we've only skimmed the surface of these carefully crafted letters, we notice some provocative patterns. For instance, only five of the seven were commended; two had nothing good said about them. Five of the seven were admonished; two had nothing bad said about them. It is extremely provocative that *every one of them* were surprised: those that thought they were doing well were not. Those that thought they were not doing well, were doing better than they thought. All of them were exhorted to improve.

And, in this particular order they profile the history of the church through the ages:

- **Ephesus** describes the apostolic Church; diligent, but neglected their devotional life.

- **Smyrna** fits the Church when persecutions began. Nothing negative was said about it; just "hang in there."

- **Pergamos** fits the Church that was married to the world under Constantine. His successors would make it the official state religion, which was disastrous spiritually.

- **Thyatira** introduced idolatry in the medieval Church, which became codified in the Roman Catholic Church. It carries an express threat of being cast into the Great Tribulation.

- **Sardis** seems to fit the Reformation and the start of denominationalism. But notice that Sardis is one of the seven that had nothing good said about it.

- **Philadelphia** is the glorious Church, the missionary Church declaring the blood of Christ. It has an express promise of being removed prior to the time of the Tribulation.

- **Laodicea** is the apostate Church.

Prophetic Profile?

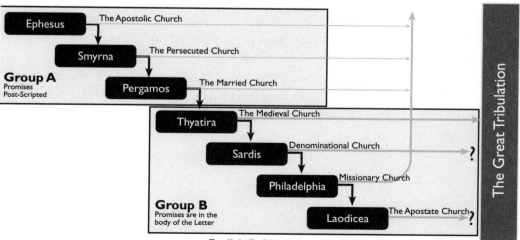

Explicit References to His Second Coming

In the first three letters, the promise to overcome is an addendum. The same promise is within the body of the last four. The last four letters are also distinctive in that they have an explicit reference to the Second Coming of Christ. So one of the possibilities is that the last four letters relate to churches alive when the Lord returns, and the first three, while historical, will have passed from the scene.

The Great Tribulation ends the life of the last four churches. The medieval church, Thyatira, is warned that if she doesn't repent, she will be thrown into the Great Tribulation. Philadelphia is promised that she will be kept from the time of the tribulation. No comment is made about the denominational church, Sardis, or the apostate church, Laodicea. One would imply that, in the absence of repenting, they too will endure the Great Tribulation, which will be characterized by a great ecumenical (but apostate) movement.

CONCLUSION

New believers will often ask, "Where should I start when studying the Bible?" There are several choices, but I often advise a new believer to undertake a serious study of the Book of Revelation. With your pastor, a good commentary, or just a concordance and a verse-by-verse study, the Book of Revelation will take you virtually into every book of the Bible—if you do it thoroughly. It will give you a strategic grasp of the Bible in its entirety like nothing else will.

The Holy Spirit promises you a special blessing if you read this book. So if you are reading your Bible, and don't know where to turn, read and study the book of Revelation. You are guaranteed a specific blessing.

When you finish that, go back to the Book of Genesis and notice how it, too, will come to life more than ever before.

In the meantime, let's take a glimpse of the rest of this fascinating book which will now layout the climax of God's dealing with the Planet Earth.

Hour 23

REVELATION 4–22
THE CONSUMMATION
OF ALL THINGS

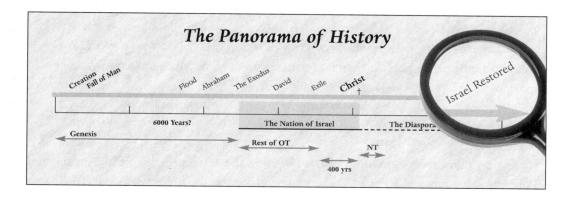

IN THIS HOUR we will explore the rest of the Book of Revelation. From chapter four on are the "things which shall be hereafter," that is, the future after the churches.

> After this I looked, and, behold, a door was opened in heaven: and the first voice which I heard was as it were of a trumpet talking with me; which said, Come up hither, and I will show thee things which must be hereafter.
>
> ... and there were seven lamps of fire burning before the throne. (Revelation 4:1, 5)

John is caught up into Heaven and into the throne room of the universe. He will be treated to a preview of the final consummation of all things.

Two things in that throne room are extremely significant: the lamp stands and the twenty-four Elders. The seven lamps of fire, which Jesus has identified as the churches which were on the earth in chapter one, are now before the throne in chapter four. Another prominent feature in chapter four is the appearance of the twenty-four Elders. These twenty-four Elders identify themselves as the kings and priests of the redeemed.

The Elders are standing on the sea of glass, which seems to correlate with the "molten sea," the laver in the Tabernacle and in the Temple. It represents the Word of God: when we were on the earth, we washed in it;[1] here, the saints are *standing on it.* (Yes, the Holy Spirit does deal in puns!)[2]

We also encounter "the four living creatures," the same cherubim we encountered in Ezekiel and Isaiah. They have the same four faces—the lion, the calf, the man, and the eagle.

Concerning the twenty-four Elders: the number twenty-four occurs in only one other instance in Scripture—when David organized the priesthood into twenty-four courses, or twenty-four divisions. And, fortunately, the twenty-four Elders also identify themselves:

> And they sung a new song, saying, Thou art worthy to take the book, and to open the seals thereof: for thou wast slain, and hast redeemed us to God by thy blood out of every kindred, and tongue, and people, and nation;
>
> And hast made us unto our God kings and priests: and we shall reign on the earth. (Revelation 5:9-10)

It is clear that these twenty-four Elders represent the redeemed. Only three personages in the Bible are kings *and* priests: Melchizedek,[3] the Messiah, and His redeemed.[4] The Elders represent the church in heaven.

Notice the sequence: the tribulation doesn't start until the Seven-sealed Scroll is opened. The Lamb doesn't receive the Seven-sealed Scroll until the Elders place their crowns on the glassy sea. And the Elders are obviously in heaven when that happens. Therefore, the church is in heaven *before* the wrath of God is poured out.

THE SEVEN-SEALED SCROLL

Chapter five has the biggest escrow closing in history: the Seven-sealed Scroll. John says,

And I saw in the right hand of him that sat on the throne a scroll written within and on the backside, sealed with seven seals. (Revelation 5:1)

From Jeremiah and other places, we know this as a title deed. The requirements to redeem a title deed were written on the outside. This seven-sealed scroll is the title deed to the earth.

And I saw a strong angel proclaiming with a loud voice, Who is worthy to open the scroll, and to loose the seals thereof?

And no man in heaven, nor in earth, neither under the earth, was able to open the scroll, neither to look thereon. And I wept much, because no man was found worthy to open and to read the scroll, neither to look thereon. (Revelation 5:2, 3)

The Book of Ruth clarifies that only a *Goel*, a kinsman redeemer, could redeem the land. Adam had forfeited his dominion of the Planet Earth, and John sobbed convulsively because no "man" (a kinsman) could be found qualified to redeem the deed. But, fortunately, Someone was found who was qualified, able, and willing.

And one of the elders saith unto me, Weep not: behold, the Lion of the tribe of Judah, the Root of David, hath prevailed to open the book, and to loose the seven seals thereof.

And I beheld, and, lo, in the midst of the throne and of the four living creatures, and in the midst of the elders, stood the Lamb as it had been slain, having seven horns and seven eyes, which are the seven Spirits of God sent forth into all the earth. (Revelation 5:5, 6)

The number seven represents completeness. Horns represent authority. Eyes represent perception. And all that is enabled by the Seven Spirits of God, the Old Testament idiom for the Holy Spirit.[5]

The sequential opening of the seven seals initiates a series of judgments: seven seals followed by seven trumpet judgments, and then seven bowls (or vials) are poured out, climaxing with the Lord Himself interrupting the Battle of Armageddon.

First Seal

As Jesus opens each seal, certain dramatic things happen. He opens the first seal:

And I saw, and behold a white horse: and he that sat on him had a bow; and a crown was given unto him: and he went forth conquering, and to conquer. (Revelation 6:2)

Many commentators jump to the conclusion that because the rider is on a white horse, he is one of the good guys, perhaps Jesus Himself. If this is Jesus Christ, He is traveling in bad company. We opt with those conservative commentators who see this first seal, the white horseman, as a *false* Christ. This is the World Leader coming forth (commonly called, "the Antichrist").

And he has a bow, but not a bow and arrow. The Greek word for *bow* used here is only used one other place: it is a token of a covenant.[6] The bow here could be the token of the very covenant which defines the Seventieth Week of Daniel.[7]

Second Seal

> And when he had opened the second seal, I heard the second living creature say, Come and see.
>
> And there went out another horse that was red: and power was given to him that sat thereon to take peace from the earth, and that they should kill one another: and there was given unto him a great sword. (Revelation 6:3-4)

The red horseman seems to echo "the wars and rumors of wars" which Jesus spoke of in His confidential briefing to His disciples.[8]

Third Seal

> And when he had opened the third seal, I heard the third living creature say, Come and see.
>
> And I beheld, and lo a black horse; and he that sat on him had a pair of balances in his hand. And I heard a voice in the midst of the four living creatures say, A measure of wheat for a penny, and three measures of barley for a penny; and see thou hurt not the oil and the wine. (Revelation 6:5-6)

Most commentators recognize this represents famine, but many don't realize how the famine is being caused—by inflation. (Most famines are not caused by a shortage of resources, but by political manipulation.)

Fourth Seal

> And when he had opened the fourth seal, I heard the voice of the fourth living creature say, Come and see.
>
> And I looked, and behold a pale horse: and his name that sat on him was Death, and Hell followed with him. And power was given unto them over the fourth part of the earth, to kill with sword, and with hunger, and with death, and with the beasts of the earth. (Revelation 6:7-8)

Don't presume that the "beasts of the earth" are necessarily four-footed mammals. They might be beasts you see under a microscope. They could even be some biological pestilence being cultivated as a terrorist weapon.

> *Don't presume that the "beasts of the earth" are necessarily four-footed mammals. They might be beasts you see under a microscope.*

Fifth Seal

And when he had opened the fifth seal, I saw under the altar the souls of them that were slain for the word of God, and for the testimony which they held: and they cried with a loud voice, saying, How long, O Lord, holy and true, dost thou not judge and avenge our blood on them that dwell on the earth?

And white robes were given unto every one of them; and it was said unto them, that they should rest yet for a little season, until their fellow servants also, and their brethren, that should be killed as they were, should be fulfilled. (Revelation 6:9-11)

All through the book of Revelation, we will read about "those that dwell on the earth." The earth dwellers are those who are not saved. They are the losers. They are the adversaries of God's program. In contrast, the remnant is saved. But we see the souls of the martyrs who have been, and will continue to be killed, during this period for the sake of the Gospel.

Sixth Seal

And I beheld when he had opened the sixth seal, and, lo, there was a great earthquake; and the sun became black as sackcloth of hair, and the moon became as blood; And the stars of heaven fell unto the earth:

And the heaven departed as a scroll when it is rolled together; and every mountain and island were moved out of their places.

And the kings of the earth, and the great men, and the rich men, hid themselves in the dens and in the rocks of the mountains; and said to the mountains and rocks, Fall on us, and hide us from the face of him that sitteth on the throne, from the wrath of the Lamb: For the great day of his wrath is come; and who shall be able to stand? (Revelation 6:12-17)

There is an interesting parallel between these six seals and the events that Jesus described in His confidential briefing to His disciples regarding His Second Coming.[9] He spoke of false Christs, wars and rumors of wars, famines and pestilences, earthquakes, and cosmic changes of all kinds.

PAUSE BETWEEN THE SIXTH AND SEVEN SEALS

After the sixth seal is opened there is a pause before the seventh seal. This is a pattern all through Revelation. Six of a group of seven things will be presented, and then there is a pause with a change of subject, or a parenthetical discussion of some kind, and then the seventh thing is presented. In this case, we have six seals, and then 144,000 Israelites are sealed in chapter seven. Chapter eight then opens with the seventh seal.

These 144,000 Israelites are uniquely sealed. That is, they are given special protection against the particular attacks upon the Jews during the tribulation. The tribulation will affect everybody, but it will focus on the Jews; that's why Jeremiah refers to this period as "the time of Jacob's trouble." Chapter seven specifically designates 12,000 from each tribe: Judah, 12,000; Reuben, 12,000; Gad, 12,000; Asher, 12,000; Nephtali, 12,000; Manassah, 12,000; Simeon, 12,000; Levi, 12,000; Issachar, 12,000; Zebulun, 12,000; Joseph, 12,000; and Benjamin, 12,000.

The Holy Spirit could not have done more to show that these are not merely symbolic. There are 144,000, 12,000 from each of the twelve tribes. (The next time someone rings your doorbell and claims to be one of the 144,000, ask them which tribe they are from!)

There are two interesting omissions: Where are the tribes of Dan and Ephraim? Here is one of the great mysteries. We learned earlier that the twelve tribes are really a baker's dozen. The tribe of Joseph is also known as Ephraim and Manasseh, his two sons. So there are actually thirteen names. The tribes are listed in the Scripture twenty times, and each time they are in a different order. Often one of the tribes is not listed for some reason. For instance, in the military marching order, the Levites are not counted because they were exempt from military duty, but twelve tribes are still listed by having Joseph split into Ephraim and Manasseh.

Throughout the Old Testament the tribe of Dan seems to be slighted by the Holy Spirit. We don't know why exactly, but we can guess it was because Dan introduced idolatry into the land. So he is not sealed in Revelation. He has to survive by his own wits, yet he does survive, because we know from Ezekiel that when the land is divided in the millennium, he inherits first. But he doesn't get the benefit of the supernatural sealing.

And where is the tribe of Ephraim? Ephraim was also a tribe through which idolatry entered the land, and they are here, just hidden. Both Manasseh and Joseph are listed; with Manasseh already mentioned, all that's left of Joseph is Ephraim. He seems slighted by this elliptical allusion.

After the parenthetical event of Chapter 7, the final seal is opened.

Seventh Seal

And when he had opened the seventh seal, there was silence in heaven about the space of half an hour. And I saw the seven angels which stood before God; and to them were given seven trumpets. (Revelation 8:1-2)

THE SEVEN TRUMPETS

The seventh seal sets the stage for the Seven Trumpet Judgments. Let's take a look at those:

The first angel sounded, and there followed hail and fire mingled with blood, and they were cast upon the earth: and the third part of trees was burnt up, and all green grass was burnt up.

And the second angel sounded, and as it were a great mountain burning with fire was cast into the sea: and the third part of the sea became blood; And the third part of the creatures which were in the sea, and had life, died; and the third part of the ships were destroyed. (Revelation 8:7-9)

According to some scientists, an asteroid hits the earth about once every ten thousand years. This passage could be describing this type of collision.

And the third angel sounded, and there fell a great star from heaven, burning as it were a lamp, and it fell upon the third part of the rivers, and upon the fountains of waters; and the name of the star is called Wormwood: and the third part of the waters became wormwood; and many men died of the waters, because they were made bitter.

And the fourth angel sounded, and the third part of the sun was smitten, and the third part of the moon, and the third part of the stars; so as the third part of them was darkened, and the day shone not for a third part of it, and the night likewise.

And I beheld, and heard an angel flying through the midst of heaven, saying with a loud voice, Woe, woe, woe, to the inhabiters of the earth by reason of the other voices of the trumpet of the three angels, which are yet to sound! (Revelation 8:10-13)

These first four trumpets are sometimes called the "judgment of the thirds," since they seem to be a parallel of a similar but more intense series in the forthcoming "bowl" judgments which begin in Chapters 15 and 16. The final three in the trumpet judgments are sometimes called the "three woes" because of the emphasis in verse 13.

The fifth trumpet is particularly strange:

> And the fifth angel sounded, and I saw a star [the word "star" is often used for an angel] fall from heaven unto the earth: and to him was given the key of the bottomless pit. And he opened the bottomless pit; and there arose a smoke out of the pit: and there came out of the smoke locusts upon the earth: and unto them was given power . . . [over] only those men which have not the seal of God in their foreheads . . .
>
> And they had a king over them, which is the angel of the bottomless pit, whose name in the Hebrew tongue is Abaddon, but in the Greek tongue hath his name Apollyon [both of these words mean destruction]. One woe is past; and, behold, there come two woes more hereafter. (Revelation 9:1-4, 11-12)

These "locusts" have a king over them; but the Bible tells us that natural locusts have no king.[10] So, obviously, these are not natural locusts, but some kind of demons.

> And I heard a voice . . . saying to the sixth angel which had the trumpet, Loose the four angels which are bound in the great river Euphrates. And the four angels were loosed, which were prepared for an hour, and a day, and a month, and a year, for to slay the third part of men.
>
> And the number of the army of the horsemen were two hundred thousand thousand . . . And the rest of the men which were not killed by these plagues yet repented not of the work of their hands. (Revelation 9:14-16, 20)

Amazingly, in spite of all these plagues coming upon the earth, there is no repentance among the earth dwellers.

True to the pattern, there is a parenthetical break after the sixth trumpet. Chapter ten deals with the mighty angel (which some see as Jesus) who presents John with a little book to digest (reminiscent of a similar instruction to Jeremiah).

Chapter eleven deals with the Temple and the two witnesses. The first two verses deal with the Temple. John is told to measure the Temple, but not the outer court, because it's given to the Gentiles for forty-two months. That's an interesting number. It is one of the several ways that the two halves of the "Seventieth Week" of Daniel are referred to. Each half is referred to as three and a half years ("time, times, and the dividing of time"), forty-two months, and 1260 days. It is the most documented period in the entire Bible.

THE TWO WITNESSES

The rest of Chapter eleven is about the two witnesses. They are empowered for 1,260 days (forty-two months). As long as they are ministering, no one can touch them because they have four powers:

1. They can call down fire from heaven.
2. They can shut heaven so it doesn't rain for 1,260 days (forty-two months).
3. They can turn water into blood.
4. They can smite the earth with plagues.

The witnesses are hated for their preaching, and the Antichrist wants to kill them. When their ministry is finished, he does kill them and lets their bodies lie in the street. The earth dwellers celebrate and send gifts to one another because the witnesses are finally dead. But after three and a half days, before the eyes of the world, these bodies will stand up and ascend into heaven. (How will the entire world watch this event? On CNN, of course!)

Who are these two witnesses? There are many conjectures, but their four powers were given specifically to only two people in the Old Testament. Elijah called down fire from heaven at Mount Carmel. He also shut the heavens so it would not rain (for precisely that same period of time: three and a half years). Moses turned water into blood and smote the earth with plagues.

I believe the witnesses will be Elijah and Moses. Both had their ministries interrupted for various reasons. And I believe there was a staff meeting discussing these arrangements at the Transfiguration.[11]

Then we have the seventh trumpet angel sound:

And the seventh angel sounded; and there were great voices in heaven, saying, The kingdoms of this world are become the kingdoms of our Lord, and of his Christ; and he shall reign for ever and ever. (Revelation 11:15)

THE DRAMA OF REDEMPTION

Chapter twelve summarizes God's plan of redemption and Satan's attempts to thwart the plan of God through a vision of the woman and the man child.

First, we see a woman with the sun and the moon under her feet and twelve stars. And she is with child. (Some people try to make that woman the Church, but if that is true, she is in trouble. She is pregnant, yet the Church is always presented as the virgin bride.)

You may remember that back in Genesis 37, Jacob identified this woman. One of Joseph's dreams involved the sun, the moon, and the twelve stars. Jacob recognized these idioms as referring to himself, his wife and their twelve sons. Then the red dragon is introduced. He has seven heads, ten horns, and seven crowns (idioms from the visions of Daniel), and he positions himself to devour the man child as soon as he is born. Verse 9 identifies the red dragon as none other than Satan.

The woman gives birth to the man child who will rule all the nations with a rod of iron, which, of course, is an idiom for Jesus Christ.[12] The woman is Israel, and actually beginning in Genesis 3, where "the seed of the woman" is the promise of the Messiah.

The man-child is caught up to God and his throne. This may include both to the ascension of Jesus in Acts 1 and also to the Rapture of the Church. (The Church is also the Body of Christ raised to God and His throne.)

The woman then flees into the wilderness for 1,260 days (there's that number again). Then follows a cosmic war between Michael and his angels, against the dragon and his angels. The dragon is cast to the earth, and he persecutes the woman for three and a half years. By now you recognize that forty-two months, 1,260 days and three and a half years are the same amount of time: It is half of the Seventieth Week of Daniel.

Revelation 12 is actually a summary and prophecy of the entire history of God's redeeming work through His chosen people. It is also a summary of Satan's war against God from Genesis throughout the Old Testament, through the Gospels and to the Cross. But subsequent chapters of Revelation show us that God will, of course, be the victor, and He will share the spoils with His redeemed.

THE TWO BEASTS

Revelation 13 presents a deadly duo of two beasts. We often hear of the "Antichrist," but it is important to recognize that it is actually a duet of two Satanic leaders. The first beast rises out of the sea, which most scholars associate with the Gentile nations. He has seven heads, ten horns (idioms drawn directly from Daniel), and each head has a crown and the name of blasphemy. One of the heads is mortally wounded, but then healed—this head wound becomes his identifier in subsequent references. (In Zechariah we find a reference to him as having his right eye darken and one arm withered.[13] We suspect those may be vestiges from his head wound.)

> *We often hear of the "Antichrist," but it is important to recognize that it is actually a duet of two Satanic leaders.*

This "beast" is empowered by the dragon for forty-two months. (There's that same time period again.) He also "overcomes" the saints. This yields an important insight. Jesus told the disciples at Caesarea Philippi: "that the gates of hell shall not prevail against His Church."[14] (*Prevail* is the same Greek word, *nikao*, as is used in Revelation 13:7.) This would appear like a contradiction. But it simply highlights that not all saints are in the Church because the Church has been removed by then. These saints comprise what scholars call the "tribulation saints," which are saved after the rapture of the church. All the earth-dwellers—those not written in the Book of Life—will worship this beast. Many of the faithful will suffer martyrdom in this period.

Then another beast is introduced, a beast out of the earth. He will later be called the "false prophet." The two beasts are a duet. This one has two horns like a lamb (symbols of authority) but he speaks like the dragon (Satan). By working miracles, he causes the earth to worship the first beast. He deceives everyone except those who are supernaturally protected. He forces people to worship an image of the first beast, an image that apparently appears to be alive. He forces people to receive a mark with either his name or number, which is the famed "6-6-6." No one will be able to buy or sell without this mark.

(This is not the debit card in your wallet. The number here in question is the number of the beast and signifies an allegiance with him. He derives this control because allegiance to him will be required to participate in electronic commerce.)

Why is the mark on the right hand or the forehead? Perhaps to identify with his distinguishing infirmity.

The Seven Bowls

After this parenthetical review, we encounter seven angels and seven bowls of God's wrath being poured out. We will sense a parallel with the plagues of Egypt.

And the first went, and poured out his bowl upon the earth; and there fell a noisome and grievous sore upon the men which had the mark of the beast, and upon them which worshiped his image.

And the second angel poured out his bowl upon the sea; and it became as the blood of a dead man: and every living soul died in the sea.

And the third angel poured out his bowl upon the rivers and fountains of waters; and they became blood. (Revelation 16:2-4)

And the fourth angel poured out his bowl upon the sun; and power was given unto him to scorch men with fire.

And the fifth angel poured out his bowl upon the seat of the beast; and his kingdom was full of darkness; and they gnawed their tongues for pain, and blasphemed the God of heaven because of their pains and their sores, and repented not of their deeds.

And the sixth angel poured out his bowl upon the great river Euphrates; and the water thereof was dried up, that the way of the kings of the east might be prepared.

And I saw three unclean spirits like frogs come]out of the mouth of the dragon, and out of

The Seven Bowls of Wrath

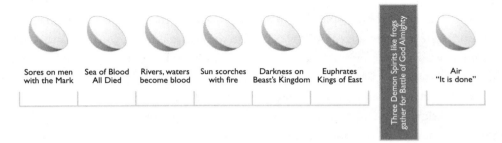

| Sores on men with the Mark | Sea of Blood All Died | Rivers, waters become blood | Sun scorches with fire | Darkness on Beast's Kingdom | Euphrates Kings of East | Three Demon Spirits like frogs gather for Battle of God Almighty | Air "It is done" |

And the seventh angel poured out his vial ino the air;
and there came a great voice out of the temple of heaven,
from the throne, saying,
It is done.
—Rev. 16:17

the mouth of the beast, and out of the mouth of the false prophet: For they are the spirits of devils, working miracles, which go forth unto the kings of the earth and of the whole world, to gather them to the battle of that great day of God Almighty. (Revelation 16:10-14)

Once again, six events are presented, and then there is a parenthetical interval: this time just one verse:

Behold, I come as a thief. Blessed is he that watcheth, and keepeth his garments, lest he walk naked, and they see his shame. (Revelation 16:15)

And then the narrative continues:
And he gathered them together into a place called in the Hebrew tongue Armageddon .(Revelation 16:16)

Then the final seventh bowl is poured out:

And the seventh angel poured out his vial into the air; and there came a great voice out of the temple of heaven, from the throne, saying, It is done. (Revelation 16:17)

It is poured "into the air." Who is the "prince of the power of the air"? Satan.[15]

(There are some provocative parallels between the trumpet judgments and the bowl—"vial"—judgments. There are numerous subtleties all through the Book of Revelation which are taken up in a more detailed study.)

THE BATTLE OF ARMAGEDDON

The famed Battle of Armageddon will take place in the Valley of Jezreel, right below Mount Megiddo, sixty miles north of Jerusalem. It has a long history of battles. In this valley, Jabin's nine nundred chariots were overwhelmed when Barak and Deborah defeated Sisera; Gideon's three hundred defeated the Midianites and the Amalekites; Samson triumphed over the Philistines; Saul was slain by Philistines; Ahaziah was slain by the arrows of Jehu; and Pharaoh Neco slew King Josiah. Saracens, Christian crusaders, Egyptians, Persians, Druses, Turks, Arabs, and even Napoleon on his disastrous march from Egypt to Syria, all encountered this valley so ideally suited for warfare.

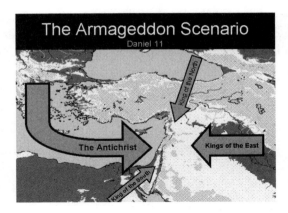

(On the other side of the Jezreel Valley from Mount Megiddo is Nazareth. As a boy, Jesus probably played on the hillside overlooking this very valley that would be the scene of the final world battle that He Himself would interrupt as God's Messiah.)

The scenario for the battle of Armageddon is outlined in Daniel 11. It is initiated by the "kings of the south," responded to by the "kings of the north," and then is joined by a western confederacy led by the Antichrist. And just about the time the Antichrist thinks he has everything under control, he quivers in his boots because the "kings of the east" make their entrance. It's a four-power conflict. If it isn't stopped, all mankind would be destroyed, but the Lord Himself will interrupt it (in chapter nineteen).

MYSTERY BABYLON DESTROYED

Chapters seventeen and eighteen detail the destruction of Mystery Babylon, the great whore who rides the beast with seven heads and ten horns. In chapter seventeen, she is "the Mother of Harlots and Abominations of the Earth," and is drunk with the blood of the saints.

In chapter eighteen, Babylon is described as the great city whose destruction in one hour is mourned by three groups of people—kings, merchants, and those who trade by sea. Apparently the foundation of "Babylon" is international trade, yet she is the epitome of false religion.

There are two women in the book of Revelation: Israel, the woman in chapter twelve, and Babylon, the woman who rides the beast in chapter seventeen. These women are deliberately contrasted. The first woman is the mother of the Man-Child; the other, the mother of harlots. One is clothed with the sun; the other with purple, scarlet and gold. One's identity is the sun, moon, and stars; the other reigns over the kings of the earth. The enemy of the woman Israel is the dragon; the enemies of the woman riding the beast are the ten kings she is riding who ultimately consume her. The first woman is hated by the world; the woman on the beast is caressed by the world. Israel is sustained by the wings of heaven; the woman riding the beast is sustained by the dragon. Israel is considered a widow and the divorced wife of Jehovah; the woman riding the beast brags, "I am no widow." The final destination of the woman in chapter twelve is the New Jerusalem; the final destination of the woman on the beast is the habitation of demons.

The destruction of Babylon is described in three pairs of chapters: Isaiah 13 and 14, Jeremiah 50 and 51, and Revelation 17 and 18. Reading them at one sitting will give you a feel for the idioms. Combining the accounts brings out the following points that indicate Babylon's destruction is yet to come.

- Many nations will attack Babylon. That hasn't happened yet. Persia conquered Babylon but didn't destroy it; they just took it over. Two centuries later, Alexander conquered it and made it his capital. He died there. It ultimately atrophied; but even today, Saddam Hussein has begun its modest rebuilding.

- Israel will be in the land and forgiven, according to Isaiah and Jeremiah.

- Babylon will finally be destroyed like Sodom and Gomorrah. That has yet to happen.

- Both Isaiah and Jeremiah repeatedly hammer the point that once it is destroyed, it will never be inhabited again; even the building materials will never be reused.

- Babylon will be destroyed during the "Day of the Lord." Both Isaiah and Jeremiah emphasize this, as does Revelation implicitly.

THE FIFTH HORSEMAN

And now we have the big climax, the fifth horseman:

> And I saw heaven opened, and behold a white horse; and he that sat upon him was called Faithful and True, and in righteousness he doth judge and make war. His eyes were as a flame of fire, and on his head were many crowns; and he had a name written, that no man knew, but he himself.
>
> And he was clothed with a vesture dipped in blood: and his name is called The Word of God. (Revelation 19:11-13)

This is the very title that John uses of Jesus in opening his Gospel.

> And the armies which were in heaven followed him upon white horses, clothed in fine linen, white and clean. And out of his mouth goeth a sharp sword, that with it he should smite the nations: and he shall rule them with a rod of iron: and he treadeth the winepress of the fierceness and wrath of Almighty God. And he hath on his vesture and on his thigh a name written, KING OF KINGS, AND LORD OF LORDS. (Revelation 19:14-16)

On a horse that is combat ready, the thigh would be a natural place to put an insignia.

THE MILLENNIAL KINGDOM

Then we get to chapter twenty, the Millennial Kingdom.

> And I saw an angel come down from heaven, having the key of the bottomless pit and a great chain in his hand. And he laid hold on the dragon, that old serpent, which is the Devil, and Satan, and bound him a thousand years, And cast him into the bottomless pit, and shut him up, and set a seal upon him, that he should deceive the nations no more, till the thousand years should be fulfilled: and after that he must be loosed a little season. (Revelation 20:1-3)

Tragically, there is a lot of controversy about the Millennium, as this specific period is called. There are many different, yet defendable, views regarding many aspects of end-time prophecies, but this common divergence—denying a literal Millennium—is particularly dangerous in that it would appear to be an attack on the very character of God! It does violence to His numerous and explicit promises and commitments that pervade both the Old and New Testaments. The Old Testament is replete with commitments for a literal Messiah ultimately ruling the world through Israel from His throne in Jerusalem. There are at least 1,845 references in the Old Testament and seventeen books give prominence to the event. The ancient rabbinical aspirations were dominated by it. In fact, this obsession obscured their recognizing the Messiah when He made His initial appearance. There are at least 318 references in 216 chapters of the New Testament, and twenty-three of its twenty-seven books give prominence to the event.

In the Millennium, the creation apparently will be physically changed according to Zechariah 4 and Isaiah 35. The curse appears to be lifted according to Isaiah 11. Creation itself is redeemed, not just you and me. The laws of entropy which apparently were introduced in Genesis 3 will be rescinded in the Millennium. And the earth will be full of the knowledge of the Lord according to Isaiah 11 and Habbakuk 2.

Yet this isn't eternity: There is still death and sin. People will own land, and the land will be fruitful. Eternity is something else entirely.

Why will Satan be loosed at the end? God is going to demonstrate that even after a thousand years of perfect rule, and even with Satan bound, man is still evil enough to rebel at his first opportunity.

THE NEW HEAVEN AND THE NEW EARTH

Revelation 21 describes the New Heaven and the New Earth.

> And I saw a new heaven and a new earth: for the first heaven and the first earth were passed away; and there was no more sea.
>
> And I John saw the holy city, new Jerusalem, coming down from God out of heaven, prepared as a bride adorned for her husband . . .
>
> And there came unto me one of the seven angels which had the seven vials full of the seven last plagues, and talked with me, saying, Come hither, I will show thee the Bride, the Lamb's wife. And he carried me away in the spirit to a great and high mountain, and showed me that great city, the holy Jerusalem, descending out of heaven from God. (Revelation 21:1-2,9-10)

Some of the features of the New Jerusalem are twelve gates named for the twelve tribes and its twelve foundations named for the twelve apostles. It is apparently a cube with twelve thousand furlongs in each of three dimensions (fifteen hundred miles in each of three directions.) There is no Temple because we are dwelling directly with God. There is no night because the Lamb of God is the light thereof. And there is the tree of life for the healing of the nations.

Chapter twenty-two closes with the promise of His coming.

> And, behold, I come quickly; and my reward is with me, to give every man according as his work shall be.
>
> I am Alpha and Omega, the beginning and the end, the first and the last. Blessed are they that do His commandments, that they may have right to the tree of life, and may enter in through the gates into the city.
>
> I Jesus have sent mine angel to testify unto you these things in the churches. I am the root and the offspring of David, and the bright and morning star.

And the Spirit and the bride say, Come. And let him that heareth say, Come. And let him that is athirst come. And whosoever will, let him take the water of life freely . . . Surely I come quickly. Amen. Even so, come, Lord Jesus!. (Revelation 22:12-17, 20)

Praise God!

Hour 24

CLOSING THOUGHTS

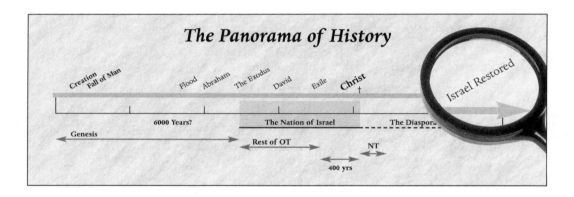

THROUGHOUT THIS ENTIRE STUDY, we have tried to focus on some central themes. The Old Testament is the account of a nation. The New Testament is the account of a Man which that nation produced. The central event of all history is that the Creator became a man. That's staggering. He died to purchase us and is alive now. The most exalted privilege is to know Him. That's what the Bible is all about.

Prophecy is the central theme of the Bible. By one scholastic reckoning, there are 8,362 predictive verses in Scripture, with 1,817 predictions on 737 subjects.[1] Actually, I think all Scripture is prophetic. Prophecy isn't just about the future: it is the "forth-telling" of God's entire plan of redemption. The Hebrew *Midrash,* a highly venerated commentary on the Old Testament, emphasizes that *prophecy is pattern, not just prediction.* The more you understand the overview of the whole, the more you will recognize how each incident, each episode, fits into a deliberate, well-designed program from beginning to end. You will discover that every detail—even the names of people and places, even the subtleties hidden "underneath" the text itself—all evidence a deliberate design by a single Source.

And what makes it intensely exciting is that there is increasing evidence that we are being drawn toward that ultimate climax! Again, let me challenge you to investigate a preposterous premise:

We are being plunged into a period of time about which the Bible says more about than any other period in history, including the time when Jesus walked the shores of Galilee and climbed the mountains of Judea.

How do you challenge this audacious statement? You have to do two things:

1. Find out what the Bible says about these things.
2. Then, find out what is going on in the world.

You won't find that on the evening news! Use the Internet; read independent alternative publications, and study the foreign press. Do your homework.

SIGNS OF HIS COMING ARE EVERYWHERE

Prophecy itself has several themes. There is, of course, Israel. If you want to know what time it is on God's calendar, look at Israel, and specifically the city of Jerusalem. Zechariah predicted that the entire world would go into the *ultimate* war over Jerusalem. Even today, the late lights are burning in every major capital of every internationally relevant country in the world as they try to figure out what to do about Jerusalem. But all attempts to deal with it are going to fail. It will be the "bone in the throat" of the entire world. There will be no peace in Jerusalem until the Prince of Peace comes.

The Temple *will* be rebuilt. Jesus, Paul, and John all made references to it being standing when Jesus returns. Several movements are afoot that are committed to bringing it about, despite the obvious obstacles.

The city of Babylon will be reestablished. Saddam Hussein has already begun rebuilding it. According to Isaiah 13 and 14 and Jeremiah 15 and 51, Babylon has to become a major center of power before the final end times.

Russia will invade the Middle East. Our best intelligence sources suggest that it may be on our near horizon.

China is rising as a major super power. Isaiah talks about it in chapter forty-nine of his book, Isaiah; John alludes to it in the Book of Revelation. It is interesting that the centroid of power on the Planet Earth began in the Mesopotamian valley, migrated from the Middle East westward to Greece, and then to Rome. In the sixteenth and seventeenth centuries, the fragments of the Roman Empire, the northern European nations, the Dutch, the English, the Spanish, the Germans, the French—all had their day in the sun. The centroid continued moving west: the twentieth century was "the American Century." But analysts today recognize that the twenty-first century is emerging to be the "Asian Century." But it won't end there: it seems the centroid of power will continue to migrate westward until it returns to where it all started, when God will set up His own kingdom in Jerusalem.

> *People all over the world are being drawn into an ecumenical religion. This composite religion will require tolerance at the expense of truth.*

Meanwhile, a European superstate is rising to power despite their troubles and problems. The desperate challenges posed by the proliferation of weapons of mass destruction—both nuclear and biochemical—and the rise of international terrorism all converge to force some form of global government. But the same nations of the Roman Empire that broke into pieces, as Daniel talked about, are being reassembled into an Empire. The missing element today is a leader, and the world's "ultimate leader" may already be in the wings awaiting his opportunity to take the stage.

In the meantime, people all over the world are being drawn into an ecumenical religion. This composite religion will require tolerance at the expense of truth. So this, too, will also be the servant of a centralized, socialist, global government that will lead the world into an ultimate tyranny.

Taking Our Spiritual Inventory

One of the clear teachings of the Bible is that there is a limit to God's forbearance. There comes a time when He has to vindicate His justice.

After the death of Solomon, when Jeroboam took over the Northern kingdom, and led them into idolatry, for a while they enjoyed the greatest prosperity they could imagine. Clearly, they felt it was the best of times.

However, it was a time of religious idolatry, social injustice, violence, and immorality. They had abandoned the Word of God from their lives. From God's point of view, it was the worst of times. It reminds us of the opening line,

> It was the best of times and it was the worst of times.
> *Charles Dickens, Tale of Two Cities*

God called the prophet Hosea to deliver His indictment to the Northern Kingdom. Hosea went to them and said, "Because you have forgotten your heritage, and you have ascribed your prosperity to others rather than the God who provided it, God is going to judge you by having your enemies wipe you out." And they did.

The parallel to our own situation is shocking. We, too, have abandoned our heritage. The revisionists are stripping all memory of our Christian founding fathers, and their commitment to truth, from our textbooks and we, too, are already reaping the whirlwind.

Immorality is taken for granted. We change marriage partners like fashion statements. We murder babies that are socially inconvenient. Our entertainment industry celebrates fornication, adultery, and every sexual aberration and form of evil you can imagine. We have become the primary world exporters of everything God abhors. Violence stalks our schoolyards as well as our cities. Most churches have withdrawn to a form of social irrelevancy. Paganism and humanism have become our official religions. Occult practices are on the rise and taught in our schools.

Our founding fathers warned us:

> I tremble for my country when I realize that God is just,
> And that His justice will not sleep forever.
> *Thomas Jefferson*

The only thing that can save our country is a return to our heritage and to put God back into our schools and our lives.

> The only thing that can save America is a grass roots revival.
> *Robert Bork, Slouching Towards Gomorrah*

THE ANSWER

But let's not forget the good news! You have something even more powerful than the ballot box: You have the prayer closet. You have a twenty-four hour hotline to the Throne Room of the universe, and God is anxious to hear from you. If you care about your children and grandchildren, you better pray that God, in His mercy, will bring us a grass roots revival. And it needs to start with the person we see in the mirror each morning.

We possess a message of extraterrestrial origin. It portrays us as objects of an unseen warfare in which we are both the pawns and the prize. Our eternal destiny depends upon our relationship with the Ultimate Victor in this cosmic conflict. Where do *you personally* stand with respect to Him? That's the real question. What is your personal relationship with the Living Lord?

HOW TO STUDY THE BIBLE

People often ask me, "How do you study the Bible?" The first rule is, never open your Bible without prayer. Bible study is not an intellectual exercise; it is a *spiritual* exercise. Study with prayer. Develop your personal relationship with the Author of the Book.

Second, set aside your presuppositions. All of us bring the baggage of previous misconceptions to a subject, and they are often wrong. Cultivate an open mind, and investigate diligently. Remember Luke's assessment of the Bereans:

These were more noble than those in Thessalonica, in that they received the word with all readiness of mind, yet searched the scriptures daily, to prove whether those things were so. (Acts 17:11)

Third, take notes. Build your own reservoir of insights right from the beginning. If you don't start systematically, you will regret it later.

Also, I suggest you start a personal journal of this ultimate adventure. You can conduct your own laboratory experiment in the supernatural!

Go to a stationary store and buy a journal: a bound book with blank, lined paper. This will be your private, confidential journal. The value of it will depend on the degree to which you can be honest with yourself as you go. If you vow, up front, to never show this to anyone, there is at least a chance you will be candid in it. You are never going to show this to anyone. It's going to be your private treasure.

The next time you find a verse in the Bible which you do not understand, go to your journal and write down the date, the reference in question, and then, honestly (and in ink), write down why this particular verse seems confusing or like a contradiction to you. Try to document the reasons you don't understand it. That's the hard part.

Once you have done that, close your journal and take the issue before the Throne of Grace. Pray something along these lines: *"Father, I'm in your Word, and you promised me that the Holy Spirit would teach me all things.² Not most things; all things. I am sincerely interested in finding out what this verse really means and here is my problem with it. I want to claim your promise to be my tutor: please show me what this verse means. In the name of the Lord Jesus Christ, Amen."*

Then watch what happens. It may not be in the next ten seconds or the next hour or even the next day. But something surprising will occur; you may be reading somewhere else in the Bible and get an insight. Or maybe you'll be listening to a radio station, or you may overhear a conversation in a restaurant; you can never predict just how the Holy Spirit will answer—but He will answer that prayer. And suddenly that verse will become so clear you may forget how puzzled you once were.

Now you should go back to your journal, turn to the page with that puzzling reference, put down the date, and how the Holy Spirit revealed to you what it meant.

You may be wondering, "That sounds great, but why all the paperwork?" I'll tell you why: The day will come when you will inevitably go through a valley of doubt, when your faith will be tested. The day will come when you are just not sure but that we all may have simply gotten carried away with "all this Bible stuff." I want you to be able to go back to your journal and examine the "footprints" of the Holy Spirit as *He* took you by the hand, verse by verse, through your difficulties. That secret journal will become one of your dearest personal treasures. The Holy Spirit will lead you to all truth, Scripture says. Take him up on that.

The other thing to do is invest in some helps and resources. If you have a hobby, you probably know more about your hobby than your profession—because it's a labor of love. And you probably have more invested in that hobby than you care to admit to! I have a suggestion: Why not make the Bible your "hobby"? Invest in it. It doesn't cost much to build a small library of resources right at home. Get a good study Bible, a good concordance, a Bible encyclopedia, and establish a study center in your own home so that when a question comes up you can personally pop right in and get it answered. You don't have to wait until the weekend and pester your pastor. You can find out yourself. It will start to make the Bible alive and real for you.

If you are computer literate, the resources available today are breathtaking. I travel on a plane with more equivalent volumes than most seminaries possess because they are all on CD-ROMs (and they are all word-searchable). On the Internet, you can get the *Blue Letter Bible*³ in English, Greek, and Hebrew (and you don't have to know those languages: The computer helps you). It's all there and it's all free.

Ben Franklin thought a person should be "a jack of all trades and *master of one.*" (He is often misquoted: he didn't say "master of none.") The cultured person, he believed, should know something about everything but everything about something. For a Christian, his specialization should be, of course, the Bible.

The most fruitful way to "come up to speed" is in a home Bible study fellowship. There's probably one in your neighborhood, or among your associates. If you can't find one, start one yourself! It is not difficult and it unquestionably is one of the richest paths to blessing you'll ever discover. And I would like to help you. There are many helpful materials available for this purpose—this survey that you are participating in right now is a candidate resource to take a group through. Contact us and we'll be glad to send you others.⁴

Ultimately, the most enduring and fruitful approach is to take a book of the Bible—any book—and go through it with a group, verse by verse, at a pace of about a chapter a week. The Lord will bless it beyond your wildest expectations. Try it. Ask anyone who has done it.

THE PRIMARY THEME OF THE BIBLE: JESUS CHRIST THE KING

Often when we get involved in peripheral issues—end time prophecy, or whatever—it is important to conclude with a focus on the key to what it is all about. I frequently will retreat to the following summary as to who He really is.⁵

Who is Jesus Christ? He is the King of the Jews. That's a *racial* statement. Make no mistake about it—he is Jewish.

He is also the King of Israel. He is a *national* King.

He is also the King of all the Ages, the King of Heaven, the King of Glory, the King of Kings, and Lord of Lords.

He was a prophet before Moses; a priest after Melchizedek; a champion like Joshua; an offering in the place of Isaac; a king from the line of David; a wise counselor even above Solomon; a beloved, rejected, and then exalted son like Joseph. And yet far more.

The heavens declare His glory and the firmament shows His handiwork. He is, was, and always will be; He is the first and the last, the Alpha and Omega, the Aleph and the Tau, the A and the Z; He is the firstfruits of them that slept.

He is the "I AM that I AM," the voice of the burning bush. He is the Captain of the Lord's Host, the conqueror of Jericho.

He is enduringly strong; entirely sincere; eternally steadfast; immortally graceful; imperially powerful; impartially merciful. In Him dwells the fullness of the Godhead bodily; the very God of very God.

He is our Kinsman Redeemer, and so He is also our Avenger of Blood. He is our City of Refuge; our Performing High Priest, our Personal Prophet, our Reigning King.

He is the loftiest idea in literature; the highest personality in philosophy; the fundamental doctrine of theology; the Supreme Problem in higher criticism. He is the Miracle of the Ages; the superlative of everything good.

You and I are the beneficiaries of a love letter written in blood on a wooden cross erected in Judea two thousand years ago. "He was crucified on a cross of wood; yet He made the hill on which it stood." By Him were all things made that were made; without Him was not anything made that was made; by Him are all things held together!

What held Him to that cross? It wasn't the nails! (At any time, He could have said, "Enough already! I'm out of here!") What held Him there was His love for you and me.

> *You and I are the beneficiaries of a love letter written in blood on a wooden cross erected in Judea two thousand years ago.*

He was born of a woman so that we could be born of God. He humbled Himself so that we could be lifted up. He became a servant so that we could be made His co-heirs. He suffered rejection so that we could become His friends. He denied Himself so that we could freely receive all things. He gave Himself so that He could bless us in every way.

He is available to the tempted and the tried; He blesses the young; He cleanses the lepers; He defends the feeble; He delivers the captives; He discharges the debtors; He forgives the sinners; He franchises the meek; He guards the besieged; He heals the sick; He provides strength to the weak; He regards the aged; He rewards the diligent; He serves the unfortunate; He sympathizes and He saves!

His offices are manifold; His reign is righteous; His promises are sure; His goodness is limitless; His light is matchless; His grace is sufficient; His love never changes; His mercy is everlasting; His Word is enough; His yoke is easy; and His burden is light!

He's indescribable; He's incomprehensible; He's irresistible; He's invincible! The Heaven of heavens cannot contain Him; man cannot explain Him; the Pharisees couldn't stand Him and found they couldn't stop Him; Pilate couldn't find any fault with Him; the witnesses couldn't agree against Him. Herod couldn't kill Him, death couldn't handle Him, and the grave couldn't hold Him!

He has always been and always will be; He had no predecessor and will have no successor. You can't impeach Him and He isn't going to resign! His name is above every name, that at the name of Yeshua, every knee shall bow, every tongue shall confess, that Jesus Christ is Lord!

His is the kingdom, the power and the glory forever and ever.

Amen!

ABOUT KOINONIA HOUSE

WHERE DO YOU GO from here? What paths are open to you to continue the ultimate adventure? A natural next step is to get an expositional commentary. Pick a book that appeals to you and go through it verse by verse with a guide. There are many available. We publish verse-by-verse commentaries, with extensive background notes, on virtually all the books of the Bible. Our commentaries are typically on audio tape (or CD-ROM), and they are accompanied by a notebook with all the details and charts and background references. And it is also now possible to accumulate university course credits all the way to the Ph.D. level.

We also publish topical Briefing Packs consisting of two tapes plus notes on selected topics. We also have one of the largest websites on the Internet: <www.khouse.org>. Besides numerous Bible study materials, we monitor ten strategic trends, and will send you a free weekly newsletter (called eNews) by email which highlights the Biblical relevance of current events, and which includes links to the websites which pertain to each area of interest.

You can also access the *Blue Letter Bible*, and it's free. (Everything that is hyperlinked on the Internet is blue; the entire Bible is hyperlinked to all the helps available.) It is available in English, Hebrew, and Greek and is searchable by reference or word. In addition to the text itself, there are commentaries (both classic and contemporary), dictionaries, encyclopedias, and all kinds of other helps. They are all word-searchable and free—anywhere in the world.

Our ministry is called Koinonia House. (*Koinonia* is the Greek word for communication, fellowship, partaking in a partnership.) We are a non-denominational (but very fundamental) ministry whose mission is to create, develop, and distribute materials to stimulate, encourage, and facilitate serious study of the Bible as the inerrant Word of God.

Give us a call at 1 (800) 546-8731 and we will send you a special gift for having survived this review.

In His Name,
Chuck Missler

ABOUT THE AUTHOR

CHUCK MISSLER DEMONSTRATED an aptitude for technical interests as a youth. He became a ham radio operator at age nine and started piloting airplanes as a teenager. While still in high school, Chuck built a digital computer in the family garage.

His plans to pursue a doctorate in electrical engineering at Stanford University were interrupted when he received a Congressional appointment to the United States Naval Academy at Annapolis. Graduating with honors, Chuck took his commission in the Air Force. After completing flight training, he met and married Nancy. Chuck joined the Missile Program and eventually became Branch Chief of the Department of Guided Missiles at Lowry Air Force Base.

Chuck made the transition from the military to the private sector when he became a systems engineer with TRW, a large aerospace firm. He then went on to serve as a senior analyst with a non-profit think tank, where he conducted projects for the intelligence community and the Department of Defense. During that time, Chuck earned a master's degree in engineering at UCLA, supplementing previous graduate work in applied mathematics, advanced statistics, and information sciences. Chuck continued his education, earning a PhD from Louisiana Baptist University.

Recruited into senior management at the Ford Motor Company in Dearborn, Michigan, Chuck established the first international computer network in 1966. He left Ford to start his own company, a computer network firm that was subsequently acquired by Automatic Data Processing (listed on the New York Stock Exchange) to become its Network Services Division.

Returning to California, Chuck found himself consulting, organizing corporate development deals, serving on the board of directors at several firms, and specializing in the rescuing of financially troubled technology companies. He brought several companies out of Chapter 11 and into profitable operation. Most noteworthy of these turnarounds was the resurrection of Western Digital in the early 1980s.

As Chuck notes, his day of reckoning came several years later when—as the result of a merger—he found himself the chairman and a major shareholder of a small, publicly owned development company known as Phoenix Group International. The firm established an $8 billion joint venture with the Soviet Union to supply personal computers to their 143,000 schools. Due to several unforeseen circumstances, including the collapse of the Soviet Union, the venture failed. Chuck and Nancy lost everything, including their home, automobiles, and insurance.

As a child Chuck had developed an intense interest in the Bible; studying it became a favorite pastime. In the 1970s, while still in the corporate world, Chuck began leading weekly Bible studies at the 30,000-member Calvary Chapel Costa Mesa in California.

Chuck had also enjoyed a longtime personal relationship with Hal Lindsey, who upon hearing of Chuck's professional misfortune, suggested to Chuck that this might be the call of God on his life, a call that would lead him into the full-time ministry. Over the years, Chuck had developed a loyal following. (Through Doug Wetmore, head of the tape ministry of Firefighters for Christ, Chuck learned that more than 7 million copies of his taped Bible studies were scattered throughout the world.) In 1991 Koinonia House became Chuck's full-time profession. Koinonia House now has offices in the U.S., Canada, the U.K., New Zealand, and Australia.

NOTES

Hour 3. Genesis 4–11: From the Fall of Man to the Tower of Babel

1. Genesis 22:13 as a prime example.

Hour 4. Genesis 12–50: Abraham, Isaac, Jacob, and Joseph

1. Hebrews 11:19.

2. Genesis 15:2.

Hour 5. Exodus–Deuteronomy

1. Hebrews 7:25.

2. Genesis 22:13.

3. Isaiah 53:2.

4. Chuck Missler, *Cosmic Codes: Hidden Messages from the Edge of Eternity,* (Koinonia House, Couer d'Alene, ID, 1999), 243.

5. Colossians 2:16, 17.

6. Acts 2.

7. John 19:33-36.

8. Numbers 14: 13-19.

9. Numbers 14: 29-35.

10. 2 Corinthians 5:21.

Hour 6. Joshua, Judges, and Ruth

1. Joshua 6; Revelation 8; Joshua 10:1-16; Revelation 13; 6: 13-17.

2. Acts 2:23.

3. Genesis 38:1-26.

4. Deuteronomy 23:2.

Hour 7. Samuel, Kings, and Chronicles

1. Luke 1:32.

2. 1 Samuel 13:14; Acts 13:22.

3. 2 Chronicles 11:13, 16.

4. 1 Kings 17; Luke 4:25; James 5:17.

5. 1 Kings 18.

6. Georg Wilhelm Friedrich Hegel, *Philosophy of History*, 1832.

7. 2 Chronicles 11:13, 16.

Hour 9. The Book of Daniel

1. Luke 19:38.

2. Luke 19:43, 44.

3. Daniel 9:27.

4. Matthew 18:22.

5. J. Barton Payne, *Encyclopedia of Biblical Prophecy* (New York: Harper & Row, 1973).

Hour 10. The Post-Exile Era: Ezra, Nehemiah, and the Inter-Testament Period

1. Sir Robert Anderson, *The Coming Prince,* (Hodder & Stoughton, 1894)

2. Herodotus of Halicarnassus, *History*, 1:191.

3. Isaiah 44:27-28.

4. Isaiah 45:1.

5. Isaiah 45:2-5.

6. Ezra 1:2-3.

7. Genesis 49:10

8. *Hanukkah* is alluded to in John 10:22.

9. Matthew 24:15.

Hour 11. Isaiah, Jeremiah, and Ezekiel

1. Isaiah 7:11-14.

2. This is the commitment that the Angel Gabriel reconfirmed to Mary when the birth of Jesus was announced to her in Luke 1:32.

3. Isaiah 9:6,7.

4. Isaiah 61:1,2; quoted in Luke 4:18-19.

5. Hosea 5:15.

6. Jeremiah 22:30.

7. Isaiah 11:11.

8. Ezekiel 36:22-24.

9. Ezekiel 39:15.

Hour 12. The Minor Prophets

1. Hosea 2:23.

2. Hosea 4:1.

3. Matthew 2:15.

4. Hosea 11:1.

5. Hosea 5:15-6:1-2.

6. Isaiah 63:1-8.

7. Hosea 12:10.

8. These are catalogued in the author's *Cosmic Codes: Hidden Messages From the Edge of Eternity*, Appendix A, Koinonia House, 1999.

9. Proverbs 30:27.

10. Amos 3:7.

11. Amos 7:1 (English translation, KJV).

12. Amos 7:2 (LXX).

13. Revelation 9:11.

14. Micah 5:2.

15. Micah 6:8.

16. Habakkuk 2:4.

17. Romans 1:17.

18. Galatians 3:11.

19. Hebrews 10:38.

20. Zechariah 14:4.

21. Zechariah 12:10.

22. Malachi 3:10.

23. Matthew 11:13; Luke 16:16.

24. John 19:34.

25. John 5:39.

Hour 13. How Sure Can We Be?

1. Matthew 27:3-5.

2. Matthew 27:6-7.

3. John 20:25.

4. John 20:26-29.

5. William D. Edwards; Wesley J. Gavel; Floyd E. Hosmer, *Journal of American Medical Association*, March 21, 1986, vol. 255, no. 11, "On the Physical Death of Jesus Christ," 1455-1463.

6. Peter Stoner, *Science Speaks* (Chicago: Moody Press, 1958).

7. Genesis 3:15.

8. John 5:39.

Hour 14. The New Testament

1. $7^{34} = 5.4 \times 10^{28}$ tries: assuming 400 million tries/second results in 4.3×10^{12} computer years.

Hour 15. The Gospels

1. The Greek of Luke 3:23 uses *nomizo*, reckoned as by law.

2. This is an application of the provision in the Torah for the daughters of Zelophehad (Numbers 27:1-11; Joshua 17:3-6) in which the father of the bride adopted her husband as his son (Ezra 2:61=Nehemiah 7:63; Numbers 32:41, cf. 1 Chronicles 2:21-23, 34-35).

3. Genesis 3:15.

4. Isaiah 7:14.

5. Psalms 45:1 (LXX) uses the Greek term for stenographer, indicating this technical term was in common Greek usage many centuries earlier.

6. John 14:26.

7. John 16:13.

8. Ruth 2:4, 5.

9. J. Vernon McGee, *Luke* (Thomas Nelson Publishers: Nashville, 1991), 8; also,

   R. Kent Hughes, *Luke,* (2 vols.), (Crossway Books: Wheaton, Ill.,1998) vol.1, 15.

10. J. Vernon McGee, *Luke,* (Thomas Nelson Publishers: Nashville, 1991) 9.

11. Luke 3:1.

12. Matthew 12:40.

13. Matthew 4; Luke 4.

14. John 2.

15. John 3.

16. John 4.

17. John 5.

18. Matthew 4, Mark 1, Luke 4, John 4.

19. Isaiah 61:1,2; However, He stopped at a critical comma: Luke 4:17-21. He omitted, "and the day of vengeance of our God."

20. Luke 5.

21. Luke 6.

22. Luke 6; Matthew 5-7.

23. Luke 7.

24. Matthew 13:10-13.

25. Matthew 13:14-16; Isaiah 6:9, 10.

26. Mark 6.

27. Matthew 10, Mark 6, Luke 9,

28. Perhaps twice that number since that counts only the men, not the women and children.

29. Matthew 14, Mark 6, John 6.

30. Mark 7.

31. Mark 7.

32. Mark 7; Matthew 15.

33. Mark 8.

34. Mark 9, Matthew 17.

35. John 7.

36. John 8.

37. Luke 10-16.

38. John 11.

39. Luke 18.

40. Matthew 20, Mark 10, Luke 18.

41. Luke 19.

42. John 12:1.

Hour 16. The Passion Week

1. John 12:1.

2. Matthew 28:1.

3. Matthew 12:40.

4. John 12:1.

5. Matt 21, Mark 11, Luke 19.

6. Matthew 26.

7. John 19, Mark 15, Luke 23.

8. Luke 23.

9. Leviticus 23:11.

10. 1 Corinthians 15:20, 23; Revelation 20:6.

11. Zechariah 9:9.

12. Leviticus 23.

13. Luke 19:39.

14. Romans 11:25.

15. Luke 19:44.

16. Matthew 26:1-5.

17. Leviticus 21:10.

18. John 19:19.

19. Mark 16.

20. Matthew 28.

21. Luke 24:13ff.

22. Luke 24:34.

23. Luke 24:33-50; John 20:24-29.

24. John 21:3-14.

25. Matthew 28:16-20.

26. 1 Corinthians 15:6.

27. Luke 24; Acts 1.

28. Acts 9, 22.

29. John 20:11-18.

30. Luke 24:13-32.

31. Luke 24:35.

32. Isaiah 52:14.

Hour 17. Acts

1. John 16:7.

2. John 14:26.

3. John 16:13.

4. Acts 1:8.

5. Revelation 7.

6. Isaiah 50:4.

7. Genesis 12:1-3.

8. This incident may have profound implications regarding the possible presence of the Ark of the Covenant and the Mercy Seat being currently in Ethiopia. 2 Chronicles 35.

9. Acts 9:4.

10. Galatians 4:15.

11. Galatians 2:11.

12. 1 Corinthians 1:12.

13. 1 Peter 1:1.

14. Acts 13:1-3.

15. Acts 13:4-12.

16. Acts 13:13.

17. Acts 14:1-7.

18. Acts 14:8-20.

19. Acts 15:7-11.

20. Acts 15:13-18. James was quoting from Amos 9:11-12.

21. Paul, in his definitive statement of doctrine we call the Book of Romans, hammers this home in chapters 9, 10, and 11. We will take this up in Hour 18.

22. Acts 17:28.

23. His farewell address is recorded in Acts 20.

24. Acts 23.

Hour 18. *The Epistle to the Romans*

1. Acts 20.

2. Donald Grey Barnhouse, *Romans*, (Eerdmans Publishing: Grand Rapids, 1964), vol. 1, 3.

3. Romans 1:1-32.

4. Romans 2:1-16.

5. Romans 2:11-29

6. Luke 15:11-32.

7. Romans 1:16.

8. Habakkuk 2:4; quoted in Romans 1:17; Galatians 3:11; Hebrews 11:38.

9. Romans 1:17.

10. Galatians 3:11.

11. Hebrews 10:38.

12. Romans 1:20-22.

13. Romans 1:26, 27.

14. Romans 1:28.

15. Romans 3.

16. Romans 4.

17. Ephesians 2:8, 9.

18. Romans 5:15-21.

19. Romans 5:20.

20. Romans 6:12.

21. Romans 7:7.

22. Romans 7:8-23.

23. Romans 7:24-25.

24. John 1:11-12.

25. Genesis 12:2-3.

26. Genesis 26:2-5.

27. Hebrews 6:13-18.

28. Luke 19:42.

29. Romans 11:25.

30. Luke 21:24.

31. Hosea 5:15.

32. Isaiah 63:1-8.

33. Romans 14:1, 2.

34. Romans 14:3.

35. Romans 14:5-6.

36. Colossians 2:16, 17.

37. Romans 15:4.

Hour 19. The Pauline Epistles

1. 1 Timothy 3:16.

2. 1 Corinthians 1:18.

3. 1 Corinthians 1:26-29.

4. 1 Corinthians 3:11-15.

5. 1 Corinthians 13:1-3.

6. 1 Corinthians 13:4-7.

7. 1 Corinthians 15:1-4.

8. 1 John 3:2.

9. 2 Corinthians 5:2; Jude 6.

10. 1 Corinthians 15:51-53.

11. Galatians 3:3.

12. Ephesians 1:4.

13. Ephesians 1:5.

14. Ephesians 1:7.

15. Ephesians 1:13-14.

16. Ephesians 2:8-10.

17. Ephesians 2:7.

18. Matthew 11:11.

19. Matthew 11:13.

20. Ephesians 3:3-6.

21. Ephesians 6:12.

22. Ephesians 6:11.

23. Philippians 1:21.

24. Philippians 3:7.

25. Philippians 4:13.

26. Philippians 4:4.

27. Philippians 2:5-8.

28. Colossians 1:16-19.

29. Colossians 1:20.

30. 2 Timothy 4:7-8.

Hour 20. The Hebrew Christian Epistles

1. Note the very first verse: "The elder unto the elect lady and her children, whom I love in the truth; and not I only, but also all they that have known the truth;. . ." Who else is loved by "all they that have known the truth"?

2. 3. 2 John 2:10.

3. Matthew 13:55; Mark 6:3.

4. John 7:3-5; Acts 1:14.

Hour 21. Eschatology

1. Acts 20:27.

2. Revelation 20.

3. Daniel 9:24-27.

4. Romans 10:12; Galatians 3:28; Colossians 3:11.

5. Revelation 7.

6. Matthew 11:11, 13.

7. Matthew 24:15; 2 Thessalonians 2:4; Revelation 11:1,2.

8. Daniel 2:44-45; 7:9-14; 12:1-3; Zechariah 14:1-15; Matthew 13:41; 24:15-31; 26:64; Mark 13:14-27; 14:62: Luke 21:25-28; Acts 1:9-11; 3:19-21; 1 Thessalonians 3:13; 2 Thessalonians 1:6-10; 2:8; 2 Peter 3:1-14; Jude 14-15; Revelation 1:7; 19:11-20; 22:7, 12, 20.

9. John 14:1-3; Romans 8:19; 1 Corinthians 1:7-8; 15:1-53; 16:22; Philippians 3:20-21; Colossians 3:4; 1 Thessalonians 1:10; 2:19; 4:13-18; 5:9, 23; 2 Thessalonians 2:1, (3); 1 Timothy 6:14; 2 Timothy 4:1; Titus 2:13; Hebrews 9:28; James 5:7-9; 1 Peter 1:7, 13; 1 John 2:28-3:2; Jude 21; Revelation 2:25; 3:10.

10. He was quoting from Daniel 12.

11. Matthew 11:11.

12. Zechariah 13:8-9.

13. Jeremiah 30:7.

14. Hosea 5:15.

15. 1 Thessalonians 5:9 and Revelation 3:10.

16. 1 Thessalonians 2:7,8.

17. *Epistle of Barnabas* (A.D. 100); Irenaeus, *Against Heresies;* Hippolytus, a disciple of Irenaeus (2nd Century); Justin Martyr, *Dialogue with Trypho,* and a recent discovery in the writings of Ephrem the Syrian (4th Century). Other references include Peter Jurieu, *The Approaching Deliverance of the Church,* 1687; Philip Doddridge's *Commentary on the New Testament,* 1738; John Gill, *Commentary on the New Testament,* 1748; James Macknight, *Commentary on the Apostolical Epistles,* 1763; Thomas Scott, *Commentary on the Holy Bible,* 1792, et al.

18. Ezekiel 38 and 39.

19. Matthew 24:15; 2 Thessalonians 2:4; Revelation 11:1, 2.

20. Isaiah 13, 14; Jeremiah 50, 51; Revelation 17, 18.

21. Daniel 2, 7; Revelation 13.

22. Daniel 11:36-45; Revelation 16:16.

23. Daniel 11:41; Isaiah 63:1-6.

Hour 22. Revelation 1-4: Letters to Seven Churches

1. Mark 13:32.

2. Revelation 1:20.

3. Hebrews 4:12.

4. Revelation 4:5.

5. John 13:13-16.

6. John 10:28, 29; Romans 8:28-39. Cf. 1 Corinthians 3:11-15.

7. 1 Corinthians 15:1-4.

Hour 23. Revelation 4-22: The Consummation of All Things

1. Ephesians 5:26.

2. There are over 200 rhetorical devices (puns, metaphors, similes, allegories, and other

types) catalogued in Appendix A of our book, *Cosmic Codes: Hidden Messages From the Edge of Eternity*, Koinonia House, Coeur d'Alene Idaho, 1999.

3. Introduced in Genesis 14:18, this strange person is amplified in Psalm 110:4 and Hebrews 5:6, 10; 6:20-7:21.

4. Revelation 1:6; 20:6.

5. Isaiah 11:2

6. Genesis 9:6.

7. Daniel 9:27.

8. Matthew 24:3ff.

9. Matthew 24:3ff.

10. Proverbs 30:27.

11. Matthew 17.

12. Psalm. 2:9; Revelation. 2:27; 12:5; 19:15.

13. Zechariah 11:17.

14. Matthew 16::18.

15. Ephesians 2:2.

Hour 24. Closing Thoughts

1. J. Barton Payne, *Encyclopedia of Biblical Prophecy,*(Harper and Row, New York, 1973).

2. Deut. 4:9; John14:26; 1 John 2:27.

3. Check out our website: www.khouse.org.

4. Koinonia House, PO Box D, Coeur d'Alene, Idaho 83816; or call us at (800) 546-8731. We would love to year from you.

5. This was inspired by the late Pastor S. D. Lochridge, and eclectically tailored over the years.